The Wisdom of JOHN MUIR

100+ Selections from the Letters, Journals, and Essays of the Great Naturalist

Compiled by **ANNE ROWTHORN**

Foreword by **BILL McKIBBEN**

WILDERNESS PRESS ... *on the trail since 1967*

The Wisdom of John Muir
100+ Selections from the Letters, Journals,
and Essays of the Great Naturalist

1st EDITION 2012
8th printing 2022

Copyright © 2012 by Anne Rowthorn

Front cover photo: John Muir at Vernal Falls, Yosemite National Park, California—
    John Muir Papers, Holt-Atherton Special Collections, University of the Pacific
    Library. © 1984 Muir-Hanna Trust
Cover design: Scott McGrew
Interior design: Annie Long
Editors: Susan Haynes and Donna Poehner

ISBN 978-0-89997-694-5 (pbk.); ISBN 978-0-89997-695-2 (ebook)

Manufactured in the United States of America

Published by: **Wilderness Press**
                 An imprint of AdventureKEEN
                 2204 First Avenue South, Suite 102
                 Birmingham, AL 35233
                 (800) 678-7006; FAX (877) 374-9016
                 info@wildernesspress.com
                 www.wildernesspress.com

Visit our website for a complete listing of our books and for ordering information.

Distributed by Publishers Group West

TABLE *of* CONTENTS

CHAPTER 12: Peace to Every Living Thing 181

Dedication

KIERAN WILLIAM
AND
HANNAH ANNE,
WITH DEAREST LOVE

Acknowledgments

I AM FILLED WITH GREAT GRATITUDE to many people who have helped bring this book to fruition. First, of course, is John Muir himself, whose magnificent writings have inspired and informed my life. I am grateful to the host of Muir scholars and biographers, present and past, who have written on John Muir's life, especially Linnie Marsh Wolfe and William Frederic Badè whose books still set a high standard of scholarship, and Muir's most recent biographers, Frederick Turner and Donald Worster. I am grateful to the Sierra Club and the Holt-Atherton Special Collections at the University of the Pacific for making available online most of John Muir's works.

Special thanks are due to my hiking companion and friend, Cynthia Shattuck, who urged me to stop talking about John Muir and to start compiling this book. I owe a tremendous debt of gratitude to three talented friends whose patient reading of the entire manuscript resulted in many valuable suggestions: David Bingham, inspired by John Muir, is a self-described "tree hugger," the founder of Salem Land Trust, and serves on numerous volunteer boards and commissions involved with community participation in environmental protection, policies, and planning; Hilary Thimmesh, OSB, President Emeritus, and former professor of English at St. John's University in Collegeville, Minnesota; and George Willauer, former professor of English at Connecticut College who taught courses on nature writers.

I am grateful to the Collegeville Institute at St. John's University in Minnesota for providing accommodation, warm fellowship, and a beautiful natural environment to begin researching the book. Especially I would like to thank the Institute staff: Director Donald Ottenhoff, Carla Durand, and Elisa Schneider.

Librarians have helped immensely in locating sometimes difficult-to-find sources, and I am especially grateful to Bev Ehresmann at the Alcuin Library at St. John's

University and Jackie Hemond of the Salem Free Public Library, in Connecticut. Bob and JoAnne Pokrinchak and Yuanjin Chen kept my temperamental computer going long enough to finish the book.

Hans Christoffersen, the editorial director of the Liturgical Press, helped me find the right publisher for this book. I have been hugely fortunate in all the support and encouragement I received from Wilderness Press, especially from editors Susan Haynes who was insightful and enthusiastic from the start, and Donna Poehner whose expertise and many fine suggestions improved the book; also for the artistry of designers Annie Long and Scott McGrew. Along with Molly Merkle, they have all been wonderful to work with.

As always, family members have provided inspiration and sanity, along with lots of laughter and joy, during the compiling of the book. They are: Virginia Rowthorn and her husband, Michael Apel, and their children, Anna and Nathaniel; Perry and Hayley Zinn-Rowthorn and their children, Jackson, Beckett, and Juliette; and Chris and Hiroe Rowthorn and their children, Kieran William and Hannah Anne.

As always, my greatest thanks are reserved for my husband, Jeffery, who first discovered John Muir with me on a weekend camping trip many years ago to Yosemite National Park. By coincidence, just last week a tattered brown paper bag dropped from that trip's hiking guide with two John Muir quotations written on it: "One is constantly reminded of the infinite lavishness and fertility of nature . . . inexhaustible abundance amid what seems enormous waste. And yet when we look at any of her operations, we learn that no particle of her material is wasted or worn out. It is eternally flowing from use to use, beauty to yet higher beauty." I had scribbled those words, and on the same scrap, Jeffery had copied another Muir quotation, "I only went out for a walk and finally concluded to stay out till sundown, for I found, I was really going in."

We are still out for that walk, and I heartily thank all who have traveled with me along the way, those mentioned here and everyone else who has been part of this joyous journey.

Foreword

THIS BOOK IS INVALUABLE BECAUSE, among many other things, it reminds us what a talented writer John Muir was. In fact, his writing was in many ways his single greatest contribution. In that glorious first summer in the Sierra, he created a new grammar and vocabulary of wildness, a rhetorical engine that powered the environmental movement for a century. He is on fire with an ecstasy that still seems new and fresh to read. It is very hard for a writer to do this without slipping into sentimental mush, but Muir knew how to combine anecdote and exclamation in a way that lets you feel the sincerity of his love for this newfound world.

Muir's writing could only explode in our minds, of course, because he was doing something so new at that time. The solitary hiking adventurer is a stock figure now, but not then. And Muir pushed it at every opportunity. Consider his accounts of climbing a whipping pine tree in the middle of a giant wind storm so he could be tossed like a sailor in a mast, or of running toward an earthquake in Yosemite Valley so he could see the sparks the boulders threw out as they descended. What excited him excited others, though most would doubtless have been too scared to emulate him.

But very few explorers of that type have done the other thing that Muir did—taking on the hard work of organizing to preserve the things he loved. Think about what an accomplishment the Sierra Club was: it basically set the template for the crusading nonprofit, fighting political battles for those who simply couldn't. And think of what it produced: great heroes like David Brower, who followed in Muir's footsteps as an adventurer but also a politico. Muir may have lost Hetch Hetchy, but he set up the group that saved the Grand Canyon!

Muir was one of those rare Americans who changed the way we see the world. He helped free our minds and our bodies—he was a liberationist par excellence, and the great wheeling freedom of his words shines through to this day. Pack a rucksack, grab an apple and a copy of this book, and go find someplace suitable to read it!

Bill McKibben

AN AUTHOR, EDUCATOR, AND ENVIRONMENTALIST, Bill McKibben is the founder of the grassroots climate-change campaign **350.org** and the author of a dozen books, including *The End of Nature, Earth,* and *The Global Warming Reader.*

Introduction

NO SINGLE AMERICAN has done more to preserve our wilderness than John Muir. A self-taught botanist, inventor, glaciologist, geologist, ornithologist, and writer, Muir had already become the American wilderness's most ardent defender by 1903 when he guided President Theodore Roosevelt on a three-day camping trip in Yosemite. Roosevelt had read Muir's book, *Our National Parks,* published in 1901, and he wanted to experience the wilderness world of which John Muir wrote so eloquently. The President left behind his Secret Service agents and stepped into the wilderness with five mules, a cook, and John Muir. It was a turning point for the conservation movement: during his term of office, Roosevelt would go on to establish 148 million acres of national forest, five national parks, and twenty-three national monuments.

Until John Muir wrote about America's mountains, valleys, deserts, forests, and canyons, wilderness was commonly considered something to be conquered, tamed, used, and exploited for commercial gain. It took Muir to promote the idea that nature had meaning, beauty, and value in itself. As Muir documented his adventures in his journals and letters to friends and turned them into articles and books, the idea of wilderness and its contribution to human health and wholeness began to change.

This book, in Muir's own words with short comments by the compiler, illustrates John Muir's tremendous appeal, including his rich and luminous images of the natural world, his sense of nature's holiness beyond doctrine or creed, his passionate protest against the scourging and degradation of the environment, his belief that all creation is an interconnected web of life, and his conviction that immersion in the natural world will heal the weary, stressed, overworked urban dweller.

The Wisdom of John Muir is a compilation of more than 100 of John Muir's most evocative writings drawn from his diaries, journals, and essays. It is designed for people who love the beauty of nature and want to read about it at its best. I hope this book will touch its readers wherever they are along the continuum of knowledge of John Muir and the natural world. It may serve as an introduction for those unfamiliar with Muir but who have grown up visiting our national parks. It will offer some close readings of Muir's texts to those who have already been exposed to his thought. The casual reader can pick up *The Wisdom of John Muir* and turn to topics of interest, or read the book through from cover to cover:

Chapter 2 offers a picture of the pristine Yosemite Valley and the Sierra Nevada Mountains before they were touched by human intervention.

If it is sheer adventure you are looking for, start with Chapter 7 to learn how Muir narrowly escaped death on frigid glaciers and icy mountaintops.

Go to Chapter 9 for John Muir's fierce defense of the environment.

To renew your own desire to experience a sense of wonder in the natural world, start with Chapter 6.

To marvel at nature's overflowing, inexhaustible abundance, read any essay in Chapter 8.

Chapter 11 opens to the reader fresh views of Alaska as experienced for millennia by First Nations peoples.

Wherever you begin or however you read this book, John Muir is bound to touch your imagination, kindle your heart, and renew your own love for Earth.

THE BOOK'S 12 CHAPTERS are arranged by themes that roughly follow the sequence of events in John Muir's life. Highlights of his life introduce each of the chapters, and brief, reflective comments accompany the selections to explain or elaborate upon their particular contexts. All the section and selection titles are taken from John Muir's own words.

On his travels, John Muir's pattern was to find a campsite after 15 to 20 miles of "tramping," have his supper of black tea and hard bread, and in the campfire's glow, record in his journal his impressions of the day just passed and write letters to friends.

This accounts for the freshness and sense of immediacy and naturalness in Muir's writing. His 60 journals and voluminous letters were solely meant for his own purposes and to share with a small circle of friends. He never intended that they would be published. His friends had other ideas. So impressed were they by Muir's vivid descriptions of the mountains and lakes, flowers, and cascading waterfalls, they tried to persuade him to turn his letters into articles. Muir was resistant. Writing for friends and family was one thing, and he enjoyed it. Writing articles took a more self-conscious effort, and every time he started to write for a wider audience, Muir felt his creative energies drying up. He would laboriously weigh each word and phrase, continuously crossing out and revising again and again. But he persevered and in 1872 he published his first article.

Writing books, Muir felt, would be completely out of the question. In a Christmas day letter to a friend in 1871, he complained, "Book-making frightens me because it demands so much artificialness and retrograding. . . . Moreover, I find that though I have a few thoughts entangled in the fibers of my mind, I possess no words into which I can shape them. . . . These mountain fires that glow in one's blood are free to all, but I cannot find the chemistry that may press them unimpaired into booksellers' bricks. True, I can proclaim that moonshine is glorious, and sunshine more glorious, that winds rage, and waters roar. . . . This is about the limit of what I feel capable of doing for the public. But for my few friends I can do more because they already know the mountain harmonies and can catch the tones I gather for them, though written in a few harsh and gravelly sentences."[1]

The influential New York publisher, Robert Underwood Johnson, who had visited Muir in Yosemite, provided a breakthrough. Johnson assured him that writing books is easy! All Muir needed to do was select his best essays and arrange them in a logical order; each essay would become a chapter. Muir did just that, and his first book, *The Mountains of California*, came out in 1894. It is a gem in prose-poetry, and it almost immediately established Muir as a commanding spokesman for the earth, as a writer who described nature's wonders so vividly, that many readers wanted to see for themselves the wild beauty Muir described so eloquently.

And now, almost 100 years after John Muir's death, we need him more than ever. Our planet is in peril. There is so much despair and darkness in our world. Climate change is remaking the global village. Storms, fires, droughts, floods, tsunamis, earthquakes, blistering temperatures, Arctic chill, the extinction of species—the earth is suffering severely. The future of human life on earth is becoming uncertain. Despite the host of scientists and ecologists exhorting us to pay attention to Mother Earth, for the most part, their warnings are ignored. We wonder why.

Have we as a people lost our link with the earth? Has our advanced technological society robbed us of the feeling of real soil under our feet or of the wind at our backs on a steep mountain trail? Have we become an indoor people? Are we more comfortable ensconced in front of the computer monitor than sitting on the beach watching the setting sun splash its dazzling palate of colors across the western sky? Have we become like Paul, the fourth-grader in San Diego referred to in Richard Louv's book *Last Child in the Woods,* who plays indoors because ". . . that's where all the electrical outlets are."[2]

Richard Louv made the startling statement that this generation of children is the first to be raised inside, enticed to stay there by their indoor comforts and their huge array of alluring toys, most of them electronic. He has named the phenomenon "nature deficit disorder" which he defines as ". . . the human costs of alienation from nature, among them: diminished use of the senses, attention difficulties, and higher rates of physical and emotional illnesses."[3]

Described in another way, Wendell Berry, the naturalist, writer, and organic farmer has said, "Our children no longer learn how to read the Great Book of Nature from their own direct experience or how to interact creatively with the seasonal transformations of the planet. They seldom learn where their water comes from or where it goes. We no longer coordinate our human celebration with the great liturgy of the heavens."[4]

Living away from direct contact with nature, humankind severs the link that for millennia has kept us close to the earth. Away from regular contact with the earth, we don't know the serenity of a dense redwood forest, neither its scents nor sounds. We don't know earth's countless species and creatures. Our children are more likely to see nature's artifacts at museums of natural history than in actual nature where the deer and the antelope play. They visit the zoo to see captive animals that have been plucked from their native habitats, or they go to aquariums where whales and dolphins have been trained to follow human commands. They are more likely to see alligators wrestled at a reptile ranch than to observe an alligator swimming freely in the Florida Everglades. Children who still play out of doors typically do so in a manicured suburban yard or a city playground rather than in the woods or along a muddy brook.

Not only are children staying indoors with all its attendant perils, their parents and grandparents are inside with them. And we can see what this lifestyle is doing to us. Rates of depression are on the rise. In l933, when the Oglala Lakota writer Luther Standing Bear made his now well-known statement that ". . . Man's heart away from nature becomes hard," he could not have imagined how true his words would become.[5]

Turned away from the natural world, we are indifferent to the many ways earth is groaning and suffering. We don't empathize with the earth, and we don't feel earth's pain. As the naturalist Robert Michael Pyle wrote in the memoir of his childhood, *The Thunder Tree,* "I believe that one of the greatest causes of the ecological crisis is the state of personal alienation from nature in which many people live. We lack the widespread intimacy with the living world. . . . fewer people organize their lives around nature, or even allow it to affect them profoundly."[6]

What is urgently needed is the restoration of the connection between the human world and the world of nature, nothing short of a conversion—a turning around—to the earth so we may see earth with fresh eyes in all its extreme beauty and fragility. This is why we need John Muir, whose writings build that essential bridge between the natural world and our imaginations. Muir's passion for the natural world evokes our own passion. Dire facts of the fate of the earth won't motivate us to rebuild and restore Mother Earth. Only a passion for "wildness," to use John Muir's word, is strong enough to inspire us to protect our beloved planet. As David Toolan wrote in *At Home in the Cosmos,*

"Loyalty to the earth: that's our mantra we have been seeking. Without love of, and loyalty to the earth, there can be no justice to the earth, no ecological ethic for our time. What we require is a new and enlarged social contract—a contract with the earth."[7]

Only love, compassion, passion, and connection to the ground of our being can dispel the darkness and heal the earth and ourselves. I live in the hope that we can turn our hearts back to the earth and, like John Muir in his time, that we in ours may let the earth become our teacher.

John Muir believed that life's most essential lessons were learned in the University of the Wilderness. He was not talking about books and lectures and learned professors, not about a Harvard or a University of California, nor about Europe's ancient halls of learning, but about the universe itself as life's elemental teacher. The supreme University of the Wilderness is the universe itself, the university that is here under our feet and all around us in the soaring mountains and golden grain, in the expanse of the high prairie, from sea to shining sea, and in every drop of dew and shower of rain. The universe is the primary teacher, artist, economist, revealer of the Divine, and healer of all. It is the dandelion poking its face up through the cracked city sidewalk, the falling autumn leaf, the rhythm of the rolling tide, the burst of spring in every tree and flower. Earth's wonders are everywhere. We need only eyes to see, ears to hear, hearts to embrace, and a passion to stand up for earth's rights. As John Muir said, "Try the mountain passes. They will kill care, save you from deadly apathy, set you free, and call forth every faculty into vigorous, enthusiastic action."[8]

chapter one

Earth-Planet, Universe

Commentary

DANIEL MUIR MADE A GOOD LIVING operating a feed and grain store in Dunbar, Scotland, a fishing and farming town on the North Sea. He and his second wife, Ann Gilrye Muir, and their growing family first lived over the store, but when income permitted, they moved to a house next door. Perhaps most people would have rested content with a stable, a profitable business, and a solid family, but not John Muir's father, Daniel.

Daniel was a complex man, driven by deep religious convictions and always seeking a better path of being faithful. From his Scottish Presbyterian roots, he sought a simpler expression of the faith more in keeping with early Christian communities. When he learned that the fledgling Disciples of Christ had established centers in Wisconsin, he decided in late 1848 to emigrate. Canada, reported to have vast open prairies suitable for farming, was a possibility, but he chose Wisconsin because of the church and because there were other Scottish families in the area.

In February of 1849 Daniel Muir set off on the six-week journey with John, age 11, Sarah, age 13, and 9-year-old David. They left behind Ann and the four other Muir children until Daniel could find suitable farmland and build a homestead.

The family sailed from Glasgow to New York City and then traveled to Buffalo where they continued their journey through the Great Lakes and then by wagon to Fountain Lake, near Portage, Wisconsin. For the next eight years, Daniel and his sons chopped away the oak and hickory forest, pulled out roots and rocks, built a simple house, planted winter wheat and corn for the draught animals and vegetables for themselves. In the winter the work was bone-chilling, and in the summer they baked under the blistering sun. As John Muir wrote in the memoir of his childhood, *The Story of My Boyhood and Youth,*

"I was put to the plough at the age of twelve, when my head reached but little above the handles, and for many years I had to do the greater part of the ploughing. It was hard work for so small a boy. . . . And as I was the eldest boy, the greater part of all the other hard work of the farm quite naturally fell on me. I had to split rails for long lines of zigzag fences. . . . Making rails was hard work and required no little skill. I used to cut and split a hundred a day from our short, knotty oak timber, swinging the axe and heavy mallet, often with sore hands, from early morning to night."[1]

Whether the children were sick or well, Daniel drove them to work from dawn to dusk. Twice John almost died—once from pneumonia and once when he was overtaken by toxic fumes from a well he was digging.

Believing that the Fountain Lake farm wasn't fertile enough, Daniel bought Hickory Hill, a new half-section of land (320 acres) five miles from Fountain Lake. As John recalled, ". . .we began all over again to clear and fence and break up the fields for a new barn, doubling all the stunting, heartbreaking, chopping, grubbing, stump-digging, rail-splitting, fence-building, barn-building, house-raising. . . ."[2]

An insatiable reader, the young John Muir was constantly borrowing books from friends and neighbors, but farm work kept him from attending school in America until entering the University of Wisconsin in 1861. Always fond of "wildness," as he called natural areas, John dreamed of the planet's most distant and wild places. Not surprisingly, the books that particularly influenced him were: *Travels in the Interior Districts of Africa* (1795) by his fellow Scot, Mungo Park, and *Personal Narrative of Travels in the Equinoctial Regions of America* (1814) by the German naturalist and explorer, Alexander von Humboldt.

The Muir children's only free time was Sunday afternoon after church, Sunday School, and farm chores. Their only vacation days were Independence Day and New Year's Day, but John and his brothers made the most of it. His father had built the boys a simple plank boat for fishing and swimming in Fountain Lake. John reveled in running through the oak groves and the grass-filled meadows. He delighted in springtime's gift of wild flowers. He was particularly fond of lilies. He knew the identity of every bird, and he awaited the arrival of migratory birds that flocked to the Muir fields. His blood quickened to the haunting call announcing the loons' return to the lake. The sights, the sounds, the music, and the scents of winter unfolding into spring were intoxicating to the naturalist-in-the-making.

For more than a decade John Muir worked his father's farms. As a diversion he taught himself algebra, geometry, and trigonometry, and, using scraps from the wood pile, he concocted all manner of inventions—clocks, door latches, water wheels, an automatic horse-feeder, a barometer, a thermometer, a hygrometer, a self-setting saw mill, and, most important to John, an "early rising machine." This unique device would, at its appointed time, usually 1 a.m., tip Muir's bed on end, rousing him to read, to study, to imagine, to invent, to dream. Muir's inventions attracted the attention of his neighbors, especially William Duncan, who urged him to exhibit them at the Wisconsin State Fair in Madison in l860. Muir won the "Ingenious Whittler's Award" and met Mrs. Jeanne C. Carr, wife of University of Wisconsin's Professor Ezra Carr. It was a fortuitous encounter. Taken by Muir's intelligence and creativity, she urged him to enroll at the university. Jeanne Carr, in a role similar to that of an older sister, was to encourage and guide John Muir for many years, both at the University of Wisconsin and in the wider, outdoor "university of the wilderness" where landscapes, waters, skies, and animals of the waters, lands, and air would teach him all he would need to know about the universe. But before he could enter full-time into the "university of the wilderness," he had many hurdles to overcome and much to understand before finding his way to become, in his words, "joyful and free."

The years between 1860 and l867 were turbulent both for the nation and for John Muir personally. The North and the South had taken up arms against each other, and for Muir these were years of moral choices, decisions about which line of work to follow, and how to nourish his independent spirit while supporting himself.

The battle cry was rising. Muir's companions from neighboring farms were enlisting in the military as were his fellow students at the University of Wisconsin. Muir was not drafted, but had he been, it is hard to say how he would have responded. Aside from some hunting he did as a farm boy, Muir had never carried a gun and he could not conceive of killing another human being. Whether wearing the blue or the gray, the end result would be the same. Killing is killing; death is death. War was an unconscionable loss of life. When Congress passed the Enrollment Act of 1863, requiring all male citizens to enlist, Muir felt he couldn't join. But where would he go and what would he do? He was 25 years old; most of his brothers and sisters had married, and his parents had moved into Portage. He was uncertain about which studies to pursue in Madison. Should he fulfill his parents' dream and become a preacher? Or his own idea of becoming a doctor? Perhaps he could support himself as a country schoolteacher as he'd done for a few months in 1862. He was certain he did not want to spend his life on a farm.

All his life, beginning in early childhood, John Muir was drawn to the wild, natural world. From the seashore of the Firth of Forth and its surrounding hills to Wisconsin's lakes and forests, the natural world had been a source of wonder and refreshment. Now he needed the clarification of thought that only the wilderness could afford him. By this time he had acquired the skills of a botanist, so nothing pleased him more than the gathering and classification of plants. In 1863 he took a long tour through the Wisconsin Dells and along the Wisconsin River to the Mississippi River gathering and identifying all kinds of plant species. Still, the gathering of specimens could not constitute his life's work, and by this time the clock was ticking. He was balancing on a thin line between desire and duty without any clearly discernable direction to his life.

Though factory work was far from his first choice of employment, in light of his gifts for invention and innovation, Muir saw it as his only way forward. Consequently, he did three stints working in factories—each of them ending in disaster. His first was for an inventor he'd met at the Wisconsin State Fair. The invention was a steam-powered ice-breaking boat, and Muir was hired as the boat's mechanic at the plant in Prairie du Chien, Wisconsin. When the boat broke up on its maiden voyage on the ice-filled Mississippi, the job abruptly ended.

In 1864, Muir and his younger brother, Daniel, went to work in a Meaford, Ontario, factory making 30,000 broom handles. When a fire burned the factory to the ground, this job ended too. By this time the Civil War was winding down, and it was now safe for Muir to return to the United States. He headed to Indianapolis, at the time a thriving manufacturing city that had doubled its population during the war. He easily found employment in a factory that manufactured wagon wheels, staves, barrels, and plow handles. He was hired to increase the factory's efficiency. As the plant's productivity increased, so also did Muir's sense of ambivalence. In May he wrote to his sister Sarah, "I feel something within, some restless fires urge me on in a way very different from my real wishes, and I suppose that I am doomed to live in some sort of noisy commercial centers. Circumstances over which I have had no control almost compel me to abandon my profession of choice [living in the natural, wild world] and to take up the business of an inventor. . . ."[3] Ten months later (March 5, 1867) while Muir was working late on the assembly line, a belt snapped, grazing the cornea of his right eye. By the time he'd struggled back to his boarding house he had lost sight in both his eyes. For weeks, condemned to a darkened room, Muir hoped and prayed that his sight would return. If his blindness continued, he feared a life in the shadow-lands, merely a bystander banished to the edge of society, never taking his full part or making his contribution, forever dependent upon the charity of others.

In April, to his immense relief, his sight began returning and he started roaming the fields on the outskirts of Indianapolis. In case he had any setbacks, he wanted to gather enough flowers and sunlight, sylvan landscapes and streams to cherish for the rest of his life. As he gathered flowers and specimens, he gathered himself.

By the first of September, after finally regaining his sight during the summer at home in Wisconsin, Muir set out for his 1,000-mile walk to the Gulf of Mexico. Leaving factory and farm, he was at last walking towards his destiny. His intention was to "make and take one more grand Sabbath three years long,"[4] fulfilling a long-cherished dream of going to Cuba and South America and traveling to the sources of the Amazon to see for himself the great araucaria tree, a long-lived coniferous tree of the Southern Hemisphere. He carried only a plant press, a New Testament, a little food, and a new diary inscribed "John Muir, Earth-planet, Universe."

Muir tramped through Kentucky, over the Cumberland Mountains, and then into

Georgia, sleeping under the stars and accepting the meals and hospitality of the people he met along the way, some of them recently freed slaves.

By the time he reached Savannah, he was low in spirits and in cash. The money he'd asked his brother, David, to send from his bank account back in Wisconsin hadn't arrived. Exhausted, Muir found a resting place in the Bonaventure cemetery a few miles from town, where he could spend a few days hoping the bank draft would arrive. Nights were hot, humid, and thick with mosquitoes. As soon as his funds from home arrived, Muir set off again on his journey. But he was feeling ill. Sickening more and more as he walked and feeling feverish by the time he reached Cedar Keys on the Gulf coast of Florida, he nonetheless obtained a job at a local saw mill. When a full-blown case of what was later identified as malaria—probably contracted in the cemetery—rendered him delirious, his kindly employers took him into their home and cared for him as his health slowly returned. As he was able, Muir worked a little but again became restless and anxious to continue his travels. When a small schooner docked at the port to pick up a load of lumber for Cuba, Muir talked to the captain and obtained passage.

Muir stayed a month on the boat anchored in Havana harbor, spending every day exploring the outskirts of the city, discovering its tropical plants, grasses, and cacti. But in the aftermath of the malaria he was still weak, and the heat and humidity dampened his desire to go further south. He dreamed of cool forests and clear crystal streams. When he saw a notice advertising $40 fares from New York to California, he boarded an orange boat in Havana for New York. Arriving in February, he had to wait two weeks for a southward-bound ship. He wrote, "I felt completely lost in the vast throngs of people, the noise of the streets, the immense size of the buildings."[5] It was a relief when the steamer left for the Isthmus of Panama.

From Colón, Muir took a train through the dense jungle to Panama's west coast, where he boarded the steamer, the *Nebraska*, among a "barbarous mob" of fortune-seekers, misfits, laborers, idealists, dreamers, and families seeking a better life.

The Beginnings of Lifelong Wanderings

FROM THE START, John Muir was drawn to "wildness," as he called the natural world. Curious and imaginative by temperament, Muir couldn't resist the urge to run away to the seashore, marsh, and fields where his soul was nurtured just as his identity as a naturalist was set on course. Escaping his father's heavy-handedness wasn't easy. The elder Muir believed that his son should stay home in his house and yard and learn his lessons well (Latin, French, English, spelling, history, and geography), especially his Biblical lessons. But Muir, who never rejected his Christian faith, found it more authentically expressed in the magnificence of creation gloriously displayed in every shining lake and towering tree. Throughout his writings, Muir frequently capitalized the "N" in nature, suggesting that to Muir, Nature was synonymous with the creative force of the universe, the impulse that calls all creation and all beings—both plant and animal—into life. By capitalizing nature, Muir animated it into a person by that name, one whose mountainous face changes expressions, whose streams "sing," and even "shout."

> When I was a boy in Scotland I was fond of everything that was wild, and all my life I've been growing seaweeds, eels and crabs in the pools among the rocks when the tide was low; and best of all to watch the waves in awful storms thundering on the black headlands and craggy ruins of the old Dunbar Castle when the sea and the sky, the waves and the clouds, were mingled together as one. We never thought of playing truant, but after I was five or six years old I ran away to the seashore or the fields almost every Saturday, and every day in the school vacations except Sundays, though solemnly warned that I must play at home in the garden and back yard, lest I should learn to think bad thoughts and say bad words. All in vain. In spite of the sure sore punishments that followed like shadows, the natural inherited wildness in our blood ran true on its glorious course as invincible and unstoppable as stars. . . .
>
> My earliest recollections of the country were gained on short walks with my grandfather when I was perhaps not over three years old. On one of these walks

grandfather took me to Lord Lauderdale's gardens, where I saw figs growing against a sunny wall and tasted some of them, and got as many apples to eat as I wished. On another memorable walk in a hayfield, when we sat down to rest on one of the haycocks I heard a sharp, prickly, stinging cry, and, jumping up eagerly, called grandfather's attention to it. He said he heard only the wind, but I insisted on digging into the hay and turning it over until we discovered the source of the strange exciting sound—a mother field mouse with half a dozen naked young hanging to her teats. This to me was a wonderful discovery. . . .

Wildness was ever sounding in our ears, and Nature saw to it that besides school lessons and church lessons some of her own lessons should be learned, perhaps with a view to the time when we should be called to wander in wildness to our heart's content. Oh, the blessed enchantment of those Saturday runaways in the prime of the spring! How our young wondering eyes reveled in the sunny, breezy glory of the hills and the sky, every particle of us thrilling and tingling with the bees and glad birds and glad streams! We… were glorious, we were free—school cares and scoldings, heart thrashings and flesh thrashings alike, were forgotten in the fullness of Nature's glad wildness. These were my first excursions—the beginnings of lifelong wanderings.

—*The Story of My Boyhood and Youth*

Everything New and Pure

HERE JOHN MUIR INTRODUCES his idea of the university—the universe—as the primary teacher of life's elemental lessons. His university was not books, classrooms, examinations, common rooms, and learned professors; all these paled in comparison with the education offered by immersion in the natural world.

This sudden plash into pure wildness—baptism in Nature's warm heart—how utterly happy it made us! Nature streaming into us, wooingly teaching her wonderful glowing lessons, so unlike the dismal grammar ashes and cinders so long thrashed into us. Here without knowing it we still were at school; every wild lesson a love lesson, not whipped but charmed into us. Oh, that glorious Wisconsin wilderness! Everything new and pure in the very prime of the spring when Nature's pulses were beating highest and mysteriously keeping time with our own! Young hearts, young leaves, flowers, animals, the winds and the streams and the sparkling lake, all wildly, gladly rejoicing together!

—*The Story of My Boyhood and Youth*

Leaving for the University of the Wilderness

JOHN MUIR'S MOST ENDURING LESSONS during his university years were those gleaned from his classmate, a botanist, named Milton Griswold. Griswold introduced him to plant biology and classification, reinforcing what Muir knew intuitively—that the natural world is not a haphazard assembly of parts, but continuous, united, and harmonious links in the web of life. As Muir was to reflect later, "…I was always fond of flowers, attracted to their external beauty and purity. Now my eyes were opened to their inner beauty, all alike revealing glorious traces of the thoughts of God, and leading on and on into the infinite cosmos."

Although I was four years at the University, I did not take the regular course of studies, but instead picked out what I thought would be most useful to me, particularly chemistry, which opened a new world, and mathematics and physics, a little Greek and Latin, botany and geology. I was far from satisfied with what I had learned, and should have stayed longer. Anyhow I wandered away on a glorious botanical and geological excursion, which has lasted nearly fifty years and is not yet completed, always happy and free, poor and rich, without thought of a diploma or of making a name, urged on and on through endless, inspiring, Godful beauty.

From the top of a hill on the north side of Lake Mendota I gained a last wistful, lingering view of the beautiful University grounds and buildings where I had spent so many hungry and happy and hopeful days. There with streaming eyes I bade my blessed Alma Mater farewell. But I was only leaving one University for another, the Wisconsin University for the University of the Wilderness.

—*The Story of My Boyhood and Youth*

Joyful and Free

TRAVELING BY RAIL TO JEFFERSONVILLE, Indiana, John Muir set off on his 1,000-mile journey via "the wildest, leafiest, and least trodden way." But where was he going? His plan was to walk to Florida, board a boat to Cuba and, perhaps, like one of the heroes of his youth, Alexander von Humboldt, he might make it to South America and up to the mystifying sources of the Amazon River. Along the way Muir found shelter where he could, often outside under the stars, sometimes with white families and former slaves who generously shared their fare with him, however meager. He spent several nights in a cemetery in Savannah and even there he enjoyed the live oak trees dripping with Spanish moss. Everything he saw delighted him, even alligators and snakes. "They dwell happily in these flowery wilds, are part of God's family. . . cared for with the same species of tenderness and love as is bestowed on angels in heaven or saints on earth"

I had long been looking from the wild woods and gardens of the Northern States to those of the warm South, and at last, all draw backs overcome, I set forth on the first day of September, 1867, joyful and free, on a thousand-mile walk to the Gulf of Mexico. Crossing the Ohio at Louisville, I steered through the big city by compass without speaking a word to any one. Beyond the city I found a road running southward, and after passing a scatterment of suburban cabins and cottages I reached the green woods and spread out my pocket map to rough-hew a plan for my journey. My plan was simply to push on in a general southward direction by the wildest, leafiest, and least trodden way I could find, promising the greatest extent of virgin forest. Folding my map, I shouldered my little bag and plant press and strode away among the old Kentucky oaks, rejoicing in splendid visions of pines and palms and tropic flowers in glorious array, not, however, without a few cold shadows of loneliness, although the great oaks seemed to spread their arms in welcome.

I have seen oaks of many species in many kinds of exposure and soil, but those of Kentucky excel in grandeur all I had ever before beheld. They are broad and dense and bright green. In the leafy bowers and caves of their long branches dwell magnificent avenues of shade, and every tree seems to be blessed with a double portion of strong exulting life. Walked twenty miles, mostly on river bottom, and found shelter in a rickety tavern.

—*A Thousand-Mile Walk to the Gulf*

Life and Death in a Graveyard

JEANNE C. CARR, John Muir's close friend who encouraged him to attend the University of Wisconsin and who served as something between a valued older sister and mentor, called this reflection a "prose-poem." Such could be said for most of Muir's writings.

I gazed at this peerless avenue [of trees] as one newly arrived from another planet, without a past or a future, alive only to the presence of the most adorned and living of the tree companies I have ever beheld. Bonaventure is called a graveyard, but its accidental graves are powerless to influence the imagination in such a depth of life. The rippling of living waters, the song of birds, the cordial rejoicing of busy insects, the calm grandeur of the forest, make it rather one of the Lord's elect and favored fields of clearest light and life. Few people have considered the natural beauty of death. Let a child grow up in nature, beholding their beautiful and harmonious blendings of death and life; their joyous, inseparable unity, and Death will be sting-less indeed to him.

LETTER TO JEANNE S. CARR, SEPTEMBER–OCTOBER, 1867

Imperishable Impressions that Vibrate Our Lives

HAVING SURVIVED THE INTERMINABLE BOGS and alligator-filled swamps of interior Florida, John Muir finally reached Cedar Keys, on the Gulf of Mexico, where he experienced an epiphany. Just the sight of the shining waters and the sea breezes recalled his happy days as a boy exploring the seaside of his Scottish home. He learned what others since have noted, which is how impressions of childhood experiences of nature can remain throughout our lifetimes, nourishing and shaping our views of the natural world.

To-day I reached the sea. While I was yet many miles back in the palmy woods, I caught the scent of the salt sea breeze which, although I had so many years lived far from sea breezes, suddenly conjured up Dunbar, its rocky coast, winds and waves; and my whole childhood, that seemed to have utterly vanished in the New World, was now restored amid the Florida woods by that one breath from the sea. Forgotten were the palms and magnolias and the thousand flowers that enclosed me. I could see only dulse [a reddish-brown seaweed] and tangle, long winged gulls, the Bass Rock in the Firth of Forth, and the old castle, schools, churches, and long country rambles in search of birds' nests. I do not wonder that the weary camels coming from the scorching African deserts should be able to scent the Nile.

How imperishable are all the impressions that ever vibrate one's life! We cannot forget anything. Memories may escape the action of will, may sleep a long time, but when stirred by the right influence, though that influence be light as a shadow, they flash into full stature and life with everything in place. For nineteen years my vision was bounded by forests, but to-day, emerging from a multitude of tropical plants, I beheld the Gulf of Mexico stretching away unbounded, except by the sky. What dreams and speculative matter for thought arose as I stood on the strand, gazing out on the burnished, treeless plain!

—*A Thousand Mile Walk to the Gulf*

chapter two

The Morning of Creation

Commentary

WHEN THE NEBRASKA passed through the Golden Gates of San Francisco on March 29, 1868, John Muir had the sense that he had arrived home. Along with his fellow passenger, an Englishman named Joseph Chilwell, he set out immediately from San Francisco by foot towards the Sierra Nevada Mountains. The pair walked south, crossed the coastal mountains into the Central Valley over Pacheco Pass. At the top Muir paused. Below was the vast grass and flower-carpeted Central Valley and in the distance the majestic Sierra Nevada peaks rising on the horizon. This was Muir's first view of the Sierras and the image that would remain forever etched in his mind. As one of his biographers said, "…suddenly there was come a glorious dawning, lighting up all previous obscurities, revealing that the apparently upward paths of his life led like a map to this place."[1]

Following the Merced River, passing through Coulterville, Chilwell and Muir reached the Yosemite foothills after a month of walking. They spent the summer working at odd jobs—breaking horses, shearing sheep, and serving as farm hands.

In l869 he became chief shepherd of Patrick Delaney's flock of 2,000 sheep, and this is what Muir considers his first summer in the Sierra. Along with Carlo, a Saint Bernard dog, he and another shepherd followed the flock to green pastures high in the mountains and eventually into Yosemite and up to Tuolumne Meadows. Every day Muir explored the mountains and streams, the waterfalls and the huge variety of plants and birds. He learned to make sourdough bread that became the staple of his diet when he was tramping. He needed the job and its money; he was fond of Pat Delaney, but he was aghast at the damage done by the sheep. "Sheep, like people, are ungovernable when hungry…almost every leaf that these hoofed locusts can reach within the radius of a mile or two has been devoured. Even the bushes are stripped bare."[2] Still, his job as a shepherd enabled Muir to get into the Sierra where he wanted to be. Here he had what was, by his own reckoning, an authentic conversion to the wilderness: "Our flesh-and-bone tabernacle seems transparent as glass to the beauty about us, as if truly an inseparable part of it, thrilling with the air and trees, streams and rocks, in the waves of the sun—a part of all nature, neither old nor young, sick nor well, but immortal. Just now I can hardly conceive of any bodily condition dependent on food or breath any more than the ground or the sky. How glorious a conversion, so complete and wholesome it is. In this newness of life we seem to have been always."[3]

These Sierra years—1868–1874—were probably the happiest years of John Muir's life and easily the most productive. Working for James Hutchins, one of the first white settlers in the Yosemite Valley, Muir operated a sawmill, using only fallen trees, and he utilized his carpentry skills to improve Hutchins's rustic hotel. Having become knowledgeable about every aspect of Yosemite, its flora and fauna and its geological features, Muir was sought out as a guide. In this role he introduced a stream of visitors to the Valley, including Ralph Waldo Emerson in 1871.

From his first weeks in Yosemite, Muir wondered how the mountains and valleys had been formed. From observations throughout the terrain he became convinced that Yosemite had been shaped and molded by glacial action, slowly moving ice that carved away whole mountainsides and created the valleys and streams. This theory challenged that of the California state geologist, Josiah D. Whitney, who contended that Yosemite had been created as a result of earthquakes. Geologists later affirmed Muir's slowly moving ice theory, but the dispute with Whitney pushed Muir to learn more by exploring the "living glaciers" of Alaska, where glacial action was more evident than in the Sierra.

During these halcyon years Muir found himself and his livelihood; he found his grounding and his sense of place; he found his sense of well-being and his home. He kept diaries and journals, which he handsomely illustrated; he wrote letters to his friends and notes to himself on scraps of paper. He recorded impressions of all he was learning, sensing, feeling, seeing, hearing, and tasting. These became the sources for most of his articles and books. His first published article, "Yosemite Glaciers," appeared in the *New York Tribune* in December, 1871. By 1874 he had completed fifteen articles for the California literary magazine, *Overland Monthly*. Muir's richly embroidered writings of these Yosemite years formed the basis for *My First Summer in the Sierra* (1911), *The Mountains of California* (1894), *The Yosemite* (1912), and, to some extent, *Our National Parks* (1901).

The passion and energy of these formative six years were the point of reference of Muir's life. As he recorded in his journal one August evening during his first summer in the Sierra, "The Forests…and lakes and meadows and glad-singing streams. . . . I should like to dwell with them forever . . . a new heaven and earth every day. . . . Creation just beginning. . . ."[4]

Arriving in the Enchanting World of the Sierra Nevada

JOHN MUIR WAS TO DRAW many times on this image of his first sight of the Sierra Nevada. It was a view that shaped his thinking and sustained him all his days to come. Of his three-month walk from San Francisco to this point, Muir wrote, "I followed the Diablo foothills along the San Jose Valley to Gilroy, thence over the Diablo Mountains to the Valley of the San Joaquin by the Pacheco Pass, thence down the valley opposite the mouth of the Merced River, thence across to San Joaquin, and up into the Sierra Nevada to the mammoth trees of Mariposa and the glorious Yosemite, thence down the Merced to this place." The curtain was raised!

> The air was perfectly delicious, sweet enough for the breath of angels; every draught of it gave a separate and distinct piece of pleasure. I do not believe that Adam and Eve ever tasted better in their balmiest nook.
>
> The last of the Coast Range foothills were in near view all the way to Gilroy. Their union with the Valley is by curves and slopes of inimitable beauty, and they were robed with the greenest grass and richest light I ever beheld, and colored and shaded with millions of flowers of every hue, chiefly of purple and golden yellow;

and hundreds of crystal rills joined songs with the larks, filling all the Valley with music like a sea, making it an Eden from end to end.

The scenery, too, and all of Nature in the pass is fairly enchanting, strange and beautiful mountain ferns, low in the dark canyons and high upon the rocky, sunlit peaks, banks of blooming shrubs, and sprinklings and gatherings of flowers, precious and pure as ever enjoyed the sweets of a mountain home. And oh, what streams are there beaming, glancing, each with music of its own, singing as they go in the shadow and light, onward upon their lovely changing pathways to the sea; and hills rise over hills, and mountains over mountains, heaving, waving, swelling, in most glorious, overpowering, unreadable majesty; and when at last, stricken with faint like a crushed insect, you hope to escape from all the terrible grandeur of these mountain powers, other fountains, other oceans break forth before you, for there, in clear view, over heaps and rows of foot hills is laid a grand, smooth outspread plain, watered by a river, and another range of peaky snow-capped mountains a hundred miles in the distance. That plain is the valley of the San Joaquin, and those mountains are the great Sierra Nevadas. The valley of the San Joaquin is the floweriest piece of world I ever walked, one vast level, even flower-bed, a sheet of flowers, a smooth sea ruffled a little by the tree fringing of the river and here and there of smaller cross streams from the mountains. . . .

—LETTER TO JEANNE C. CARR, JULY 26, [1868]

A New Earth Every Day

IT WAS JOHN MUIR'S VIEW that all of nature was a revelation of a dynamic God who is continuously creating the universe. Although Muir grew far beyond his father's orthodox theology, he remained steeped in the language of the Bible, which he had memorized as a boy. "A New Heaven and a New Earth Every Day," is an echo of The Revelation to John, Chapter 21, verse 1, "Then I saw a new heaven and a new earth."

Another glorious Sierra day, warm, crisp, fragrant, clear—On the way back to our Tuolumne camp, I enjoyed the scenery if possible more than when it first came to view. Every feature already seems familiar as if I had lived here always. I never weary gazing at the wonderful Cathedral [Peak]. It has more individual character than any other rock or mountain I ever saw, excepting perhaps the Yosemite South Dome. The forests, too, seem kindly familiar, and the lakes and meadows and glad singing streams. I should like to dwell with them forever. Here with bread and water I should be content. . . . Bathed in such beauty, watching the expressions ever varying on the faces of the mountains, watching the stars, which here have a glory that the lowlander never dreams of, watching the circling seasons, listening to the songs of the waters and winds and birds, would be endless pleasure.

And what glorious cloud-lands I should see, storms and calms—a new heaven and a new earth every day, aye and new inhabitants. . . . And why should this appear extravagant? It is only common sense, a sign of health, genuine, natural, all-awake health. One would be at an endless Godful play, and what speeches and music and acting and scenery and lights!—sun, moon, stars, auroras. Creation just beginning, the morning stars "still singing together and all the [creatures] of God shouting for joy."

—JOURNAL ENTRY, JULY 27, 1868

A Window Opening into Heaven

ALL OF JOHN MUIR'S FIRST SUMMER in the Sierra was an epiphany, and during his hike to Lake Tenaya he was close to ecstasy. As he recounted, ". . . every crystal, every flower a window opening into heaven, a mirror reflecting the Creator. . . . In the midst of such beauty, pierced with its rays, one's body is all one tingling palate."

Up and away to Lake Tenaya—another big day, enough for a lifetime. The rocks, the air, everything speaking with audible voice or silent; joyful, wonderful, enchanting, banishing weariness and sense of time. No longing for anything now or hereafter as we go home into the mountain's heart. The level sunbeams are touching the fir-tops, every leaf shining with dew. Am holding an easterly course, the deep canyon of Tenaya Creek on the right hand, Mt. Hoffman on the left, and the lake straight ahead about ten miles distant, the summit of Mt. Hoffman about three thousand feet above me, Tenaya Creek four thousand feet below and separated from the shallow, irregular valley, along which most of the way lies, by smooth domes and wave-ridges. Many mossy emerald bogs, meadows, and gardens in rocky hollows to wade and saunter through—and what fine plants they give me, what joyful streams I have to cross, and how many views are displayed of the Hoffman and Cathedral Peak masonry, and what a wondrous breadth of shining granite pavement to walk over for the first time about the shores of the lake! On I sauntered in freedom complete; body without weight as far as I was aware; now wading through starry parnassia [evergreen] bogs, now through gardens shoulder deep in larkspur and lilies, grasses and rushes, shaking off showers of dew; crossing piles of crystalline moraine boulders, bright mirror pavements, and cool, cheery streams going to Yosemite; crossing bryanthus [red heather] carpets and the scoured pathways of avalanches, and thickets of snow-pressed ceanothus [a woody shrub]; then down a broad, majestic stairway into the ice-sculptured lake-basin.

The snow on the high mountains is melting fast, and the streams are singing bank-full, swaying softly through the level meadows and bogs, quivering with sun-spangles, swirling in pot-holes, resting in deep pools, leaping, shouting in wild, exulting energy over rough boulder dams, joyful, beautiful in all their forms. No Sierra landscape that I have seen holds anything truly dead or dull, or any trace of what in manufactories is called rubbish or waste; everything is perfectly clean and pure and full of divine lessons. This quick, inevitable interest attaching to everything seems marvelous until the hand of God becomes visible; then it seems reasonable that what interests Him may well interest us. When we try to pick out anything by itself, we find it hitched to everything else in the universe. One fancies a heart like our own must be beating in every crystal and cell, and we feel like stopping to speak to the plants and animals as friendly fellow-mountaineers. Nature as a poet, an enthusiastic workingman, becomes more and more visible the farther and higher we go; for the mountains are fountains—beginning places, however related to sources beyond mortal ken.

—JOURNAL ENTRY, JULY 27, 1868

The Sun's Glorious Greeting

THIS SELECTION COMES FROM John Muir's first book, *The Mountains of California*, published in 1894 when he was 56 years old. Drawn from journals he never intended to publish, the book is an extended homage to the mountains, glaciers, forests, and valleys, flora and fauna of the Sierra. Some of Muir's favorite flowers mentioned here were varieties of heather, reminiscent of the heather on the hills of his native Scotland.

How glorious a greeting the sun gives the mountains! To behold this alone is worth the pains of any excursion a thousand times over. The highest peaks burned like islands in a sea of liquid shade. Then the lower peaks and spires caught the glow, and long lances of light, streaming through many a notch and pass, fell thick on the frozen meadows. The majestic form of Ritter was full in sight, and I pushed rapidly on over rounded rock-bosses and pavements, my iron-shod shoes making a clanking sound, suddenly hushed now and then in rugs of bryanthus [red heather], and sedgy lake-margins soft as moss. Here, too, in this so-called "land of desolation," I met cassiope [mountain heather], growing in fringes among the battered rocks. Her blossoms had faded long ago, but they were still clinging with happy memories to the evergreen sprays, and still so beautiful as to thrill every fiber of one's being. Winter and summer, you may hear her voice, the low, sweet melody of her purple bells. No evangel among all the mountain plants speaks Nature's love more plainly than cassiope. Where she dwells, the redemption of the coldest solitude is complete.

The very rocks and glaciers seem to feel her presence, and become imbued with her own fountain sweetness. All things were warming and awakening. Frozen rills began to flow, the marmots came out of their nests in boulder-piles and climbed sunny rocks to bask, and the dun-headed sparrows were flitting about seeking their breakfasts. The lakes seen from every ridge-top were brilliantly rippled and spangled, shimmering like the thickets of the low Dwarf Pines. The rocks, too, seemed responsive to the vital heat—rock-crystals and snow-crystals thrilling alike. I strode on exhilarated, as if never more to feel fatigue, limbs moving of themselves, every sense unfolding like the thawing flowers, to take part in the new day harmony.

Now came the solemn, silent evening. Long, blue, spiky shadows crept out across the snow-fields, while a rosy glow, at first scarce discernible, gradually deepened and suffused every mountain-top, flushing the glaciers and the harsh crags above them. This was the alpenglow, to me one of the most impressive of all the terrestrial manifestations of God. At the touch of this divine light, the mountains seemed to kindle to a rapt, religious consciousness, and stood hushed and waiting like devout worshipers. Just before the alpenglow began to fade, two crimson clouds came streaming across the summit like wings of flame, rendering the sublime scene yet more impressive; then came darkness and the stars.

—*The Mountains of California*

Deep Summer Joy

EVERY MOMENT IS AN OPPORTUNITY to be awake to the overpowering beauty of nature.

Go where you may, you everywhere find the lawn divinely beautiful, as if Nature had fingered and adjusted every plant this very day. The floating grass panicles are scarcely felt in brushing through their midst. . . . Parting the grasses and looking

more closely you may trace the branching of their shining stems, and note the marvelous beauty of their mist of flowers, the glumes and pales exquisitely penciled,
the yellow dangling stamens, and feathery pistils. Beneath the lowest leaves you
discover a fairy realm of mosses, … their precious spore-cups poised daintily on polished shafts, curiously hooded, or open, showing the richly ornate peristomas worn
like royal crowns. Creeping liverworts are here also in abundance, and several rare
species of fungi, exceedingly small, and frail, and delicate, as if made only for beauty.
Caterpillars, black beetles, and ants roam the wilds of this lower world, making their
way through miniature groves and thickets like bears in a thick wood.

   And how rich, too, is the life of the sunny air! Every leaf and flower seems
to have its winged representative overhead. Dragon-flies shoot in vigorous zigzags
through the dancing swarms, and a rich profusion of butterflies … make a fine addition to the general show. … Humming-birds, too, are quite common here, and the
robin is always found along the margin of the stream, or out in the shallowest portions of the sod, and sometimes the grouse and mountain quail, with their broods of
precious fluffy chickens. Swallows skim the grassy lake from end to end, fly-catchers
come and go in fitful flights from the tops of dead spars, while woodpeckers swing
across from side to side in graceful festoon curves—birds, insects, and flowers all in
their own way telling a deep summer joy.

—*The Mountains of California*

In the Morning

JOHN MUIR MAY HAVE CARRIED in his mind the hymn, written in 1848, by the
Irish poet, Cecil Frances Alexander, "All Things Bright and Beautiful." Her words reso-
nant with those of John Muir, "All things bright and beautiful,/all creatures great and
small,/all things wise and wonderful: the Lord God made them all./Each little flower
that opens, /each little bird that sings,/God made their glowing colors, and made their

tiny wings./The purple-headed mountains,/the river running by, /the sunset and the morning that brightens up the sky. . . ."

> In the morning everything is joyous and bright, the delicious purple of the dawn changes softly to daffodil yellow and white; while the sunbeams pouring through the passes between the peaks give a margin of gold to each of them. Then the spires of the firs in the hollows of the middle region catch the glow, and your camp grove is filled with light. The birds begin to stir, seeking sunny branches on the edge of the meadow for sun-baths after the cold night, and looking for their breakfasts, every one of them as fresh as a lily and as charmingly arrayed. Innumerable insects begin to dance, the deer withdraw from the open glades and ridge-tops to their leafy hiding-places in the chaparral, the flowers open and straighten their petals as the dew vanishes, every pulse beats high, every life-cell rejoices, the very rocks seem to tingle with life, and God is felt brooding over everything great and small.
>
> —*The Mountains of California*

In the Cool of the Evening

BY THE TIME JOHN MUIR wrote this letter, he had been discovered as a writer, and he spent several months each year in Oakland and San Francisco writing for various journals. He felt neither comfortable nor healthy living in the city and pined for the mountains. This extract from a long letter records his joyful return. Still, he had a presentiment that the intense Yosemite phase of his life might be over, for he wrote in the same letter, "No one of the rocks seems to call me now, nor any of the distant mountains. Surely this Merced and Tuolumne chapter of my life is done."

> In the cool of evening, I caught Brownie [his mule] and cantered across to the Tuolumne; the whole way being fragrant and golden with hemizonia [sunflower-like wildflowers of the Sierra foothills]. . . . Few nights of my mountain nights have

been more eventful than that of my ride in the woods from Coulterville, when I made my reunion with the winds and pines. It was eleven o'clock when we reached Black's ranch. I was weary and soon died in sleep. How cool and vital, and re-creative was the hale young mountain air! On, higher, higher, up into the holy of holies of the woods. Pure, white, lustrous clouds overshadowed the massive congregations of silver fir and pine. We entered, and a thousand living arms were waved in solemn blessing. An affinity of mountain life. How complete is the absorption of one's life into the spirit of mountain woods!

—LETTER TO JEANNE C. CARR, SEPTEMBER, 1874

An Evening under the Stars and Moon

HERE IS AN ACCOUNT of an evening spent at the foot of Upper Yosemite Falls. Although Muir was thoroughly drenched in the spray, he was captivated by the beauty of the night, the waterfalls, and the stars.

In the afternoon I came up the mountain here with a blanket and a piece of bread to spend the night in prayer among the spouts of the fall. . . . Silver from the moon illumines this glorious creation which we term falls and has laid a magnificent double prismatic bow at its base. This tissue of the falls is delicately filmed on the outside like the substance of spent clouds, and the stars shine dimly through it. In the solid shafted body of the falls is a vast number of passing caves, black and deep, with close white convolving spray for sills and shooting comet shoots above and down their sides like lime crystals in a cave, and every atom of the magnificent being, from the thin silvery crest that does not dim the stars to the inner arrowy hardened shafts that strike onward like thunderbolts in sound and energy, all is life and spirit, every bolt and spray feels the hand of God. O the music that is blessing me now! . . . . The notes of this night's song echo in every fiber and all the grandeur of form is engraved. . . .

—LETTER TO JEANNE C. CARR, [APRIL 3, 1871]

A Picturesque Snow Storm

MUIR'S EMBROIDERED WORDS draw images in our minds of what it was like being snowbound in Yosemite.

On November 28th came one of the most picturesque snow storms I have ever seen. It was a tranquil day in Yosemite. About midday a close-grained cloud grew in the middle of the valley, blurring the sun; but rocks and trees continued to caste shadow. In a few hours the cloud-ceiling deepened and gave birth to a rank down-growth of silky streamers. These cloud-weeds were most luxuriant about the Cathedral Rocks, completely hiding all their summits. Then heavier masses, hairy outside with a dark nucleus, appeared, and foundered almost to the ground. Toward night all cloud and rock distinctions were blended out, rock after rock disappeared, El Capitan, the Domes and the Sentinel, and all the brows about Yosemite Falls were wiped out, and the whole valley was filled with equal, seamless gloom. There was no wind and every rock and tree and grass blade had a hushed, expectant air. The fullness of time arrived, and down came the big flakes in tufted companies of full grown flowers. Not jostling and rustling like autumn leaves or blossom showers of an orchard whose castaway flakes are hushed into any hollow for a grave, but they journeyed down with gestures of confident life, alighting upon predestined places on rock and leaf, like flocks of linnets or showers of summer flies. Steady, exhaust-less, innumerable. The trees, and bushes, and dead brown grass were flowered far beyond summer, bowed down in blossom and all the rocks were buried. Every peak and dome, every niche and tablet had their share of snow. And blessed are the eyes that beheld morning open the glory of that one dead storm. In vain did I search for some special separate mass of beauty on which to rest my gaze. No island ap-peared throughout the whole gulf of the beauty. The glorious crystal sediment was everywhere. From wall to wall of our beautiful temple, from meadow to sky was one finished unit of beauty, one star of equal ray, one glowing sun, weighed in the celestial balances and found perfect.

—"YOSEMITE IN WINTER," *New York Tribune*, JANUARY 1, 1872

chapter three

The Power of Beauty

Commentary

JOHN MUIR NEVER CONSIDERED HIMSELF a trail-blazer; he did not take his many talents, or his sharp intellect, very seriously. He was kind and friendly but not effusive. He was neither a hermit nor a recluse, yet he carried little more than the clothes on his back. He was generous. He had time for people, and he enjoyed their company, but he was completely at home in the forests by himself. His companions were what he called "plant people," and sometimes "plant saints," "flower people," and "animal people." He felt a relationship between himself and the birds and mammals, even lizards and insects. He observed the order and integrity of their lives and how they cared for their young.

John Muir hadn't planned the direction of his life, yet when he reached the Sierras he knew intuitively that he had found the path that was right for him. Reflecting back, he recorded in his journal, "I only went out for a walk and finally concluded to stay out till sundown, for going out, I found, was really going in."[1]

Going out and staying out day and night, season into season, through storms and sunshine, in driving rain and cold and searing heat, Muir was overpowered by the beauty and splendor of the natural world. Such grandeur, Muir reasoned, could only have been created by God, and it reflected God's bounty. Like a perfectly tranquil pond with nary a ripple touching its surface as the sun approaches the horizon in the evening just before the still of night descends when every rock, every tree, every line of hills is piercingly reflected, so the creating God of the universe is reflected. Or, as John Muir paused and noted, "How wonderful the power of . . . beauty! Gazing awe-stricken, I might have left everything for it. . . . Beauty beyond thought everywhere, beneath, above, made and being made forever."[2] Furthermore, Muir saw the world as constantly being created, its forces moving in cycles, ever rising and falling. "This grand show is eternal. It is always sunrise somewhere, the dew is never dried at once; a shower is forever falling; vapor is ever rising. Eternal sunrise, eternal sunset, eternal dawn and gloaming, on sea and continents and islands, each in its turn, as the round earth turns."[3]

Raised as a Christian, Muir never renounced his orthodox roots. Many of his writings have biblical overtones, and he even borrowed some scriptural phrases in his writings. Still, Muir's writings stress not a Trinitarian god, but God who is revealed in numberless ways. For John Muir the path to the Divine was a wide-open window; everything in nature was a source of Divine revelation. As he wrote in a letter to a friend in 1872, ". . . fresh truth [is] gathered and absorbed from pines and waters and deep singing winds. . . . Rocks and waters are words of God and so are men. We all flow from one fountain Soul. All are expressions of one Love. God does not appear, and flow out, only from narrow chinks and round bored wells here and there in favored races and places, but He flows in grand undivided currents, shoreless and boundless over creeks and forms and all kinds of civilizations and peoples and beasts, saturating all."[4]

Muir often capitalized the words nature, beauty, love, soul, and universe, just as he capitalized the word god. For him the perfect synonym for God was Beauty. Whether as seen carving the lines of the mountains with glaciers, in the star-filled night, or in crashing waterfalls, all was Beauty. He said everything in Nature, "From form to form, beauty to beauty, ever changing, never resting, all are speeding on with love's enthusiasm, singing with the stars the eternal song of creation."[5] Transformed by the power of beauty himself, John Muir wanted others to be also. "I am hopelessly and forever a mountaineer. . . . I care only to entice people to look at Nature's loveliness."[6]

Nature's Cathedral

ON THIS LATE SUMMER DAY, John Muir had hiked across the Tuolumne River, over meadows, and through heavily wooded forests to Cathedral Peak, which to him was more wondrous than the finest of Europe's Gothic cathedrals.

How often I have gazed at it [Cathedral Peak] from the tops of hills and ridges, and through openings in the forests on my many short excursions, devoutly wondering, admiring, longing! This I may say is the first time I have been at church in California, led here at last, every door graciously opened for the poor lonely worshiper. In our best times everything turns into religion, all the world seems a church and the mountains altars. And lo, here at last in front of the Cathedral [Peak] is blessed cassiope [mountain heather] ringing her thousands of sweet-toned bells, the sweetest church music I ever enjoyed. Listening, admiring, until late in the afternoon I compelled myself to hasten away. . . .

—JOURNAL ENTRY, SEPTEMBER 7, 1868

The Power of Beauty

JOHN MUIR RECORDED IN HIS JOURNAL this description of the Merced Valley during his first week of working as a sheepherder. He had no interest in pursuing sheepherding, but ". . . money was scarce and I couldn't see how a bread supply was to be kept up. While I was anxiously brooding on the bread problem, so troublesome to wanderers, and trying to believe that I might learn to live like the wild animals, gleaning nourishment here and there from seeds, berries, etc., sauntering and climbing in joyful independence of money or baggage, Mr. Delaney, a sheep-owner, for whom I had worked a few weeks, called on me, and offered to engage me to go with his shepherd and flock to the headwaters of the Merced and Tuolumne rivers—the very region I had most in mind. I was in the mood to accept work of any kind that would take me into the mountains whose treasures I had tasted last summer in the Yosemite region." Dazzled by the beauty of the Sierra Mountains, Muir said, "Gaze-stricken, I might have left everything for it." He did just that!

. . . a magnificent section of the Merced Valley at what is called Horseshoe Bend came full in sight—a glorious wilderness that seemed to be calling with a thousand songful voices. Bold, down-sweeping slopes, feathered with pines and clumps of manzanita [berry-bearing shrubs] with sunny, open spaces between them, make up most of the foreground; the middle and background present fold beyond fold of finely modeled hills and ridges rising into mountain-like masses in the distance, all covered with a shaggy growth of chaparral, mostly adenostoma [small flowering shrubs with stiff leaves], planted so marvelously close and even that it looks like soft, rich plush without a single tree or bare spot. As far as the eye can reach it extends, a heaving, swelling sea of green as regular and continuous as that produced by the heaths of Scotland. The sculpture of the landscape is as striking in its main lines as in its lavish richness of detail; a grand congregation of massive heights with the river shining between, each carved into smooth, graceful folds without leaving a single rocky angle exposed, as if the delicate fluting and ridging fashioned out of metamorphic slates had been carefully sandpapered. The whole landscape showed design, like man's noblest sculptures. How wonderful the power of its beauty! Gazing awe-stricken, I might have left everything for it. Glad, endless work would then be mine tracing the forces that have brought forth its features, its rocks and plants and animals and glorious weather. Beauty beyond thought everywhere, beneath, above, made and being made forever. I gazed and gazed and longed and admired until the dusty sheep and packs were far out of sight, made hurried notes and a sketch, though there was no need of either, for the colors and lines and expression of this divine landscape-countenance are so burned into mind and heart they surely can never grow dim.

—JOURNAL ENTRY, JUNE 5, 1869

A Peaceful Joyful Stream of Beauty

THERE IS THE SAYING OF AN UNKNOWN ZEN MASTER, "Knock on the sky and listen to the sound." John Muir knocked, listened, observed, and took into the core of his being everything that was natural and beautiful. All his senses were awake; he was enfolded in nature's grasp.

> Half cloudy, half sunny, clouds lustrous white. The tall pines crowded along the top of the Pilot Peak Ridge look like six-inch miniatures exquisitely outlined on the satiny sky. . . . And so this memorable month ends, a stream of beauty unmeasured, no more to be sectioned off by almanac arithmetic than sun-radiance or the currents of seas and rivers—a peaceful, joyful stream of beauty. Every morning, arising from the death of sleep, the happy plants and all our fellow animal creatures great and small, and even the rocks, seemed to be shouting, "Awake, awake, rejoice, rejoice, come love us and join in our song. Come! Come!" Looking back through the stillness and romantic enchanting beauty and peace of the camp grove, this June seems the greatest of all the months of my life, the most truly, divinely free, boundless like eternity, immortal. Everything in it seems equally divine—one smooth, pure, wild glow of Heaven's love, never to be blotted or blurred by anything past or to come.
>
> —JOURNAL ENTRY, JUNE 30, 1869

Opening a Thousand Windows

GOD'S FIRST REVELATION is through every aspect of the natural world—days and seasons, the sun rising and setting, rivers and ravens, mountains and plains, forests and ferns, winds and storms, stars splashed across the evening sky—everything that is and was; all creatures that walk, swim, crawl on Earth and fly in the realms above, in Muir's words are "opening a thousand windows to show us God."

> Oh, these vast, calm, measureless mountain days, inciting at once to work and rest! Days in whose light everything seems equally divine, opening a thousand windows to show us God. Nevermore, however weary, should one faint by the way who gains

the blessings of one mountain day; whatever his fate, long life, short life, stormy or calm, he is rich forever.

—JOURNAL ENTRY, JUNE 23, 1869

Enduring Beauty

AFTER DAYS OF NEAR STARVATION, Mr. Delaney, the sheep-owner, arrived at the sheep camp with provisions for the shepherds. Now with all his senses tingling, Muir records the beauty of a golden summer day in the High Sierra.

…hunger vanishes, we turn our eyes to the mountains, and tomorrow we go climb-ing cloud-ward. Never while anything is left of me shall this first camp be forgotten. It has fairly grown into me, not merely as memory pictures, but as part and parcel of mind and body alike. The deep hopper-like hollow, with its majestic trees through which all the wonderful nights the stars poured their beauty. The flowery wildness of the high steep slope toward Brown's Flat, and its bloom-fragrance descending at the close of the still days. The embowered river-reaches with their multitude of voices making melody, the stately flow and rush and glad exulting on-sweeping currents caressing the dipping sedge-leaves and bushes and mossy stones, swirl-ing in pools, dividing against little flowery islands, breaking gray and white here and there, ever rejoicing, yet with deep solemn undertones recalling the ocean— the brave little bird ever beside them, singing with sweet human tones among the waltzing foam-bells, and like a blessed evangel explaining God's love. And the Pilot Peak Ridge, its long withdrawing slopes gracefully modeled and braided, reaching from climate to climate, feathered with trees that are the kings of their race, their ranks nobly marshaled to view, spire above spire, crown above crown, waving their long, leafy arms, tossing their cones like ringing bells—blessed sun-fed mountain-eers rejoicing in their strength, every tree tuneful, a harp for the winds and the sun. The hazel and buckthorn pastures of the deer, the sun-beaten brows purple and yellow with mint and golden-rods, carpeted with chamaebatia [an aromatic evergreen shrub], humming with bees.

And the dawns and sunrises and sun downs of these mountain days—the rose light creeping higher among the stars, changing to daffodil yellow, the level beams bursting forth, streaming across the ridges, touching pine after pine, awakening and warming all the mighty host to do gladly their shining day's work. The great sun-gold noons, the alabaster cloud-mountains, the landscape beaming with consciousness like the face of a god. The sunsets, when the trees stood hushed awaiting their good-night blessings. Divine, enduring, unwastable wealth.

—JOURNAL ENTRY, JULY 7, 1869

Illilouette Falls

JOHN MUIR'S FAVORITE WATERFALL in Yosemite was none of the classic, famous falls—the Upper Yosemite, Bridal Veil, nor Vernal Fall. It was the modest and lovely Illilouette, because as he explained, it is a ". . . singular form and beauty, flashing up and dancing in large flame-shaped masses, wavering at times, then steadying, rising and falling in accord with the shifting forms of the water. . . . the color changed not at all. Nothing in clouds or flowers, on bird-wings or the lips of shells, could rival it in fineness. It was the most divinely beautiful mass of yellow light I ever beheld—one of nature's precious sights that come to us but once in a lifetime."

One of the finest things I ever saw in Yosemite or elsewhere I found on the brow of this beautiful fall [the Illilouette]. It was in the Indian summer, when the leaf colors were ripe and the great cliffs and domes were transfigured in the hazy golden air. I had wandered up the rugged talus-dammed canyon of the Illilouette, admiring the wonderful views to be had there of the great Half Dome and the Liberty Cap, the foliage of the maples, dogwoods, rubus tangles, etc., the late goldenrods and asters, and the extreme purity of the water, which in motionless pools on this stream is almost perfectly invisible. The voice of the fall was now low, and the grand flood had waned to floating gauze and thin-broidered folds of linked and arrowy lace-work. When I reached the fall, slant sun-beams were glinting across the head of it, leaving all the rest in shadow; and on the illumined brow a group of yellow spangles were playing, of singular form and beauty, flashing up and dancing in large flame-shaped masses, wavering at times, then steadying, rising and falling in accord with the shifting forms of the water. But the color changed not at all. Nothing in clouds or flowers, on bird-wings or the lips of shells, could rival it in fineness. It was the most divinely beautiful mass of yellow light I ever beheld—one of nature's precious sights that come to us but once in a lifetime.

—"THE TREASURES OF YOSEMITE," *Century Magazine*, AUGUST, 1890

A Beautiful Crystal Hill

IMAGINE IT IS A FRIGID JANUARY in snow-covered Yosemite. Muir was so taken with the beauty of the frozen falls that created a cone as ice froze around the water-flow, he scarcely noticed the bone-chilling temperatures nor considered the fragility of the ice-crater. Against his better judgment, he sought to get as close as possible to the delicate and beautiful crystal hill.

Anxious to learn what I could about the structure of this curious ice-hill, I tried to climb it, carrying an ax to cut footsteps. Before I had reached the base of it I was met by a current of spray and wind that made breathing difficult. I pushed on backward, however, and soon gained the slope of the hill, where by creeping close to the surface most of the blast was avoided. Thus I made my way nearly to the summit, halting at times to peer up through the wild whirls of spray, or to listen to the sublime thunder beneath me, the whole hill sounding as if it were a huge, bellowing, exploding drum. I hoped that by waiting until the fall was blown aslant I should be able to climb to the lip of the crater and get a view of the interior; but a suffocating blast, half air, half water, followed by the fall of an enormous mass of ice from the wall, quickly discouraged me. The whole cone was jarred by the blow, and I was afraid its side might fall in. Some fragments of the mass sped past me dangerously near; so I beat a hasty retreat, chilled and drenched, and laid myself on a sunny rock in a safe place to dry.

Throughout the winter months the spray of the upper Yosemite Fall is frozen while falling thinly exposed and is deposited around the base of the fall in the form of a hollow truncated cone, which sometimes reaches a height of five hundred feet or more, into the heart of which the whole volume of the fall descends with a tremendous roar as if pouring down the throat of a crater. In the building of this ice-cone part of the frozen spray falls directly to its place, but a considerable portion is first frozen upon the face of the cliff on both sides of the fall, and attains a thickness of a foot or more during the night. When the sun strikes this ice-coating it is expanded and cracked off in masses weighing from a few pounds to several tons, and is built into the walls of the cone; while in windy, frosty weather, when the fall is swayed from side to side, the cone is well drenched, and the loose ice-masses and dust are all firmly frozen together. The thundering, reverberating reports of the falling ice-masses are like those of heavy cannon. They usually occur at intervals of a few minutes, and are the most strikingly characteristic of the winter sounds of the valley, and constant accompaniments of the best sunshine. While this stormy building is in progress the surface of the cone is smooth and pure white, the whole presenting the appearance of a beautiful crystal hill wreathed with folds of spray which are oftentimes irised.

—"THE TREASURES OF YOSEMITE," *Century Magazine,* AUGUST, 1890

One Grand Canyon of Canyons

AFTER THE CIVIL WAR, The Gilded Age brought great economic growth to the United States, quickly transforming it into a modern industrial nation. The production of steel rose dramatically, and the nation's forests were sacked for such natural resources, such as as timber, gold, and silver. Ten million immigrants flocked across oceans to work the nation's farms, mills, and factories. In l869, John Muir's first recorded summer in the Sierra, the Pacific Railroad and the Central Pacific Railroad met at Promontory Point in Utah, where a golden spike was driven in, indicating that the nation—from East to West—was linked by 3,500 miles of iron rails and wooden ties. It now took six days to move goods from the resource-rich West to the East.

Concerned about the toll such rapid growth was taking on the nation's forests, President Grover Cleveland's Secretary of the Interior, Hoke Smith, requested the National Academy of Sciences form a forestry commission to review the status of the American forests. In l896, led by Harvard botany professor Charles Sprague Sargent, John Muir joined the prestigious group of scientists and conservationists, which included Gifford Pinchot, to survey the forests of Yellowstone, South Dakota's Black Hills, Idaho, Oregon, Washington, the Cascades, the mountains of southern California, and the southern Sierra Nevada. The trip opened up new territory to Muir, and he was particularly impressed by the Grand Canyon of the Colorado River, which he described as "one grand canyon of canyons."

The Colorado River rises in the heart of the continent on the dividing ranges and ridges between the two oceans, drains thousands of snowy mountains through narrow or spacious valleys, and thence through canyons of every color, sheer-walled and deep, all of which seem to be represented in this one grand canyon of canyons.

It is very hard to give anything like an adequate conception of its size; much more of its color, its vast wall-sculpture, the wealth of ornate architectural buildings that fill it, or, most of all, the tremendous impression it makes. . . . So tremendous a chasm would be one of the world's greatest wonders even if, like ordinary canyons cut in sedimentary rocks, it were empty and its walls were simple. But instead of being plain, the walls are so deeply and elaborately carved into all sorts of recesses—

alcoves, cirques, amphitheaters, and side canyons—that, were you to trace the rim closely around on both sides, your journey would be nearly a thousand miles long. Into all these recesses the level, continuous beds of rock in ledges and benches, with their various colors, run like broad ribbons, marvelously beautiful and effective even at a distance of ten or twelve miles. And the vast space these glorious walls inclose, instead of being empty, is crowded with gigantic architectural rock forms gorgeously colored and adorned with towers and spires like works of art.

Looking down from this level plateau, we are more impressed with a feeling of being on the top of everything than when looking from the summit of a mountain. From side to side of the vast gulf, temples, palaces, towers, and spires come soaring up in thick array half a mile or nearly a mile above their sunken, hidden bases, some to a level with our standpoint, but none higher. And in the inspiring morning light all are so fresh and rosy-looking that they seem new-born; as if, like the quick-growing crimson snowplants of the California woods, they had just sprung up, hatched by the warm, brooding, motherly weather.

—Steep Trails

Leaf Shadows

NOTHING ESCAPED JOHN MUIR'S ATTENTION. We can imagine him pausing as the hush of the day recedes and the shadows lengthen, his eyes resting upon a single rock—the delicacy of the shadows thrown on it by the oak tree, their slight movement in the gentle breeze, then swirling, dancing, jumping as the wind picks up. It is a moment in time, so ephemeral, so eternal.

Pure sunshine all day. How beautiful a rock is made by leaf shadows! Those of the live oak are particularly clear and distinct, and beyond all art in grace and delicacy, now still as if painted on stone, now gliding softly as if afraid of noise, now dancing, waltzing in swift, merry swirls, or jumping on and off sunny rocks in quick dashes like wave embroidery on seashore cliffs. How true and substantial is this shadow beauty, and with what sublime extravagance is beauty thus multiplied!

—JOURNAL ENTRY, JUNE 19, 1869

Reflections of the Creator

THE BEAUTY OF CREATION flowed through all of John Muir's senses, into his heart, and out through his hand, as every evening he recorded in his journal his impressions of the day. It was as if the Creator was silently moving Muir's hand across the page.

The myriads of flowers tingeing the mountain-top do not seem to have grown out of the dry, rough gravel of disintegration, but rather they appear as visitors, a cloud of witnesses to Nature's love in what we in our timid ignorance and unbelief call howling desert. The surface of the ground, so dull and forbidding at first sight, besides being rich in plants, shines and sparkles with [varieties of minerals and] crystals: mica, hornblende, feldspar, quartz, tourmaline. The radiance in some places is so great as to be fairly dazzling, keen lance rays of every color flashing, sparkling in glorious abundance, joining the plants in their fine, brave beauty-work—every crystal, every flower a window opening into heaven, a mirror reflecting the Creator.

From garden to garden, ridge to ridge, I drifted enchanted, now on my knees gazing into the face of a daisy, now climbing again and again among the purple and azure flowers of the hemlocks, now down into the treasuries of the snow, or gazing afar over domes and peaks, lakes and woods, and the billowy glaciated fields of the upper Tuolumne, and trying to sketch them. In the midst of such beauty, pierced with its rays, one's body is all one tingling palate. Who wouldn't be a mountaineer! Up here all the world's prizes seem nothing.

—JOURNAL ENTRY, JULY 26, 1869

chapter four

Trees of Life

Commentary

JOHN MUIR LIKED EVERYTHING about trees—their scent, their height, the sound of the wind rustling through their branches, the shade they provide in summer. He respected them for their age and resilience and for the homes they provide for birds, squirrels, and insects.

The Harvard botanist and close friend of Muir, Charles Sprague Sargent, said of him, "Few men I have known loved trees as deeply and intelligently as John Muir.... No one has studied the Sierra trees as living beings more deeply and continuously than Muir, and no one in writing about them has brought them as close to other lovers of nature."[1]

Muir was fond of the oaks of his Wisconsin childhood and the palmettos he was introduced to on his 1,000-mile walk to the Gulf. The thick forests of Japan, Siberia, and the Caucasus impressed him. Close to the end of his life, he fulfilled a long-held desire of visiting the great araucaria trees of South America and the baobabs of Africa. Still, Muir was convinced that the finest trees in the world were in the Sierra Nevada, where his favorites were the sugar pine and the giant sequoia.

Just observing trees wasn't enough for Muir; he had to get close to them, to experience them. He was a tree-hugger! In Muir's view, the best way to experience trees was to climb them, to sway in the wind with them, and to view the landscape from their heights.

Also significant during the 1880s was John Muir's family tree, which was adding a few branches. In 1874, while he was spending the winter in Oakland writing articles for the *Overland Monthly*, he met a charming friend of Jeanne and Ezra Carr, Louie Wanda Strenzel. Louie was the 27-year-old daughter of John Theophil Strenzel, a Polish immigrant physician, who owned a prosperous fruit farm in Martinez, California. Muir visited the family when he wasn't traveling and corresponded with them when he was away. He cannot be accused of making hasty decisions, for it took him another five years to propose to Louie. The couple was married on April 14, 1880 on the Strenzel farm. The wedding gift from Louie's family was their own house (they built another one on the property for themselves). John bought farmland adjoining his in-laws' farm.

Aside from short trips to Alaska, the Grand Canyon, Yellowstone, and the forests and deserts of Nevada and Utah, Muir spent a lot of time at home on the ranch between the years of 1880 and 1889. On March 25, 1881, his daughter Wanda was born; his second daughter, Helen, arrived on January 23, 1886.

Not long after John and Louie married, John took over the management of his new family's farm, and by all accounts, he was highly successful. The farm cultivated a large variety of grapes, apples, pears, plums, and oranges. Muir improved the farm's efficiency and was one of the first California fruit growers to ship his produce to Hawaii.

When John Muir left his father's Wisconsin farms, the one line of work he said he would never pursue was farming. So what had changed? We can only speculate. Muir was now a family man with a wife and children to support, and there may have been other factors that made farming different this time around. San Francisco Bay didn't have anything like the harsh Wisconsin winters, so farming was both easier and more profitable. Also by this time there was more in John Muir's life than farming. He was writing articles and developing his reputation as a mountaineer and a conservationist; he was becoming a popular lecturer around the Bay Area. He also took frequent, if shorter, journeys into the wilderness. All these gave him some relief from the farm's regular routines. John Muir was a farmer—and so much more.

Louie seems to have understood her husband's need to be away, and when he seemed burdened with farm responsibilities, she would often suggest that he refresh himself in the mountains. During his travels he wrote frequently to Louie and his daughters, and in reviewing the letters he and Louie exchanged, no trace of resentment on her part is detected. She appears to have completely accepted and even encouraged her husband's adventurous spirit.

American Forests! The Glory of the World!

IN 1889 WHEN JOHN MUIR met Enos Mills, who was influential in the establishment of Rocky Mountain National Park in l915, the two conservationists recognized each other as like-minded people. The lanky Kansan farmer's son had the same kind of rebirth in the Colorado Rockies as John Muir experienced when he first saw the Sierra. They shared a passion for preserving the natural world, and they both loved trees. Mills wrote, "The ancients told many wonderful legends concerning the tree, and claimed for it numerous extraordinary qualities. Modern experience is finding some of these legends to be almost literal truth, and increasing knowledge of the tree shows that it has many of those high qualities for which it was anciently revered. Though people no longer think of it as the Tree of Life, they are beginning to realize that the tree is what enables [us]… to live comfortably and hopefully upon this beautiful world."

> The forests of America must have been a great delight to God; for they were the best he ever planted. The whole continent was a garden, and from the beginning it seemed to be favored above all the other wild parks and gardens of the globe. To prepare the ground, it was rolled and sifted in seas with infinite loving deliberation and forethought, lifted into the light, submerged and warmed over and over again, pressed and crumpled into folds and ridges, mountains and hills, sub-soiled with heaving volcanic fires, ploughed and ground and sculptured into scenery and soil with glaciers and rivers—every feature growing and changing from beauty to beauty, higher and higher. And in the fullness of time it was planted in groves, and belts, and broad, exuberant, mantling forests, with the largest, most varied, most fruitful, and most beautiful trees in the world. Bright seas made its border with wave embroidery and icebergs; gray deserts were outspread in the middle of it, mossy tundras on the north, savannas on the south, and blooming prairies and plains; while lakes and rivers shone through all the vast forests and openings, and happy birds and beasts gave delightful animation. Everywhere, everywhere over all the

blessed continent, there were beauty, and melody, and kindly, wholesome, foodful abundance.

These forests were composed of about five hundred species of trees, all of them in some way useful, ranging in size from twenty-five feet in height and less than one foot in diameter at the ground to four hundred feet in height and more than twenty feet in diameter—lordly monarchs proclaiming the gospel of beauty like apostles. For many a century after the ice-ploughs were melted, nature fed them and dressed them every day; working like a man, a loving, devoted, painstaking gardener; fingering every leaf and flower and mossy furrowed bole; bending, trimming, modeling, balancing, painting them with the loveliest colors; bringing over them now clouds with cooling shadows and showers, now sunshine; fanning them with gentle winds and rustling their leaves; exercising them in every fiber with storms, and pruning them; loading them with flowers and fruit, loading them with snow, and ever making them more beautiful as the years rolled by. Wide-branching oak and elm in endless variety, walnut and maple, chestnut and beech, ilex and locust, touching limb to limb, spread a leafy translucent canopy along the coast of the Atlantic over the wrinkled folds and ridges of the Alleghenies—a green billowy sea in summer, golden and purple in autumn, pearly gray like a steadfast frozen mist of interlacing branches and sprays in leafless, restful winter.

To the southward stretched dark, level-topped cypresses in knobby, tangled swamps, grassy savannas in the midst of them like lakes of light, groves of gay sparkling spice-trees, magnolias and palms, glossy-leaved and blooming and shining continually.

To the northward, over Maine and the Ottawa, rose hosts of spiry, resiny evergreens—white pine and spruce, hemlock and cedar, shoulder to shoulder, laden with purple cones, their myriad needles sparkling and shimmering, covering hills and swamps, rocky headlands and domes, ever bravely aspiring and seeking the sky; the ground in their shade now snow-clad and frozen, now mossy and flowery; beaver meadows here and there, full of lilies and grass; lakes gleaming like eyes, and a silvery embroidery of rivers and creeks watering and brightening all the vast glad wilderness.

Thence westward were oak and elm, hickory and tupelo, gum and liriodendron, sassafras and ash, linden and laurel, spreading on ever wider in glorious exuberance over the great fertile basin of the Mississippi, over damp level bottoms, low dimpling hollows, and round dotting hills, embosoming sunny prairies and cheery park openings, half sunshine, half shade; while a dark wilderness of pines covered the region around the Great Lakes. Thence still westward swept the forests to right and left around grassy plains and deserts a thousand miles wide: irrepressible hosts of spruce and pine, aspen and willow, nut-pine and juniper, cactus and yucca, caring nothing for drought, extending undaunted from mountain to mountain, over mesa and desert, to join the darkening multitudes of pines that covered the high Rocky ranges and the glorious forests along the coast of the moist and balmy Pacific, where new species of pine, giant cedars and spruces, silver firs and sequoias, kings of their race, growing close together like grass in a meadow, poised their brave domes and spires in the sky three hundred feet above the ferns and the lilies that enameled the ground; towering serene through the long centuries, preaching God's forestry fresh from heaven. Here the forests reached their highest development. Hence they went wavering northward over icy Alaska, brave spruce and fir, poplar and birch, by the coasts and the rivers, to within sight of the Arctic Ocean. American forests! The glory of the world! . . . With such variety, harmony, and triumphant exuberance, even nature, it would seem, might have rested content with the forests of North America, and planted no more.

—*Our National Parks*

Pruning by Rain

WISCONSIN'S WEATHER was harsher than in Muir's native Scotland, but he loved it all—the cold, the snow, the storms, even nature's method of tree-pruning. "This sudden change of the leafless woods to glowing silver was, like the great aurora, spoken of for years, and is one of the most beautiful of the many pictures that enriches my life."

Nature has many ways of thinning and pruning and trimming her forests—light-ning-strokes, heavy snow, and storm-winds to shatter and blow down whole trees here and there or break off branches as required. The results of these methods I have observed in different forests, but only once have I seen pruning by rain. The rain froze on the trees as it fell and grew so thick and heavy that many of them lost a third or more of their branches. The view of the woods after the storm had passed and the sun shone forth was something never to be forgotten. Every twig and branch and rugged trunk was encased in pure crystal ice, and each oak and hickory and willow became a fairy crystal palace. Such dazzling brilliance, such effects of white light and irised light glowing and flashing I had never seen before, nor have I since.

—*The Story of My Boyhood and Youth*

Sugar Pines

THE SUGAR PINE, one of John Muir's favorite trees, is the largest and tallest species of pine in the world; it is second only in size to the giant sequoia. The cones of the sugar pine are the longest in the world. In favorable conditions, sugar pines may live 500–600 years.

Native Americans harvested sugar pine nuts and ate the sweet sap from the pine's trunk, which is how the tree got its name. Muir liked this sap better than maple syrup. He also called the sugar pine the "noblest pine yet discovered, surpassing all others not merely in size but also in kingly beauty and majesty." He echoes the phrase from the biblical book of Proverbs in the final line of this selection, "Her children [referring to sugar pines and their defenders] will rise up and call her blessed." (Proverbs 31:28a)

No lover of trees will ever forget his first meeting with the sugar pine. In most co-niferous trees there is a sameness of form and expression which at length becomes wearisome to most people who travel far in the woods. But the sugar pines are as free from conventional forms as any of the oaks. No two are so much alike as to hide their individuality from any observer. Every tree is appreciated as a study in itself and proclaims in no uncertain terms the surpassing grandeur of the species. The branches, mostly near the summit, are sometimes nearly forty feet long, feathered richly all around with short, leafy branchlets, and tasseled with cones a foot and a half long. And when these superb arms are outspread, radiating in every direction, an immense crown-like mass is formed which, poised on the noble shaft and filled with sunshine, is one of the grandest forest objects conceivable. But though so wild and unconventional when full-grown, the sugar pine is a remarkably regular tree in youth, a strict follower of coniferous fashions, slim, erect, tapering, symmetrical, ev-ery branch in place. At the age of fifty or sixty years this shy, fashionable form begins to give way. Special branches are thrust out away from the general outlines of the trees and bent down with cones. Henceforth it becomes more and more original and independent in style, pushes boldly aloft into the winds and sunshine, growing ever more stately and beautiful, a joy and inspiration to every beholder.

Unfortunately, the sugar pine makes excellent lumber. It is too good to live, and is already passing rapidly away before the woodman's axe. Surely out of all of the abounding forest wealth of Oregon a few specimens might be spared to the world, not as dead lumber, but as living trees. A park of moderate extent might be set apart and protected for public use forever, containing at least a few hundreds of each of these noble pines, spruces, and firs. Happy will be the men who, having the power and the love and benevolent forecast to do this, will do it. They will not be forgotten. The trees and their lovers will sing their praises, and generations yet unborn will rise up and call them blessed.

—Steep Trails

King Sequoia

THE SIZE AND AGE OF THE SEQUOIA evoked in John Muir a sense of awe that never left him. He recorded in his diary that sequoias are ". . . antediluvian monuments through which we gaze in contemplation as through windows into the deeps of primeval time."

> Behold the King of glory, King Sequoia! Behold! Behold! Seems all I can say. Some time ago I left all for Sequoia and have been and am at his feet, fasting and praying for light, for is he not the greatest light in the woods, in the world? Where are such columns of sunshine, tangible, accessible, terrestrialized? Well may I fast, not from bread, but from business, book-making, duty-going, and other trifles, and great is my reward already. . . .
>
> —LETTER TO JEANNE C. CARR, AUTUMN, 1870

The Big Tree

JOHN MUIR'S DESCRIPTION of his favorite tree, the sequoia, is without peer. Even after seeing other big trees of the world, the araucaria of South America and the baobab of Africa, he maintained that the sequoia is the "The King of the forest, the noblest of a noble race."

> The Big Tree (Sequoia gigantea) is Nature's forest masterpiece, and, so far as I know, the greatest of living things. It belongs to an ancient stock, as its remains in old rocks show, and has a strange air of other days about it, a thoroughbred look inherited from the long ago-the Auld Lang Syne of trees. Once the genus was common, and with many species flourished in the now desolate Arctic regions, in the interior of North America, and in Europe, but in long, eventful wanderings from climate to climate only two species have survived the hardships they had to encounter, the gigantea and sempervirens [coastal redwoods], the former now restricted to the

western slopes of the Sierra, the other to the Coast Mountains, and both to California, excepting a few groves of Redwood which extend into Oregon. The Pacific Coast in general is the paradise of conifers. Here nearly all of them are giants, and display a beauty and magnificence unknown elsewhere. The climate is mild, the ground never freezes, and moisture and sunshine abound all the year. Nevertheless it is not easy to account for the colossal size of the Sequoias. The largest are about three hundred feet high and thirty feet in diameter. Who of all the dwellers of the plains and prairies and fertile home forests of round-headed oak and maple, hickory and elm, ever dreamed that earth could bear such growths—trees that the familiar pines and firs seem to know nothing about, lonely, silent, serene, with a physiognomy almost godlike; and so old, thousands of them still living had already counted their years by tens of centuries when Columbus set sail from Spain and were in the vigor of youth or middle age when the star led the Chaldean sages to the infant Savior's cradle! As far as man is concerned they are the same yesterday, to-day, and forever, emblems of permanence.

No description can give any adequate idea of their singular majesty, much less their beauty. Excepting the sugar-pine, most of their neighbors with pointed tops seem to be forever shouting Excelsior, while the Big Tree, though soaring above them all, seems satisfied, its rounded head, poised lightly as a cloud, giving no impression of trying to go higher. Only in youth does it show like other conifers a heavenward yearning, keenly aspiring with a long quick-growing top. Indeed the whole tree for the first century or two, or until a hundred to a hundred and fifty feet high, is arrowhead in form, and, compared with the solemn rigidity of age, is as sensitive to the wind as a squirrel tail. The lower branches are gradually dropped as it grows older, and the upper ones thinned out until comparatively few are left. These, however, are developed to great size, divide again and again, and terminate in bossy rounded masses of leafy branchlets, while the head becomes dome-shaped. Then poised in fullness of strength and beauty, stern and solemn in mien, it glows with eager, enthusiastic life, quivering to the tip of every leaf and branch and far-reaching root, calm as a granite dome, the first to feel the touch of the rosy beams of the morning, the last to bid the sun good-night. . . .

The Big Tree keeps its youth far longer than any of its neighbors. Most silver firs are old in their second or third century, pines in their fourth or fifth, while the Big Tree growing beside them is still in the bloom of its youth, juvenile in every feature at the age of old pines, and cannot be said to attain anything like prime size and beauty before its fifteen hundredth year, or under favorable circumstances become old before its three thousandth. Many, no doubt, are much older than this. On one of the Kings River giants, thirty-five feet and eight inches in diameter exclusive of bark, I counted upwards of four thousand annual wood-rings, in which there was no trace of decay after all these centuries of mountain weather. There is no absolute limit to the existence of any tree. Their death is due to accidents, not, as of animals, to the wearing out of organs. Only the leaves die of old age, their fall is foretold in their structure; but the leaves are renewed every year and so also are the other essential organs—wood, roots, bark, buds. . . . Nothing hurts the Big Tree. I never saw one that was sick or showed the slightest sign of decay. It lives on through indefinite thousands of years until burned, blown down, undermined, or shattered by some tremendous lightning stroke. No ordinary bolt ever seriously hurts Sequoia. In all my walks I have seen only one that was thus killed outright. . . . I have seen silver firs two hundred feet high split into long peeled rails and slivers down to the roots, leaving not even a stump, the rails radiating like the spokes of a wheel from a hole in the ground where the tree stood. But the Sequoia, instead of being split and slivered, usually has forty or fifty feet of its brash knotty top smashed off in short chunks about the size of cord-wood, the beautiful rosy red ruins covering the ground in a circle a hundred feet wide or more. . . . It is a curious fact that all the very old Sequoias have lost their heads by lightning. "All things come to him who waits" [well-known English proverb later popularized by President Woodrow Wilson]. But of all living things Sequoia is perhaps the only one able to wait long enough to make sure of being struck by lightning.

Thousands of years it stands ready and waiting, offering its head to every passing cloud as if inviting its fate, praying for heaven's fire as a blessing; and when at last the old head is off, another of the same shape immediately begins to grow on. Every bud and branch seems excited, like bees that have lost their queen, and tries hard to repair the damage. Branches that for many centuries have been growing out horizontally at once turn upward and all their branchlets arrange themselves with reference to a new top of the same peculiar curve as the old one. Even the small subordinate branches halfway down the trunk do their best to push up to the top and help in this curious head-making.

The great age of these noble trees is even more wonderful than their huge size, standing bravely up, millennium in, millennium out, to all that fortune may bring them, triumphant over tempest and fire and time, fruitful and beautiful, giving food and shelter to multitudes of small fleeting creatures dependent on their bounty. . . . No other known tree approaches the Sequoia in grandeur, height and thickness being considered, and none as far as I know has looked down on so many centuries or opens such impressive and suggestive views into history. . . . Great trees and groves used to be venerated as sacred monuments and halls of council and worship.

Under the huge trees up come the small plant people, putting forth fresh leaves and blossoming in such profusion that the hills and valleys would still seem gloriously rich and glad were all the grand trees away. . . . In the midst of this glad plant work the birds are busy nesting, some singing at their work, some silent, others, especially the big pileated woodpeckers, about as noisy as backwoodsmen building their cabins. Then every bower in the groves is a bridal bower, the winds murmur softly overhead, the streams sing with the birds, while from far-off waterfalls and thunder-clouds come deep rolling organ notes.

—*Our National Parks*

Wind Storm in the Forest

LONG BEFORE ANOTHER Wisconsin conservationist, Aldo Leopold, coined the phrase "thinking like a mountain" in his book *A Sand County Almanac* (1949), John Muir climbed a tree in gale-force winter winds to help him think like a tree. He wanted to feel its sway, listen to wind rippling its leaves and bending its trunk; he wanted the view from the top and the aroma of the tree's fresh scent. Finally the storm abated and the setting sun filled the sky, and Muir offered an evening benediction, taken from the Gospel according to John 14: 27, "Peace I leave with you, my peace I give you."

> The mountain winds, like the dew and rain, sunshine and snow, are measured and bestowed with love on the forests to develop their strength and beauty. . . . The snow bends and trims the upper forests every winter, the lightning strikes a single tree here and there, while avalanches mow down thousands at a swoop as a gardener trims out a bed of flowers. But the winds go to every tree, fingering every leaf and branch and furrowed bole; not one is forgotten; the Mountain Pine towering with outstretched arms on the rugged buttresses of the icy peaks, the lowliest and most retiring tenant of the dells; they seek and find them all, caressing them tenderly, bending them in lusty exercise, stimulating their growth, plucking off a leaf or limb as required, or removing an entire tree or grove, now whispering and cooing through the branches like a sleepy child, now roaring like the ocean; the winds blessing the forests, the forests the winds, with ineffable beauty and harmony as the sure result. . . .
>
> One of the most beautiful and exhilarating storms I ever enjoyed in the Sierra occurred in December, 1874, when I happened to be exploring one of the tributary valleys of the Yuba River. The sky and the ground and the trees had been thoroughly rain-washed and were dry again. The day was intensely pure, one of those incomparable bits of California winter, warm and balmy and full of white sparkling sunshine, redolent of all the purest influences of the spring, and at the same time enlivened

with one of the most bracing wind-storms conceivable. Instead of camping out, as I usually do, I then chanced to be stopping at the house of a friend. But when the storm began to sound, I lost no time in pushing out into the woods to enjoy it.

I heard trees falling for hours at the rate of one every two or three minutes; some uprooted, partly on account of the loose, water-soaked condition of the ground; others broken straight across. . . . The force of the gale was such that the most steadfast monarch of them all rocked down to its roots with a motion plainly perceptible when one leaned against it. Nature was holding high festival, and every fiber of the most rigid giants thrilled with glad excitement.

I drifted on through the midst of this passionate music and motion, across many a glen, from ridge to ridge; often halting in the lee of a rock for shelter, or to gaze and listen. Even when the grand anthem had swelled to its highest pitch, I could distinctly hear the varying tones of individual trees—Spruce, and Fir, and Pine, and leafless Oak—and even the infinitely gentle rustle of the withered grasses at my feet. Each was expressing itself in its own way—singing its own song, and making its own peculiar gestures—manifesting a richness of variety to be found in no other forest I have yet seen.

Toward midday, after a long, tingling scramble . . . I gained the summit of the highest ridge in the neighborhood; and then it occurred to me that it would be a fine thing to climb one of the trees to obtain a wider outlook and get my ear close to the Aeolian music of its topmost needles. But under the circumstances the choice of a tree was a serious matter. One whose instep was not very strong seemed in danger of being blown down, or of being struck by others in case they should fall; another was branchless to a considerable height above the ground, and at the same time too large to be grasped with arms and legs in climbing; while others were not favorably situated for clear views. After cautiously casting about, I made choice of the tallest of a group of Douglas Spruces that were growing close together like a tuft of grass, no one of which seemed likely to fall unless all the rest fell with it. Though comparatively young, they were about 100 feet high, and their lithe, brushy tops were rocking and swirling in wild ecstasy. Being accustomed to climb trees in making botanical studies, I experienced no difficulty in reaching the top of this one, and never before did I enjoy so noble an exhilaration of motion. The slender tops fairly flapped and swished in the passionate torrent, bending and swirling backward and forward, round and round, tracing indescribable combinations of vertical and horizontal curves, while I clung with muscles firm braced, like a bobolink on a reed.

The view from here must be extremely beautiful in any weather. Now my eye roved over the piney hills and dales as over fields of waving grain, and felt the light running in ripples and broad swelling undulations across the valleys from ridge to ridge, as the shining foliage was stirred by corresponding waves of air. Oftentimes these waves of reflected light would break up suddenly into a kind of beaten foam, and again, after chasing one another in regular order, they would seem to bend forward in concentric curves, and disappear on some hillside, like sea-waves on a shelving shore. The quantity of light reflected from the bent needles was so great as to make whole groves appear as if covered with snow, while the black shadows beneath the trees greatly enhanced the effect of the silvery splendor. . . .

The sounds of the storm corresponded gloriously with this wild exuberance of light and motion. The profound bass of the naked branches and boles booming like waterfalls; the quick, tense vibrations of the pine-needles, now rising to a shrill, whistling hiss, now falling to a silky murmur; the rustling of laurel groves in the dells, and the keen metallic click of leaf on leaf—all this was heard in easy analysis when the attention was calmly bent.

The varied gestures of the multitude were seen to fine advantage, so that one could recognize the different species at a distance of several miles by this means alone, as well as by their forms and colors, and the way they reflected the light. All seemed strong and comfortable, as if really enjoying the storm, while responding to its most enthusiastic greetings. . . .

I kept my lofty perch for hours, frequently closing my eyes to enjoy the music by itself, or to feast quietly on the delicious fragrance that was streaming past.

The fragrance of the woods was less marked than that produced during warm rain, when so many balsamic buds and leaves are steeped like tea; but, from the chafing of resiny branches against each other, and the incessant attrition of myriads of needles, the gale was spiced to a very tonic degree. And besides the fragrance from these local sources there were traces of scents brought from afar. For this wind came first from the sea, rubbing against its fresh, briny waves, then distilled through the redwoods, threading rich ferny gulches, and spreading itself in broad undulating currents over many a flower-enameled ridge of the coast mountains, then across the golden plains, up the purple foot-hills, and into these piney woods with the varied incense gathered by the way.

Winds are advertisements of all they touch, however much or little we may be able to read them; telling their wanderings even by their scents alone. We all travel the milky way together, trees and men; but it never occurred to me until this storm-day, while swinging in the wind, that trees are travelers, in the ordinary sense. They make many journeys, not extensive ones, it is true; but our own little journeys, away and back again, are only little more than tree-wavings—many of them not so much.

When the storm began to abate, I dismounted and sauntered down through the calming woods. The storm-tones died away, and, turning toward the east, I beheld the countless hosts of the forests hushed and tranquil, towering above one another on the slopes of the hills like a devout audience. The setting sun filled them with amber light, and seemed to say, while they listened, "My peace I give unto you."

As I gazed on the impressive scene, all the so-called ruin of the storm was forgotten, and never before did these noble woods appear so fresh, so joyous, so immortal.

—The Mountains of California

Music of the Treetops

ROBERT UNDERWOOD JOHNSON, the associate editor of *Century Magazine*, helped Muir begin his writing career by telling him it was easy to write a book. All that was required was the stringing together of previously published articles. Muir did just that in his first book, from which this description of the silver pine comes. This essay comes from the book's longest chapter, in which the silver pine is just one of the seventeen trees profiled. It is illustrative of Muir's penetrating understanding of trees in all their phases and seasons.

I have oftentimes feasted on the beauty of these noble [silver pine] trees when they were towering in all their winter grandeur, laden with snow—one mass of bloom; in summer, too, when the brown, staminate clusters hang thick among the shimmering needles, and the big purple bursare ripening in the mellow light; but it is during cloudless wind-storms that these colossal pines are most impressively beautiful. Then they bow like willows, their leaves streaming forward all in one direction, and, when the sun shines upon them at the required angle, entire groves glow as if every leaf were burnished silver. The fall of tropic light on the royal crown of a palm is a truly glorious spectacle, the fervid sun-flood breaking upon the glossy leaves in long lance-rays, like mountain water among boulders. But to me there is something more impressive in the fall of light upon these silver pines. It seems beaten to the finest dust, and is shed off in myriads of minute sparkles that seem to come from the very heart of the trees, as if, like rain falling upon fertile soil, it had been absorbed, to reappear in flowers of light.

This species also gives forth the finest music to the wind. After listening to it in all kinds of winds, night and day, season after season, I think I could approximate to my position on the mountains by this pine-music alone. If you would catch the tones of separate needles, climb a tree. They are well tempered, and give forth no uncertain sound, each standing out, with no interference excepting during heavy gales; then you may detect the click of one needle upon another, readily distinguishable from their free, wing-like hum. . . .

The Silver Pine seems eager to shoot aloft. Even while it is drowsing in autumn sun-gold, you may still detect a skyward aspiration. But the Sugar Pine seems too unconsciously noble, and too complete in every way, to leave room for even a heavenward care.

—*The Mountains of California*

chapter five

Companions and Fellow Mortals

Commentary

LIKE MOST FARM BOYS of their era, the Muir brothers enjoyed hunting. They shot ducks, muskrats, hares, rabbits, prairie chickens, and hawks. One day John's brother, David, spotted a doe and her fawn, aimed his rifle and shot the fawn. Seeing the injured, startled creature dance about in confusion for a few seconds, then bound off through the woods, sink down on her knees and die, the boys were so traumatized they never again shot a deer, and John regretted his "thoughtless, childhood past." "Surely a better time must be drawing nigh when godlike human beings will become truly humane, and learn to put their animal fellow mortals in their hearts instead of on their backs or in their dinners."[1]

Living close to draft animals and cattle on the farm, Muir saw that they experienced a full a range of emotion, just like human beings. They delighted in their young; they showed their weariness after prolonged effort; they mourned the deaths of their fellow animals. Muir's heart was broken over the death of Nob, the family horse that John's father pushed relentlessly on a 24-mile trip on a blistering summer day. "She was the most faithful, intelligent, playful, affectionate, human-like horse I ever knew."

Animals are "fellow mortals"; each has its place on Earth, even those least appreciated by human beings, such as snakes, lizards, and ants. Muir recalls looking into the eyes of a copperhead and feeling a sense of kinship with it. He admired the industriousness of the pika, mammal of the high mountains, that neatly cuts grasses and alpine plants, dries them in the sun, and stores them for winter in rock caves. He admired the Douglas squirrel that runs gracefully through the treetops. Muir was especially fond of birds, and as a farm boy he knew every bird by its appearance and its voice. He considered the passenger pigeon a particularly handsome bird. Larger than a mourning dove but similar in appearance, passenger pigeons numbered in the hundreds of millions, perhaps the most numerous bird on the planet. Flying flocks covered a 300-mile swath of sky, darkening the land below as they passed. Every spring huge colonies nested in the Wisconsin fields of the Muir farms. John Muir surely would have been pained had he known that the the species became extinct in the year of his death. Later in the High Sierra, Muir developed an affection for the sweet-voiced water ouzel, a bird the size of a robin that flutters gracefully in the spray of water falls. Muir enjoyed watching the solitary water ouzel dive straight into rushing water to retrieve an insect and then appear to be dancing on the water pools below.

While Muir liked all animals, he maintained that the forests and mountains should only be host to indigenous animals. He saw the damage done by domestic sheep—"four-hoofed-locusts"—on the high meadows surrounding Yosemite his first summer in the Sierras and felt they therefore had no place there. Wild sheep, on the other hand, were indigenous to the area and left little scarring on the landscape.

Upon arriving in Wisconsin, the Muirs were given a cat and a dog they named Watch. Muir was especially fond of dogs. In 1869 when he worked as a sheep farmer, he was assisted by an amiable Saint Bernard, Carlo, and in 1880 he made the acquaintance of Stickeen, the brave little dog with whom Muir was trapped on a glacier as a storm threatened their lives. For years Muir told the story of this small, black dog on an Alaskan glacier. "He enlarged my life, extended its boundaries. . . . His heart beating in accord with the univeral heart of Nature."[2] Furthermore, "Any glimpse into the life of an animal quickens our own and makes it so much larger and better in every way. Those who dwell in the wilderness are sure to learn their kinship with animals and gain some sympathy with them…. Stickeen's homely clay was celestial fire, had in it a little of everything that is in man; he was a horizontal man-child, his heart beating in accord with the universal heart of Nature. He had his share of hopes, fears, joys, griefs, imagination, memory, soul as well as body—and surely a share of that immortality which cheers the best saint that ever walked. . . ."[3]

All life is created for its own good, and while life feeds on life, and all flesh-eating animals kill animals lower on the food chain, only human beings have the arrogance to assume that animals were created for them. Muir felt that it would be a more harmonious world if the human being understood what it meant to be a partner in creation. He wrote, "This star, our own good earth, made many a successful journey around the heavens ere man was made, and whole kingdoms of creatures enjoyed existence and returned to dust ere man appeared to claim them. After human beings have also played their part in Creation's plan, they too may disappear without any general burning or extraordinary commotion whatever."[4]

Humanity's Place in the Cosmos

DO ANIMALS HAVE RIGHTS? John Muir certainly thought so. Throughout all his writings he refers to animals as "people," and as "gentle fellow mortals," as in this selection. He maintained every life is for its own sake, not for usefulness to human beings, and that every being—whether plant or animal—has its unique place in the cosmos.

> The world, we are told, was made especially for man, a presumption not supported by all the facts. A numerous class of men are painfully astonished whenever they find anything, living or dead, in all God's universe, which they cannot eat or render in some way what they call useful to themselves. They have precise dogmatic insight of the intentions of the Creator, and it is hardly possible to be guilty of irreverence in speaking of their God any more than of heathen idols . . .
>
> How about those man-eating animals—lions, tigers, alligators—which smack their lips over raw man? Or about those myriads of noxious insects that destroy labor and drink his blood? . . .
>
> It never seems to occur to these far-seeing teachers that Nature's object in making animals and plants might possibly be first of all the happiness of each one of them, not the creation of all for the happiness of one. Why should man value himself as more than a small part of the one great unit of creation? And what creature of all

that the Lord has taken the pains to make is not essential to the completeness of that unit—the cosmos?

The universe would be incomplete without man; but it would also be incomplete without the smallest trans-microscopic creature that dwells beyond our conceited eyes and knowledge. From the dust of the earth, from the common elementary fund. . . . they are earth-born companions and our fellow mortals.

—A Thousand Mile Walk to the Gulf

Kinship with the Oxen Team and Cows

NOT HAVING GROWN UP in close proximity to animals in Scotland, when Muir's family moved to the Wisconsin farm, Muir learned to appreciate the individuality and character of all the farm animals, especially those with which he had the most contact, the oxen team and the newly born calves.

Coming direct from school in Scotland . . . getting acquainted with the animals about us was a never-failing source of wonder and delight. At first my father, like nearly all the backwoods settlers, bought a yoke of oxen to do the farm work, and as field after field was cleared, the number was gradually increased until we had five yoke. These wise, patient, plodding animals did all the plowing, logging, hauling, and hard work of every sort for the first four or five years, and, never having seen oxen before, we looked at them with the same eager freshness of conception as we did at the wild animals. We worked with them, sympathized with them in their rest and toil and play, and thus learned to know them far better than we should had we been only trained scientific naturalists. We soon learned that each ox and cow and calf had individual character. Old white-faced Buck, one of the second yoke of oxen we owned, was a notably sagacious fellow. He seemed to reason sometimes almost like ourselves. In the fall we fed the cattle lots of pumpkins and had to split them open so that mouthfuls could be readily broken off. But Buck never waited for us to come to his help. The others, when they were hungry and impatient, tried to break through the hard rind with their teeth, but seldom with success if the pumpkin was full grown. Buck never wasted time in this mumbling, slavering way, but crushed them with his head. He went to the pile, picked out a good one, like a boy choosing an orange or apple, rolled it down on to the open ground, deliberately kneeled in front of it, placed his broad, flat brow on top of it, brought his weight hard down and crushed it, then quietly arose and went on with his meal in comfort. Some would call this "instinct," as if so-called "blind instinct" must necessarily make an ox stand on its head to break pumpkins when its teeth got sore, or when nobody came with an axe to split them. Another fine ox showed his skill when hungry by opening all the fences that stood in his way to the corn-fields.

The humanity we found in them came partly through the expression of their eyes when tired, their tones of voice when hungry and calling for food, their patient plodding and pulling in hot weather, their long-drawn-out sighing breath when exhausted and suffering like ourselves, and their enjoyment of rest with the same grateful looks as ours. We recognized their kinship also by their yawning like ourselves when sleepy and evidently enjoying the same peculiar pleasure at the roots of their jaws; by the way they stretched themselves in the morning after a good rest; by learning languages—Scotch, English, Irish, French, Dutch—a smattering of each as required in the faithful service they so willingly, wisely rendered; by their intelligent, alert curiosity, manifested in listening to strange sounds; their love of play; the attachments they made and their mourning, long continued, when a companion was killed. . . .

We learned less from the cows, because we did not enter so far into their lives, working with them, suffering heat and cold, hunger and thirst, and almost deadly weariness with them; but none with natural charity could fail to sympathize with them in their love for their calves, and to feel that it in no way differed from the divine mother-love of a woman in thoughtful, self-sacrificing care; for they would brave every danger, giving their lives for their offspring. Nor could we fail to sympathize with their awkward, blunt-nosed baby calves, with such beautiful, wondering eyes looking out on the world and slowly getting acquainted with things, all so strange to them, and awkwardly learning to use their legs, and play and fight.

—*The Story of My Boyhood and Youth*

Reflection after the Death of Nob

THE POIGNANCY OF JOHN MUIR'S affection for Nob stretches across the years and touches our hearts. Reading this sad account of the needless death of his beloved horse, we feel Muir's pain and wonder that his father could have been so careless and heartless.

Nob was a great pet and favorite with the whole family, quickly learned playful tricks, came running when we called, seemed to know everything we said to her, and had the utmost confidence in our friendly kindness. . . .

My father was a steadfast enthusiast on religious matters, and, of course, attended almost every sort of church-meeting, especially revival meetings. They were occasionally held in summer, but mostly in winter when the sleighing was good and plenty of time available. One hot summer day father drove Nob to Portage and back, twenty-four miles over a sandy road. It was a hot, hard, sultry day's work, and she had evidently been over-driven in order to get home in time for one of these meetings. I shall never forget how tired and wilted she looked that evening when I unhitched her; how she drooped in her stall, too tired to eat or even to lie down. Next morning it was plain that her lungs were inflamed; all the dreadful symptoms were just the same as my own when I had pneumonia. Father sent for a Methodist minister, a very energetic, resourceful man, who was a blacksmith, farmer, butcher, and horse-doctor as well as minister; but all his gifts and skill were of no avail. Nob was doomed. We bathed her head and tried to get her to eat something, but she couldn't eat, and in about a couple of weeks we turned her loose to let her come around the house and see us in the weary suffering and loneliness of the shadow of death. She tried to follow us children, so long her friends and workmates and play-mates. It was awfully touching. She had several hemorrhages, and in the forenoon of her last day, after she had had one of her dreadful spells of bleeding and gasping for breath, she came to me trembling, with beseeching, heartbreaking looks, and after I had bathed her head and tried to soothe and pet her, she lay down and gasped and died. All the family gathered about her, weeping, with aching hearts. Then dust to dust.

She was the most faithful, intelligent, playful, affectionate, human-like horse I ever knew, and she won all our hearts. Of the many advantages of farm life for boys one of the greatest is the gaining a real knowledge of animals as fellow-mortals, learning to respect them and love them, and even to win some of their love. Thus godlike sympathy grows and thrives and spreads far beyond the teachings of churches and schools. . . .

—The Story of My Boyhood and Youth

A Terrible, Beautiful Reptile

SNAKES WERE ALMOST UNKNOWN to the Muir brothers in Scotland. Arriving in Wisconsin they had to learn which snakes were poisonous and which were harmless. But learn they did, and John Muir appreciated that these much maligned creatures were worthy of respect and had their own sort of beauty.

At first we were afraid of snakes, but soon learned that most of them were harmless. The only venomous species seen on our farm were the rattlesnake and the cop-perhead, one of each. . . . We discovered the copperhead when we were ploughing, and we saw and felt at the first long, fixed, half-charmed, admiring stare at him that he was an awfully dangerous fellow. Every fiber of his strong, lithe, quivering body, his burnished copper-colored head, and above all his fierce, able eyes, seemed to be overflowing full of deadly power, and bade us beware. And yet it is only fair to say that this terrible, beautiful reptile showed no disposition to hurt us until we threw clods at him and tried to head him off from a log fence into which he was trying to escape. We were barefooted and of course afraid to let him get very near, while we vainly battered him with the loose sandy clods of the freshly ploughed field to hold him back until we could get a stick. Looking us in the eyes after a moment's pause, he probably saw we were afraid, and he came right straight at us, snapping and looking terrible, drove us out of his way, and won his fight.

—*The Story of My Boyhood and Youth*

Lament for the Passenger Pigeon

PASSENGER PIGEONS, once exceedingly plentiful, were used as cheap food by slaves and European immigrants and as bait by fishermen. These beautiful, graceful birds were entirely extinct by 1914, the year of John Muir's death. On September 1, 1914, Martha, the last known passenger pigeon, died in the Cincinnati Zoo.

It was a great memorable day when the first flock of passenger pigeons came to our farm, calling to mind the story we had read about them when we were at school in Scotland. Of all God's feathered people that sailed the Wisconsin sky, no other bird seemed to us so wonderful. The beautiful wanderers flew like the winds in flocks of millions from climate to climate in accord with the weather, finding their food—acorns, beechnuts, pine-nuts, cranberries, strawberries, huckleberries, juniper berries, hackberries, buckwheat, rice, wheat, oats, corn—in fields and forests thousands of miles apart. I have seen flocks streaming south in the fall so large that they were flowing over from horizon to horizon in an almost continuous stream all day long, at the rate of forty or fifty miles an hour, like a mighty river in the sky, widening, contracting, descending like falls and cataracts, and rising suddenly here and there in huge ragged masses like high-plashing spray. How wonderful the distances they flew in a day—in a year—in a lifetime! They arrived in Wisconsin in the spring just after the sun had cleared away the snow, and alighted in the woods to feed on the fallen acorns that they had missed the previous autumn. A comparatively small flock swept thousands of acres perfectly clean of acorns in a few minutes, by moving straight ahead with a broad front. All got their share, for the rear constantly became the van by flying over the flock and alighting in front, the entire flock constantly changing from rear to front, revolving something like a wheel with a low buzzing wing roar that could be heard a long way off. In summer they feasted on wheat and oats and were easily approached as they rested on the trees along the sides of the field after a good full meal, displaying beautiful iridescent colors as they moved their necks backward and forward when we went very near them. The breast of the male is a fine rosy red, the lower part of the neck behind and along the sides changing from the red of the breast to gold, emerald green and rich crimson. The general color of the upper parts is grayish blue, the under parts white. The extreme length of the bird is about seventeen inches; the finely modeled slender tail about eight inches, and extent of wings twenty-four inches. The females are scarcely less beautiful.

—*The Story of My Boyhood and Youth*

The Bravest of all Sierra Mountaineers

HAVING SPENT HIS FIRST SUMMER in the Sierra working as a shepherd and noticing the tremendous damage they made to the vegetation of Tuolumne Meadows, John Muir had nothing good to say about the "four-hoofed locusts." By comparison with wild sheep, "The domestic sheep, in a general way, is expressionless, like a dull bundle of something only half alive, while the wild is as elegant and graceful as a deer, every movement manifesting admirable strength and character. The tame is timid; the wild is bold. The tame is always more or less ruffled and dirty; while the wild is as smooth and clean as the flowers of his mountain pastures."

The wild sheep ranks highest among the animal mountaineers of the Sierra. Possessed of keen sight and scent, and strong limbs, he dwells secure amid the loftiest summits, leaping unscathed from crag to crag, up and down the fronts of giddy precipices, crossing foaming torrents and slopes of frozen snow, exposed to the wildest storms, yet maintaining a brave, warm life, and developing from generation to generation in perfect strength and beauty. . . .

Compared with the best-known domestic breeds, we find that our wild species is much larger, and, instead of an all-wool garment, wears a thick overcoat of hair like that of the deer, and an undercovering of fine wool. The hair, though rather coarse, is comfortably soft and spongy, and lies smooth, as if carefully tended with comb and brush. The predominant color during most of the year is brownish-gray, varying to bluish-gray in the autumn; the belly and a large, conspicuous patch on the buttocks are white; and the tail, which is very short, like that of a deer, is black, with a yellowish border. The wool is white, and grows in beautiful spirals down out of sight among the shining hair, like delicate climbing vines among stalks of corn. . . .

Their resting-places seem to be chosen with reference to sunshine and a wide outlook, and most of all to safety. Their feeding-grounds are among the most beautiful of the wild gardens, bright with daisies and gentians and mats of purple bryanthus, lying hidden away on rocky headlands and canyon sides, where sunshine is abundant, or down in the shady glacier valleys, along the banks of the streams and lakes, where the plushy sod is greenest. Here they feast all summer, the happy wanderers, perhaps relishing the beauty as well as the taste of the lovely flora on which they feed.

When the winter storms set in, loading their highland pastures with snow, then, like the birds they gather and go to lower climates, usually descending the eastern flank of the range to the rough, volcanic table-lands and treeless ranges of the Great Basin adjacent to the Sierra. They never make haste, however, and seem to have no dread of storms, many of the strongest only going down leisurely to bare, wind-swept ridges, to feed on bushes and dry bunch-grass, and then returning up into the snow.

Man is the most dangerous enemy of all, but even from him our brave mountain-dweller has little to fear in the remote solitudes of the High Sierra. . . . And when we consider here how rapidly entire species of noble animals, such as the elk, moose, and buffalo, are being pushed to the very verge of extinction, all lovers of wildness will rejoice with me in the rocky security of Ovis montana, the bravest of all the Sierra mountaineers.

—*The Mountains of California*

Our Sympathy is Widened

THE DAY MUIR HIKED to Mt. Hoffman, the highest peak he had yet reached in the Sierra, his senses were tingling. As his eyes surveyed the 360-degree view, Muir wrote, "What glorious landscapes are about me, new plants, new animals, new crystals, and multitudes of new mountains far higher than Hoffman, towering in glorious array along the axis of the range, serene, majestic, snow-laden, sundrenched, vast domes and ridges shining below them, forests, lakes, and meadows in the hollows, the pure blue bell-flower sky brooding them all—a glory day of admission into a new realm of wonders as if Nature had wooingly whispered, "Come higher." On this wondrous day Muir discovered the industrious high-altitude mammal, the pika.

I caught sight, for the first time, of the curious pika, or little chief hare, that cuts large quantities of lupines and other plants and lays them out to dry in the sun for hay, which it stores in underground barns to last through the long, snowy winter. Coming upon these plants freshly cut and lying in handfuls here and there on the rocks has a startling effect of busy life on the lonely mountain-top. These little haymakers, endowed with brain stuff something like our own—God up here looking after them—what lessons they teach, how they widen our sympathy!

—JOURNAL ENTRY, JULY 26, 1869

The Sure-Footed, Fearless Chipmunk

THE SIERRA CHIPMUNK was reminiscent of a smaller member of the species John Muir first admired in the oak openings of the Wisconsin farm of his boyhood. Chipmunks are, ". . . exceedingly interesting little fellows, full of odd, funny ways, and without being true squirrels, have most of their accomplishments without their aggressive quarrelsomeness. I never weary watching them as they frisk about in the bushes gathering seeds and berries."

The cheery little chipmunk. . . . I never weary watching as they frisk about in the bushes gathering seeds and berries, like song sparrows poising daintily on slender twigs, and making even less stir than most birds of the same size. Few of the Sierra animals interest me more; they are so able, gentle, confiding, and beautiful, they take one's heart, and get themselves adopted as darlings. Though weighing hardly more than field mice, they are laborious collectors of seeds, nuts, and cones, and are therefore well fed, but never in the least swollen with fat or lazily full. On the contrary, of their frisky, birdlike liveliness there is no end. They have a great variety of notes corresponding with their movements, some sweet and liquid like water dripping with tinkling sounds into pools. They seem dearly to love teasing a dog, coming frequently almost within reach, then frisking away with lively chipping, like sparrows, beating time to their music with their tails, which at each chip describe half circles from side to side. Not even the Douglas squirrel is surer-footed or more fearless. I have seen them running about on sheer precipices of the Yosemite walls seemingly holding on with as little effort as flies, and as unconscious of danger, where, if the slightest slip were made, they would have fallen two or three thousand feet. How fine it would be could we mountaineers climb these tremendous cliffs with the same sure grip!

—JOURNAL ENTRY, JULY 31, 1869

Deer—The Very Poetry of Manners and Motion

THE MANY SPECIES OF DEER inhabit every continent except Antarctica. Beautiful and graceful, to John Muir, deer represented the "very poetry of manners and motion."

A fine blacktailed deer went bounding past camp this morning. A buck with wide spread of antlers, showing admirable vigor and grace. Wonderful the beauty, strength, and graceful movements of animals in wildernesses, cared for by Nature only. . . . Deer, like all wild animals, are as clean as plants. The beauties of their gestures and attitudes, alert or in repose, surprise yet more than their bounding exuberant strength. Every movement and posture is graceful, the very poetry of manners and motion. Mother Nature is too often spoken of as in reality no mother at all. Yet how wisely, sternly, tenderly she loves and looks after her children in all sorts of weather and wildernesses. The more I see of deer the more I admire them as mountaineers. They make their way into the heart of the roughest solitudes with smooth reserve of strength, through dense belts of brush and forest encumbered with fallen trees and boulder piles, across canyons, roaring streams, and snow-fields, ever showing forth beauty and courage.

Over nearly all the continent the deer find homes. In the Florida savannas [tropical grasslands] and hummocks [rounded knolls], in the Canada woods, in the far north, roaming over mossy tundras, swimming lakes and rivers and arms of the sea from island to island washed with waves, or climbing rocky mountains, everywhere healthy and able, adding beauty to every landscape—a truly admirable creature. . . .

—JOURNAL ENTRY, JULY 22, 1869

Master-Spirit of the Treetop

WHIMSICALLY, JOHN MUIR heads this letter to Jeanne C. Carr, "Squirrelville, Sequoia County," and in place of a date (probably sometime in the fall of 1870), he wrote, "Nut-Time." He respected the plucky little Douglas squirrel for its intelligence, hardiness, and the fact that it ate the sap of the mighty sequoia tree. Muir wrote this letter just before turning in to his open-air bed of pine boughs under the stars.

> There goes Squirrel Douglas, the master-spirit of the tree-top. It has just occurred to me how his belly is buffy brown and his back silver gray. Ever since the first Adam of his race saw trees and burrs, his belly has been rubbing upon buff bark, and his back has been combed with silver needles. Would that some of you wise— terribly wise—social scientists might discover some method of living as true to nature as the buff people of the woods, running free as the winds and waters among the burrs and filbert thickets of these leafy, motherly woods.
>
> The sun is set and the star candles are being lighted to show me and Douglas squirrel to bed.
>
> —LETTER TO JEANNE C. CARR, AUTUMN, 1870

Look into Nature's Warm Heart

THE WATER OUZEL, also known as the American dipper, likes a habitat of cold, rocky, fast-moving streams. So that it can dip, this remarkable bird is equipped with an extra eyelid, allowing it to see underwater, and scales that cover its nostrils when submerged;

thus it can complement its usual diet of insects with small fish and tadpoles. John Muir took the time to observe all the graceful motions of the water ouzel and to listen to its lilting song. It was to him, ". . . a window[to] look into Nature's warm heart."

> The water ouzel, in his rocky home amid foaming waters . . . of all the singers I like him the best. He is a plainly dressed little bird, about the size of a robin, with short, crisp, but rather broad wings, and a tail of moderate length, slanted up, giving him, with his nodding, bobbing manners, a wrennish look. He is usually seen fluttering about in the spray of falls and the rapid cascading portions of the main branches of the rivers. These are his favorite haunts; but he is often seen also on comparatively level reaches and occasionally on the shores of mountain lakes, especially at the beginning of winter, when heavy snowfalls have blurred the streams with sludge. Though not a water-bird in structure, he gets his living in the water, and is never seen away from the immediate margin of streams. He dives fearlessly into rough, boiling eddies and rapids to feed at the bottom, flying under water seemingly as easily as in the air. Sometimes he wades in shallow places, thrusting his head under from time to time in a nodding, frisky way that is sure to attract attention. His flight is a solid whir of wing-beats like that of a partridge, and in going from place to place along his favorite string of rapids he follows the windings of the stream, and usually alights on some rock or snag on the bank or out in the current, or rarely on the dry limb of an overhanging tree, perching like a tree bird when it suits his convenience. He has the oddest, neatest manners imaginable, and all his gestures as he flits about in the wild, dashing waters bespeak the utmost cheerfulness and confidence. He sings both winter and summer, in all sorts of weather—a sweet, fluty melody, rather low, and much less keen and accentuated than from the brisk vigor of his movements one would be led to expect.
>
> How romantic and beautiful is the life of this brave little singer on the wild mountain streams, building his round bossy nest of moss by the side of a rapid or fall, where it is sprinkled and kept fresh and green by the spray! No wonder he sings

well, since all the air about him is music; every breath he draws is part of a song, and he gets his first music lessons before he is born; for the eggs vibrate in time with the tones of the waterfalls. Bird and stream are inseparable, songful and wild, gentle and strong—the bird ever in danger in the midst of the stream's mad whirlpools, yet seemingly immortal. And so I might go on, writing words, words, words; but to what purpose? Go see him and love him, and through him as through a window look into Nature's warm heart.

—*Our National Parks*

chapter six

Renew Yourself in Nature

Commentary

IN 1871 WHEN RALPH WALDO EMERSON visited Yosemite, John Muir was convinced that if he could only persuade the elderly Transcendentalist to leave his park hotel
and his party of traveling companions in order to spend a few nights sleeping under the
stars, breathing in the fresh, pure mountain air, his health would improve and his spirits
be revived. Emerson's protective companions said that it would never do for Emerson
to lie out in the open air. Muir countered that it is hotels, dust, and the stale air of the
indoors that causes the spread of viruses, "not the pure night air under the clear starry
night." But, he noted, "His party, full of indoor philosophy, failed to see the natural
beauty and fullness of promise of my wild plans."[1]

From his own experience, John Muir understood the natural world as the great
healer of mind, body, and soul. Tired, stressed, and claustrophobic after months in San
Francisco and Oakland writing his first articles for the *Overland Monthly*, John Muir longed
to be outside again. He had eaten an irregular diet of restaurant food, and his health
was beginning to suffer; by his own description, he was "shrunken and lean." It was late
summer in 1874; the hard city pavement and the urban air were tiring him. He glimpsed
a tender branch of goldenrod struggling for life as it pushed its way through a crack in
the pavement. It was struggling to be free and to breath fresh sweet air, and so was he!
Muir left the city and headed for Coulterville, where he got his mule, Brownie, and made
his way up to the mountains "where I made my reunion with the winds and pines. It was
eleven o'clock when we reached Black's ranch. I was weary and soon died in sleep. How
cool and vital and recreative was the hale young mountain air. On higher, higher up into
the holy of holies of the woods! Pure white lustrous clouds overshadowed the massive
congregations of silver fir and pine. We entered, and a thousand living arms were waved

in solemn blessing. An infinity of mountain life. How complete is the absorption of one's life into the spirit of mountain woods. No one can love or hate an enemy here, for no one can conceive of such a creature as an enemy."[2]

As America moved rapidly from an agrarian to a modern, industrial economy and people flocked to cities to earn their livelihoods in factories, escaping, even for short periods, to the mountains and forests was, in Muir's view, essential. The journal articles he wrote between 1871 and 1874 attempted to coax the overworked, overstressed urban worker to get out to experience nature's therapy. It's free, it's open to all. Getting into the wilderness, they would find their true inner homeland and quiet their souls. When these articles were collected into Muir's book *Our National Parks* in 1901, the first paragraph of the book opened with, "The tendency nowadays to wander in wildernesses is delightful to see. Thousands of tired, nerve-shaken, over-civilized people are beginning to find out that going to the mountains is going home; that wildness is a necessity; and that mountain parks and reservations are useful not only as fountains of timber and irrigating rivers, but as fountains of life. Awakening from the stupefying effects of the vice of over-industry and the deadly apathy of luxury, they are trying as best they can to mix and enrich their own little ongoings with those of Nature, and to get rid of rust and disease. Briskly venturing and roaming, some are washing off sins and cobweb cares of the devil's spinning in all-day storms on mountains; sauntering in resiny pinewoods or in gentian meadows, brushing through chaparral, bending down and parting sweet, flowery sprays; tracing rivers to their sources, getting in touch with the nerves of Mother Earth."

But many Americans had left their farms and were grateful to be living in cities and there were city dwellers who had never left their concrete streets and sidewalks. Some were fearful about the thought of being in the wild and sleeping outside in the elements. It took John Muir quite a bit of convincing to get them outside, but he believed their health and wellbeing depended upon it. "No need to worry about bears," he assured them. "Bears are peaceful people and mind their own business. Poor fellows, they have been poisoned, trapped, and shot at until they have lost confidence in brother man, and it is not easy to make their acquaintance."[3] Furthermore, he continued, "No

American wilderness that I know of is so dangerous as a city home . . . one should go to the woods for safety, if for nothing else."[4]

Finally, Muir offered some advice for the society-sick traveler, "If you are traveling for health, play truant to doctors and friends, fill your pocket with biscuits, and hide in the hills, lave in its [Merced River] waters, tan in its gold, bask in its flower-shine, and your baptisms will make you a new creature indeed. Or, choked in the sediments of society, so tired of the world, here will your hard doubts disappear, your carnal incrustations melt off, and your soul breathe deep and free in God's shoreless atmosphere of beauty and love."[5]

Nature is a Good Mother

"NATURE IS A GOOD MOTHER," comes from a well-known essay entitled, "Wild Wool," first published as an article in the *Overland Monthly* in 1875. It is a statement of Muir's conviction that the regular, untrammeled forces of nature are sufficient to provide for all her creatures—feathers for birds, hard shells for beetles, fur for bears, and that each creature is perfectly clothed for its niche in the environment. Even the squirrel, he says, wears socks and mittens and carries a broad furry tail to use as a blanket. Using the example of sheep, Muir says that wild sheep, unlike their domestic cousins, have a thick undercoat that repels snow and rain. The purpose of the essay is to counter what Muir contended was ". . . the barbarous notion [that] is almost universally entertained by civilized man, that there is in all the manufactures of Nature something essentially coarse which can and must be eradicated by human culture." To sum up: Nature knows best!

> Nature is a good mother, and sees well to the clothing of her many bairns [children]—birds with smoothly impreceted feathers, beetles with shining jackets, and bears with shaggy furs. In the tropical south, where the sun warms like a fire, they are allowed to go thinly clad; but in the snowy northland she takes care to clothe warmly. The squirrel has socks and mittens, and a tail broad enough for a

blanket; the grouse is densely feathered down to the ends of his toes; and the wild sheep, besides his undergarment of fine wool, has a thick overcoat of hair that sheds off both the snow and the rain. Other provisions and adaptations in the dresses of animals, relating less to climate than to the more mechanical circumstances of life, are made with the same consummate skill that characterizes all the love work of Nature. Land, water, and air, jagged rocks, muddy ground, sand beds, forests, underbrush, grassy plains, etc., are considered in all their possible combinations while the clothing of her beautiful wildlings is preparing. No matter what the circumstances of their lives may be, she never allows them to go dirty or ragged. The mole, living always in the dark and in the dirt, is yet as clean as the otter or the wave-washed seal; and our wild sheep, wading in snow, roaming through bushes, and leaping among jagged storm-beaten cliffs, wears a dress so exquisitely adapted to its mountain life that it is always found as unruffled and stainless as a bird.

—Steep Trails

We Dream of Bread

JOHN MUIR AND HIS SHEEPHERDING PARTNER were hungry. Pat Delaney, their boss, was many days late in delivering camp provisions of flour, beans, bacon, dried peaches, potatoes, molasses, sugar, potatoes, and onions. When the flour for making sourdough bread was gone and Mr. Delaney still hadn't arrived, Muir wrote this reflection on the eating habits of Native people, wishing that, like them, he could be more self-sufficient, eating from food sources naturally available. This is part of one of Muir's best-known essays, entitled "Bread Famine," which also contains his recipe for California sourdough bread which, along with tea, was Muir's dietary stable.

Rather weak and sickish this morning, and all about a piece of bread. Can scarce command attention to my best studies, as if one couldn't take a few days' saunter in the Godful woods without maintaining a base on a wheat-field and grist-mill.

Like caged parrots we want a cracker, any of the hundred kinds—the remainder biscuit of a voyage around the world would answer well enough, nor would the wholesomeness of saleratus biscuit be questioned. Bread without flesh is a good diet, as on many botanical excursions I have proved. Tea also may easily be ignored. Just bread and water and delightful toil is all I need—not unreasonably much, yet one ought to be trained and tempered to enjoy life in these brave wilds in full independence of any particular kind of nourishment. That this may be accomplished is manifest, as far as bodily welfare is concerned, in the lives of people of other climes. The Eskimo, for example, gets a living far north of the wheat line, from oily seals and whales. Meat, berries, bitter weeds, and blubber, or only the last, for months at a time; and yet these people all around the frozen shores of our continent are said to be hearty, jolly, stout, and brave. We hear, too, of fish-eaters, carnivorous as spiders, yet well enough as far as stomachs are concerned, while we are so ridiculously helpless, making wry faces over our fare, looking sheepish in digestive distress amid rumbling, grumbling sounds that might well pass for smothered baas. We have a large supply of sugar, and this evening it occurred to me that these belligerent stomachs might possibly, like complaining children, be coaxed with candy. Accordingly the frying-pan was cleansed, and a lot of sugar cooked in it to a sort of wax, but this stuff only made matters worse.

. . . . Our stomachs, like tired muscles, are sore with long squirming. Once I was very hungry in the Bonaventure graveyard near Savannah, Georgia, having fasted for several days; then the empty stomach seemed to chafe in much the same way as now, and a somewhat similar tenderness and aching was produced, hard to bear, though the pain was not acute. We dream of bread, a sure sign we need it. Like the Indians, we ought to know how to get the starch out of fern and saxifrage stalks, lily bulbs, pine bark, etc. Our education has been sadly neglected for many generations. Wild rice would be good. I noticed a leersia [a course grass] in wet meadow edges, but the seeds are small. Acorns are not ripe, nor pine nuts, nor filberts. The inner bark of pine or spruce might be tried. Drank tea until half intoxicated. Man seems to crave a stimulant when anything extraordinary is going on, and this is the only one I use.

—JOURNAL ENTRY, JULY 7, 1869

The Influences of Pure Nature

JOHN MUIR WAS ATTRACTED to the rich variety of life found in Yosemite's matchless glacial meadows. No cultivated garden can compare, nor have the healing power of a glacial meadow. Muir described glacial meadows as ". . . smooth, level, silky lawns, lying embedded in the upper forests, on the floors of the valleys. . . . They are nearly as level as the lakes whose places they have taken, and present a dry, even surface free from rock-heaps, mossy bogginess, and the frowsy roughness of rank, coarse-leaved, weedy, and shrubby vegetation. The sod is close and fine, and so complete that you cannot see the ground; and at the same time so brightly enameled with flowers and butterflies that it may well be called a garden-meadow. . . . [Their flowers and grasses] respond to the touches of every breeze, rejoicing in pure wildness, blooming and fruiting in the vital light."

Go where you may, you everywhere find the lawn divinely beautiful, as if Nature had fingered and adjusted every plant this very day. The floating grass panicles are scarcely felt in brushing through their midst, so fine are they, and none of the flowers have tall or rigid stalks. In the brightest places you find three species of gentians with different shades of blue, daisies pure as the sky, silky leaved ivesias [variety of wild flowers found in the American West] with warm yellow flowers, several species of orthocarpus [also known as "owl's clover"] with blunt, bossy spikes, red and purple and yellow; the alpine goldenrod, penstemon, [commonly known as "beard tongue" for the fuzzy texture of its petals] and clover, fragrant and honeyful, with their colors massed and blended. Parting the grasses and looking more closely you may trace the branching of their shining stems, and note the marvelous beauty of their mist of flowers, the glumes and pales exquisitely penciled, the yellow dangling stamens, and feathery pistils. Beneath the lowest leaves you discover a fairy realm of mosses . . . their precious spore-cups poised daintily on polished shafts, curiously hooded, or open, showing the richly ornate petals worn like royal crowns. Creeping liverworts [moss-like plants growing in damp, dark places] are here also in abundance, and several rare species of fungi, exceedingly small, and frail, and delicate, as if made only for beauty. Caterpillars, black beetles, and ants roam the wilds of this lower world, making their way through miniature groves and thickets like bears in a thick wood.

And how rich, too, is the life of the sunny air! Every leaf and flower seems to have its winged representative overhead. Dragon-flies shoot in vigorous zigzags through the dancing swarms, and a rich profusion of butterflies . . . make a fine addition to the general show. Many of these last are comparatively small at this elevation, and as yet almost unknown to science; but every now and then a familiar vanessa or papilio [species of butterfly] comes sailing past. Humming-birds, too, are quite common here, and the robin is always found along the margin of the stream, or out in the shallowest portions of the sod, and sometimes the grouse and mountain quail, with their broods of precious fluffy chickens. Swallows skim the grassy lake from end to end, fly-catchers come and go in fitful flights from the tops of dead spars, while woodpeckers swing across from side to side in graceful festoon curves—birds, insects, and flowers all in their own way telling a deep summer joy.

The influences of pure nature seem to be so little known as yet, that it is generally supposed that complete pleasure of this kind, permeating one's very flesh and bones, unfits the student for scientific pursuits in which cool judgment and observation are required. But the effect is just the opposite. Instead of producing a dissipated condition, the mind is fertilized and stimulated and developed like sun-fed plants. All that we have seen here enables us to see with surer vision the fountains among the summit-peaks to the east whence flowed the glaciers that ground soil for the surrounding forest; and down at the foot of the meadow the moraine which formed the dam which gave rise to the lake that occupied this basin before the meadow was made; and around the margin the stones that were shoved back and piled up into a rude wall by the expansion of the lake ice during long bygone winters; and along the sides of the streams the slight hollows of the meadow which mark those portions of the old lake that were the last to vanish.

I would fain ask my readers to linger awhile in this fertile wilderness, to trace its history from its earliest glacial beginnings, and learn what we may of its wild inhabitants and visitors. How happy the birds are all summer and some of them all winter; how the pouched marmots drive tunnels under the snow, and how fine and brave a life the slandered coyote lives here, and the deer and bears!

—*The Mountains of California*

No Pain Here

JOHN MUIR ONLY TOOK THE JOB as sheepherder for the opportunity it offered him to spend every day in the high mountains. Finishing his camp chores, he commented, "By the time the sun is fairly above the mountain-tops I am beyond the flock, free to rove and revel in the wilderness all the big immortal days." This is an account of such a day.

No pain here, no dull empty hours, no fear of the past, no fear of the future. These blessed mountains are so compactly filled with God's beauty, no petty personal hope or experience has room to be. Drinking this champagne water is pure pleasure, so is breathing the living air, and every movement of limbs is pleasure, while the whole body seems to feel beauty when exposed to it as it feels the camp-fire or sunshine, entering not by the eyes alone, but equally through all one's flesh like radiant heat, making a passionate ecstatic pleasure glow not explainable. One's body then seems homogeneous throughout, sound as a crystal.

—JOURNAL ENTRY, JULY 20, 1869

A Thousand Yellowstone Wonders Are Calling

BY 1885 WHEN JOHN MUIR visited the United States' first national park, established in 1872, he had been on a quest to discover as much of America's wilderness as possible. He had already explored most of California's mountains, and he had completed three trips to Alaska.

Well-traveled as he was, Muir was not prepared for the majesty of Yellowstone—its geysers, hot springs, steaming pots of sulfurous mud, and his favorite, the spectacular waterfall of the Grand Canyon of the Yellowstone, which infused his whole being with awe. "With few exceptions, the traveler . . . finds that, however much the scenery and vegetation in different countries may change, Mother Earth is ever familiar and the same. But here the very ground is changed, as if belonging to some other world. The walls of the canyon from top to bottom burn in a perfect glory of color, confounding and dazzling when the sun is shining—white, yellow, green, blue, vermilion, and various other shades of red indefinitely blending. All the earth hereabouts seems to be paint. Millions of tons of it lie in sight, exposed to wind and weather as if of no account, yet marvelously fresh and bright, fast colors not to be washed out or bleached out by either sunshine or storms. The effect is so novel and awful, we imagine that even a river might be afraid to enter such a place. But the rich and gentle beauty of the vegetation is reassuring . . . forests and gardens extend their treasures in smiling confidence on either side, nuts and berries ripen well . . . blind fears vanish, and the grand gorge seems a kindly, beautiful part of the general harmony, full of peace and joy and good will."

We see Nature working with enthusiasm like a man, blowing her volcanic forges like a blacksmith blowing his smithy fires, shoving glaciers over the landscapes like a carpenter shoving his planes, clearing, plowing, harrowing, irrigating, planting, and sowing broadcast like a farmer and gardener, doing rough work and fine work, planting sequoias and pines, rosebushes and daisies; working in gems, filling every crack and hollow with them; distilling fine essences; painting plants and shells, clouds, mountains, all the earth and heavens, like an artist—ever working toward beauty higher and higher. Where may the mind find more stimulating, quickening pasturage? A thousand Yellowstone wonders are calling, "Look up and down and round about you!" And a multitude of still, small voices may be heard directing you to look through all this transient, shifting show of things called "substantial" into the truly substantial, spiritual world whose forms flesh and wood, rock and water, air and sunshine, only veil and conceal, and to learn that here is heaven and the dwelling-place of the angels.

The sun is setting; long, violet shadows are growing out over the woods from the mountains along the western rim of the park; the Absaroka range is baptized in the divine light of the alpenglow [reddish glow seen near sunset and sunrise on summits of mountains], and its rocks and trees are transfigured. Next to the light of the dawn on high mountain tops, the alpenglow is the most impressive of all the terrestrial manifestations of God.

Now comes the gloaming. The alpenglow is fading into earthy, murky gloom, but do not let your town habits draw you away to the hotel. Stay on this good fire-mountain and spend the night among the stars. Watch their glorious bloom until the dawn, and get one more baptism of light. Then, with fresh heart, go down to your work, and whatever your fate, under whatever ignorance or knowledge you may afterward chance to suffer, you will remember these fine, wild views, and look back with joy to your wanderings in the blessed old Yellowstone Wonderland.

—Our National Parks

Wander Here a Whole Summer

IN THE 1890S THE RAILROAD had reached what is now West Glacier, the eastern entrance to what would become Glacier National Park (the tenth national park, established in l910). From there visitors could take a stage coach in to Lake McDonald. While he may have been unrealistic about how much time visitors could take to visit wild places, John Muir believed that any amount of time spent in nature would lengthen one's lifespan.

> Wander here a whole summer, if you can. Thousands of God's wild blessings will search you and soak you as if you were sponge, and the big days will go by un-counted. If you are business-tangled, and so burdened with duty that only weeks can be got out of the heavy-laden year, then go to the Flathead Reserve; for it is easily and quickly reached by the Great Northern Railroad. Get off the track at Belton Station [now West Glacier], and in a few minutes you will find yourself in the midst of what you are sure to say is the best care-killing scenery on the continent—beautiful lakes derived straight from glaciers, lofty mountains steeped in lovely nemophila-blue skies and clad with forests and glaciers, mossy, ferny waterfalls in their hollows, nameless and numberless, and meadowy gardens abounding in the best of every-thing. When you are calm enough for discriminating observation, you will find the king of the larches, one of the best of the Western giants, beautiful, picturesque, and regal in port, easily the grandest of all the larches in the world. . . .
>
> Lake McDonald, full of brisk trout, is in the heart of this forest, and Avalanche Lake is ten miles above McDonald, at the feet of a group of glacier-laden mountains. Give a month at least to this precious reserve. The time will not be taken from the sum of your life. Instead of shortening, it will indefinitely lengthen it and make you truly immortal. Nevermore will time seem short or long, and cares will never again fall heavily on you, but gently and kindly as gifts from heaven.
>
> —*Our National Parks*

Reflections on a Nighttime Walk in the Thin White Light

AS JOHN MUIR WALKED DOWN from upper Yosemite Falls thoroughly soaked by their spray, he became reflective. The little bush he passed, the spray from the falls, and even the grains of sand he rested on as he wrote his letter—all he saw as fellow beings, companion travelers.

> How little do we know of ourselves, of our profoundest attractions and repulsions, of our spiritual affinities! How interesting does man become, considering his relations to the spirit of this rock and water! How significant does every atom of our world become amid the influences of those beings unseen, spiritual, angelic mountaineers that so throng these pure mansions of crystal foam and purple granite!
>
> I cannot refrain from speaking to this little bush at my side and to the spray-drops that come to my paper and to the individual sands of the slope I am sitting upon.
>
> Well, I must go down now. . . . Farewell to you and to all beings about us! I shall have a glorious walk down the mountain in the thin white light, over the open brows grayed with selaginella [wild white flowers that appear in the early spring] and through thick black shadow caves in the live oaks all stuck full of snowy lances of moonlight.
>
> —LETTER TO JEANNE C. CARR, APRIL 3, 1871

Stand Beside Me

MUIR DESCRIBED HIS IMPRESSIONS of a winter hike in the High Sierra. "I reached the top of the ridge in four or five hours, and through an opening in the woods the most imposing wind-storm effect I ever beheld came full in sight; unnumbered mountains rising sharply into the cloudless sky, their bases solid white, their sides plashed with snow, like ocean rocks with foam, and on every summit a magnificent silvery banner." He engaged all the senses and invites the reader to do the same, to live in this moment now.

> Fancy yourself standing beside me on this Yosemite Ridge [Fern Ledge]. There is a strange garish glitter in the air and the gale drives wildly overhead, but you feel

nothing of its violence, for you are looking out through a sheltered opening in the woods, as through a window. In the immediate foreground there is a forest of silver fir their foliage warm yellow-green, and the snow beneath them strewn with their plumes, plucked off by the storm; and beyond broad, ridgy, canyon-furrowed, dome-dotted middle ground, darkened here and there with belts of pines, you behold the lofty snow laden mountains in glorious array, waving their banners with jubilant enthusiasm as if shouting aloud for joy. They are twenty miles away, but you would not wish them nearer, for every feature is distinct and the whole wonderful show is seen in its right proportions, like a painting on the sky.

And now after this general view, mark how sharply the ribs and buttresses and summits of the mountains are defined, excepting the portions veiled by the banners; how gracefully and nobly the banners are waving in accord with the throbbing of the wind flood; how trimly each is attached to the very summit of its peak like a streamer at a mast-head; how bright and glowing white they are, and how finely their fading fringes are penciled on the sky! See how solid white and opaque they are at the point of attachment and how filmy and translucent toward the end, so that the parts of the peaks past which they are streaming look dim as if seen through a veil of ground glass. And see how some of the longest of the banners on the highest peaks are streaming perfectly free from peak to peak across intervening notches or passes, while others overlap and partly hide one another.

—*The Yosemite*

Renew Yourself in Nature's Eternal Beauty

JOHN MUIR CLIMBED MOUNT SHASTA at least three times; on one occasion he came close to losing his life. This account is taken from a trip he made with his artist friend, William Keith, in 1888. Refreshing and enriching though the trip may have been, Muir was dismayed at the signs of destruction he observed through logging, burning, and over-grazing. "The great wilds of our country, once held to be boundless and inexhaust-ible, are being rapidly invaded and overrun in every direction, and everything destruc-tible in them is being destroyed. How far destruction may go it is not easy to guess. Every landscape, low and high, seems doomed to be trampled and harried. Even the sky is not safe from scathe—blurred and blackened with the smoke of fires that devour the woods." Muir urged his readers to see America's natural wonders before they were gone.

Arctic beauty and desolation, with their blessings and dangers, all may be found here, to test the endurance and skill of adventurous climbers; but far better than climbing the mountain is going around its warm, fertile base, enjoying its bounties like a bee circling around a bank of flowers. The distance is about a hundred miles, and will take some of the time we hear so much about—a week or two—but the benefits will compensate for any number of weeks. Perhaps the profession of doing good may be full, but every body should be kind at least to himself. Take a course of good water and air, and in the eternal youth of Nature you may renew your own. Go quietly, alone; no harm will befall you. . . .

One may make the trip on horseback, or in a carriage, even; for a good level road may be found all the way round, by Shasta Valley, Sheep Rock, Elk Flat, Huck-leberry Valley, Squaw Valley, following for a considerable portion of the way the old Emigrant Road, which lies along the east disk of the mountain, and is deeply worn by the wagons of the early gold-seekers, many of whom chose this northern route as perhaps being safer and easier, the pass here being only about six thousand feet above sea level. But it is far better to go afoot. Then you are free to make wide wa-verings and zigzags away from the roads to visit the great fountain streams of the rivers, the glaciers also, and the wildest retreats in the primeval forests, where the best plants and animals dwell, and where many a flower-bell will ring against your knees, and friendly trees will reach out their fronded branches and touch you as you pass. One blanket will be enough to carry, or you may forego the pleasure and bur-den altogether, as wood for fires is everywhere abundant. Only a little food will be required. Berries and plums abound in season, and quail and grouse and deer—the magnificent shaggy mule deer as well as the common species.

As you sweep around so grand a center, the mountain itself seems to turn, displaying its riches like the revolving pyramids in jewelers' windows. One glacier after another comes into view, and the outlines of the mountain are ever changing, though all the way around, from whatever point of view, the form is maintained of a grand, simple cone with a gently sloping base and rugged, crumbling ridges separating the glaciers and the snowfields more or less completely. The play of colors, from the first touches of the morning sun on the summit, down the snowfields and the ice and lava until the forests are aglow, is a never-ending delight, the rosy lava and the fine flushings of the snow being ineffably lovely. Thus one saunters on and on in the glorious radiance in utter peace and forgetfulness of time.

—Steep Trails

Emerson's Visit to Yosemite

RALPH WALDO EMERSON WAS ONE of John Muir's heroes, and he often carried a book of his essays with him on his travels. Muir, young, energetic, and idealistic at age 33, had eagerly awaited the visit of Emerson to the park in the spring of 1871. The celebrated Transcendentalist essayist and poet was 68, and, as Muir said, he was nearing "the sunset of his life." Muir felt convinced that if he could only take Emerson off camping for a few days his health and spirits would be rejuvenated, but the 12-member party of his fellow travelers from Boston was protective, fearing that "Mr. Emerson might take cold." So the visit wasn't what Muir had envisioned it would be, and he was left with a sense of sadness and incompleteness when Emerson departed.

Muir continued to admire Emerson and Thoreau as kindred spirits, and when he visited Boston in 1893, he went to Concord to visit their graves: "Went through lovely, ferny, flowery woods and meadows to the hill cemetery and laid flowers on Thoreau's and Emerson's graves. I think it is the most beautiful graveyard I ever saw. It is on a hill perhaps one hundred and fifty feet high in the woods of pine, oak, beech, maple, etc., and all the ground is flowery. Thoreau lies with his father, mother, and brother not far from Emerson and Hawthorne. Emerson lies between two white pine trees, one at his head, the other at [his] feet. . . . Sweet kindly Mother Earth has taken them back to her bosom whence they came. I did not imagine I would be so moved at sight of the resting places of these grand men as I found I was, and I could not help thinking how glad I would be to feel sure that I would also rest here."

> During my first years in the Sierra I was ever calling on everybody within reach to admire them, but I found no one half warm enough until Emerson came. I had read his essays, and felt sure that of all men he would best interpret the sayings of these noble mountains and trees. Nor was my faith weakened when I met him in Yosemite. He seemed as serene as a sequoia, his head in the empyrean; and forgetting his age, plans, duties, ties of every sort, I proposed an immeasurable camping trip back in the heart of the mountains. He seemed anxious to go, but considerately mentioned his party. I said: "Never mind. The mountains are calling; run away, and let [go of] plans and parties and dragging lowland duties. . . . We'll go up a canyon singing your own song, "Good-bye, proud world! I'm going home, in divine earnest. Up there lies a new heaven and a new earth; let us go to the show." But alas, it was too late—too near the sundown of his life. The shadows were growing long, and he leaned on his friends. His party, full of indoor philosophy, failed to see the natural beauty and fullness of promise of my wild plan, and laughed at it in good-natured ignorance, as if it were necessarily amusing to imagine that Boston people might be led to accept Sierra manifestations of God at the price of rough camping. Anyhow, they would have none of it, and held Mr. Emerson to the hotels and trails.
>
> After spending only five tourist days in Yosemite he was led away, but I saw him two days more; for I was kindly invited to go with the party as far as the Mariposa big trees. I told Mr. Emerson that I would gladly go to the sequoias with him, if he

would camp in the grove. He consented heartily, and I felt sure that we would have at least one good wild memorable night around a sequoia camp-fire. Next day we rode through the magnificent forests of the Merced basin, and I kept calling his attention to the sugar pines, quoting his wood-notes, "Come listen what the pine tree says," etc., pointing out the noblest as kings and high priests, the most eloquent and commanding preachers of all the mountain forests, stretching forth their century-old arms in benediction over the worshiping congregations crowded about them. He gazed in devout admiration, saying but little, while his fine smile faded away.

Early in the afternoon, when we reached Clark's Station, I was surprised to see the party dismount. And when I asked if we were not going up into the grove to camp they said: "No; it would never do to lie out in the night air. Mr. Emerson might take cold; and you know, Mr. Muir, that would be a dreadful thing." In vain I urged, that only in homes and hotels were colds caught, that nobody ever was known to take cold camping in these woods, that there was not a single cough or sneeze in all the Sierra. Then I pictured the big climate-changing, inspiring fire I would make, praised the beauty and fragrance of sequoia flame, told how the great trees would stand about us transfigured in the purple light, while the stars looked down between the great domes; ending by urging them to come on and make an immortal Emerson night of it. But the house habit was not to be overcome, nor the strange dread of pure night air, though it is only cooled day air with a little dew in it. So the carpet dust and unknowable reeks were preferred. And to think of this being a Boston choice! Sad commentary on culture and the glorious Transcendentalism!

. . . . I again urged Emerson to stay. "You are yourself a sequoia," I said. "Stop and get acquainted with your big brethren." But he was past his prime, and was now as a child in the hands of his affectionate but sadly civilized friends, who seemed as full of old-fashioned conformity as of bold intellectual independence. It was the afternoon of the day and the afternoon of his life, and his course was now westward down all the mountains into the sunset. . . . I felt lonely, so sure had I been that Emerson of all men would be the quickest to see the mountains and sing them. Gazing awhile on the spot where he vanished, I sauntered back into the heart of the grove, made a bed of sequoia plumes and ferns by the side of a stream, gathered a store of firewood, and then walked about until sundown. The birds, robins, thrushes, warblers, etc., that had kept out of sight, came about me, now that all was quiet, and made cheer. After sundown I built a great fire, and as usual had it all to myself. And though lonesome for the first time in these forests, I quickly took heart again—the trees had not gone to Boston, nor the birds; and as I sat by the fire, Emerson was still with me in spirit, though I never again saw him in the flesh.

—*Our National Parks*

Softly Comes Night to the Mountains

THIS ESSAY IS FROM JOHN MUIR'S first published work, for which he was paid $200—a large amount of money at the time. It was pieced together from letters sent to his friends.

How softly comes night to the mountains. Shadows grow upon all the landscape; only the Hoffman Peaks are open to the sun. Down in this hollow it is twilight, and my two domes, more impressive, than in a broad day, seem to approach me. They are not vast and over-spiritual . . . but comprehensible and companionable, and susceptible of human affinities. The darkness grows, and all of their finer sculpture dims. Now the great arches and deep curves sink also, and the whole structure is massed in black against the starry sky.

I have set fire to two pine logs, and the neighboring trees are coming to my charmed circle of light. The two-leaved pine, with sprays and tassels innumerable, the silver fir, with magnificent fronded whorls of shining boughs, and the graceful nodding spruce, dripping with cones, and seeming yet more spiritual in this campfire light. Grandly do my logs give back their light, slow gleaned from the suns of a hundred summers, garnered beautifully away in dotted cells and in beads of amber gum; and, together with this out-gust of light, seems to flow all the other riches of their life, and their living companions are looking down as if to witness their perfect and beautiful death. But I am weary and must rest. Good-night to my two logs and two lakes, and to my two domes high and black on the sky, with a cluster of stars between.

"YOSEMITE GLACIERS," *New York Tribune,* DECEMBER 5, 1871

chapter seven

Storms, Danger, and Survival

Commentary

JOHN MUIR WAS CURIOUS! He did not always use good judgment. On the continuum between caution and danger, Muir consistently veered towards danger.

The time Muir wanted to know how water felt as it tumbled down Upper Yosemite Falls, he climbed as close as possible to the falls so he could hear, see, smell, and feel the water. He slipped on a wet rock, fell, and knocked himself out. Coming to, he brushed himself off and continued his hike. When he wanted to know how a tree felt when it was blowing in a storm, he located what he thought was a sturdy mountain pine and climbed it. "I kept my lofty perch for hours, frequently closing my eyes to enjoy the music [of the forest] or feast quietly on the delicious fragrance that was streaming past."[1]

Muir was relentless and never spared himself. When he was tired, he tramped on for a few miles more; late in the day, he pushed himself up one more mountain. When he was hungry, he munched on a dry crust and sipped his cold, black tea. Winds, rain, snow storms, cold—John Muir seemed indifferent to them all.

A Dangerous Hike in the High Sierra

DESIRE TO BE AS CLOSE as possible to natural phenomena usually overcame John Muir's sense of caution. During his first summer in the Sierra, Muir explored Yosemite Creek, taking a few risks to do so. "My only fear was that a flake of the granite, which in some places showed joints more or less open and running parallel with the face of the cliff, might give way. After withdrawing from such places, excited with the view I had got, I would say to myself, 'Now don't go out on the verge again.' But in the face of Yosemite scenery cautious remonstrance is vain; under its spell one's body seems to go where it likes with a will over which we seem to have scarce any control."

> [Descending into a gorge of the Merced River] I took off my shoes and stockings and worked my way cautiously down alongside the rushing flood, keeping my feet and hands pressed firmly on the polished rock. The booming, roaring water, rushing past close to my head, was very exciting. I had expected that the sloping apron would terminate with the perpendicular wall of the valley, and that from the foot of it, where it is less steeply inclined, I should be able to lean far enough out to see the forms and behavior of the fall all the way down to the bottom. But I found that there was yet another small brow over which I could not see, and which appeared to be too steep for mortal feet. Scanning it keenly, I discovered a narrow shelf about three inches wide on the very brink, just wide enough for a rest for one's heels. But there seemed to be no way of reaching it over so steep a brow. At length, after careful scrutiny of the surface, I found an irregular edge of a flake of the rock some distance back from the margin of the torrent. If I was to get down to the brink at all that rough edge, which might offer slight finger holds, was the only way. But the slope beside it looked dangerously smooth and steep, and the swift roaring flood beneath, overhead, and beside me was very nerve-trying. I therefore concluded not to venture farther, but did nevertheless. Tufts of artemisia were growing in clefts of the rock near by, and I filled my mouth with the bitter leaves, hoping they might help to prevent giddiness. Then, with a caution not known in ordinary circumstances, I crept down safely to the little ledge, got my heels well planted on it, then shuffled in a horizontal direction twenty or thirty feet until close to the outplunging current, which, by the time it had descended thus far, was already white. Here I obtained a perfectly free view down into the heart of the snowy, chanting throng of comet-like streamers, into which the body of the fall soon separates.
>
> While perched on that narrow niche I was not distinctly conscious of danger. The tremendous grandeur of the fall in form and sound and motion, acting

at close range, smothered the sense of fear, and in such places one's body takes keen care for safety on its own account. How long I remained down there, or how I returned, I can hardly tell. Anyhow I had a glorious time, and got back to camp about dark, enjoying triumphant exhilaration soon followed by dull weariness. Hereafter I'll try to keep from such extravagant, nerve-straining places. Yet such a day is well worth venturing for. My first view of the High Sierra, first view looking down into Yosemite. . . .

—*My First Summer in the Sierra*

Nerve-Shaken on Mount Ritter

JOHN MUIR PUSHED HIMSELF to the limits of safety and his own endurance as illustrated on his climb up Mount Ritter in October of 1872. It was a difficult climb, and, by Muir's own admission, it was probably too late in the season and too cold and dark at night. Nonetheless, he took the risk and may have been the first mountaineer to reach Ritter's summit.

Mount Ritter is king of the mountains of the middle portion of the High Sierra. . . . As far as I know, it had never been climbed. . . . Its height above sea-level is about 13,300 feet, and it is fenced round by steeply inclined glaciers, and cañons of tremendous depth and ruggedness, which render it almost inaccessible. But difficulties of this kind only exhilarate the mountaineer. . . .

My general plan was simply this: to scale the canyon wall, cross over to the eastern flank of the range, and then make my way southward to the northern spurs of Mount Ritter in compliance with the intervening topography; for to push on directly southward from camp through the innumerable peaks and pinnacles that adorn this portion of the axis of the range, however interesting, would take too much time, besides being extremely difficult and dangerous at this time of year.

All my first day was pure pleasure; simply mountaineering indulgence, crossing the dry pathways of the ancient glaciers, tracing happy streams, and learning the habits of the birds and marmots in the groves and rocks. Before I had gone a mile from camp, I came to the foot of a white cascade that beats its way down a rugged gorge in the canyon wall, from a height of about nine hundred feet, and pours its throbbing waters into the Tuolumne. . . . Passing a little way down over the summit until I had reached an elevation of about 10,000 feet, I pushed on southward toward a group of savage peaks that stand guard about Ritter on the north and west, groping my way, and dealing instinctively with every obstacle as it presented itself. Here a huge gorge would be found cutting across my path, along the dizzy edge of which I scrambled until some less precipitous point was discovered where I might safely venture to the bottom and then, selecting some feasible portion of the opposite wall, reascend with the same slow caution. Massive, flat-topped spurs alternate with the gorges, plunging abruptly from the shoulders of the snowy peaks. . . . In so wild and so beautiful a region was spent my first day. . . .

Now came the solemn, silent evening. Long, blue, spiky shadows crept out across the snow-fields, while a rosy glow, at first scarce discernible, gradually deepened and suffused every mountain-top, flushing the glaciers and the harsh crags above them. This was the alpenglow, to me one of the most impressive of all the terrestrial manifestations of God. At the touch of this divine light, the mountains seemed to kindle to a rapt, religious consciousness, and stood hushed and waiting like devout worshipers. Just before the alpenglow began to fade, two crimson clouds came streaming across the summit like wings of flame, rendering the sublime scene yet more impressive; then came darkness and the stars.

Icy Ritter was still miles away, but I could proceed no farther that night. I found a good camp-ground on the rim of a glacier basin about 11,000 feet above the sea. . . .

I made my bed in a nook of the pine-thicket, where the branches were pressed and crinkled overhead like a roof, and bent down around the sides. These are the

best bedchambers the high mountains afford—snug as squirrel-nests, well venti-
lated, full of spicy odors, and with plenty of wind-played needles to sing one asleep.
I little expected company, but, creeping in through a low side-door, I found five or
six birds nestling among the tassels. The night-wind began to blow soon after dark;
at first only a gentle breathing, but increasing toward midnight to a rough gale that
fell upon my leafy roof in ragged surges like a cascade, bearing wild sounds from
the crags overhead. The waterfall sang in chorus, filling the old ice-fountain with its
solemn roar, and seeming to increase in power as the night advanced—fit voice for
such a landscape. I had to creep out many times to the fire during the night, for it
was biting cold and I had no blankets. Gladly I welcomed the morning star.

    The dawn in the dry, wavering air of the desert was glorious. Everything en-
couraged my undertaking and betokened success. There was no cloud in the sky,
no storm-tone in the wind. Breakfast of bread and tea was soon made. I fastened a
hard, durable crust to my belt by way of provision, in case I should be compelled to
pass a night on the mountain-top; then, securing the remainder of my little stock
against wolves and wood-rats, I set forth free and hopeful. . . .

    All along my course thus far, excepting when down in the canyons, the land-
scapes were mostly open to me, and expansive, at least on one side. . . . Rugged
spurs, and moraines, and huge, projecting buttresses began to shut me in. . . . On the
southern shore of a frozen lake, I encountered an extensive field of hard, granular
snow, up which I scampered in fine tone, intending to follow it to its head, and cross
the rocky spur against which it leans, hoping thus to come direct upon the base of
the main Ritter peak. The surface was pitted with oval hollows, made by stones and
drifted pine-needles that had melted themselves into the mass by the radiation of
absorbed sun-heat. These afforded good footholds, but the surface curved more
and more steeply at the head, and the pits became shallower and less abundant,
until I found myself in danger of being shed off like avalanching snow. I persisted,
however, creeping on all fours, and shuffling up the smoothest places on my back,
as I had often done on burnished granite, until, after slipping several times, I was

compelled to retrace my course to the bottom, and make my way around the west end of the lake, and thence up to the summit of the divide between the head waters of Rush Creek and the northernmost tributaries of the San Joaquin.

Arriving on the summit of this dividing crest, one of the most exciting pieces of pure wilderness was disclosed that I ever discovered in all my mountaineering. There, immediately in front, loomed the majestic mass of Mount Ritter, with a glacier swooping down its face nearly to my feet, then curving westward and pouring its frozen flood into a dark blue lake, whose shores were bound with precipices of crystalline snow; while a deep chasm drawn between the divide and the glacier separated the massive picture from everything else. I could see only the one sublime mountain, the one glacier, the one lake; the whole veiled with one blue shadow—rock, ice, and water close together without a single leaf or sign of life. After gazing spellbound, I began instinctively to scrutinize every notch and gorge and weathered buttress of the mountain, with reference to making the ascent. The entire front above the glacier appeared as one tremendous precipice, slightly receding at the top, and bristling with spires and pinnacles set above one another in formidable array. Massive lichen-stained battlements stood forward here and there, hacked at the top with angular notches, and separated by frosty gullies and recesses that have been veiled in shadow ever since their creation; while to right and left, as far as I could see, were huge, crumbling buttresses, offering no hope to the climber. The head of the glacier sends up a few finger-like branches through narrow couloirs [deep mountain gorges]; but these seemed too steep and short to be available, especially as I had no ax with which to cut steps, and the numerous narrow-throated gullies down which stones and snow are avalanched seemed hopelessly steep, besides being interrupted by vertical cliffs; while the whole front was rendered still more terribly forbidding by the chill shadow and the gloomy blackness of the rocks.

Descending the divide in a hesitating mood, I picked my way across the yawning chasm at the foot, and climbed out upon the glacier. There were no meadows now to cheer with their brave colors, nor could I hear the dun-headed sparrows, whose cheery notes so often relieve the silence of our highest mountains. The only sounds were the gurgling of small rills down in the veins and crevasses of the glacier, and now and then the rattling report of falling stones, with the echoes they shot out into the crisp air.

I could not distinctly hope to reach the summit from this side, yet I moved on across the glacier as if driven by fate. Contending with myself, the season is too far spent, I said, and even should I be successful, I might be storm-bound on the mountain; and in the cloud-darkness, with the cliffs and crevasses covered with snow, how could I escape? No; I must wait till next summer. I would only approach the mountain now, and inspect it, creep about its flanks, learn what I could of its history, holding myself ready to flee on the approach of the first storm-cloud. But we little know until tried how much of the uncontrollable there is in us, urging across glaciers and torrents, and up dangerous heights, let the judgment forbid as it may.

I succeeded in gaining the foot of the cliff on the eastern extremity of the glacier, and there discovered the mouth of a narrow avalanche gully, through which I began to climb, intending to follow it as far as possible, and at least obtain some fine wild views . . . I thus made my way into a wilderness of crumbling spires and battlements, built together in bewildering combinations, and glazed in many places with a thin coating of ice, which I had to hammer off with stones. The situation was becoming gradually more perilous; but, having passed several dangerous spots, I dared not think of descending; for, so steep was the entire ascent, one would inevitably fall to the glacier in case a single misstep were made. Knowing, therefore, the tried danger beneath, I became all the more anxious concerning the developments to be made above, and began to be conscious of a vague foreboding of what actually befell; not that I was given to fear, but rather because my instincts, usually so positive and true, seemed vitiated in some way, and were leading me astray. At length, after attaining an elevation of about 12,800 feet, I found myself at the foot of a sheer drop in the bed of the avalanche channel I was tracing, which seemed absolutely to bar further progress. It was only about forty-five or fifty feet high, and somewhat roughened by fissures and projections; but these seemed so slight and insecure, as footholds, that I tried hard to avoid the precipice altogether, by scaling the wall of the channel on either side. But, though less steep, the walls were smoother than the obstructing rock, and repeated efforts only showed that I must either go right ahead or turn back. The tried dangers beneath seemed even greater than that of the cliff in front; therefore, after scanning its face again and again, I began to scale it, picking my holds with intense caution. After gaining a point about halfway to the top, I was suddenly brought to a dead stop, with arms outspread, clinging close to the face of the rock, unable to move hand or foot either up or down. My doom appeared fixed. I must fall. There would be a moment of bewilderment, and then a lifeless rumble down the one general precipice to the glacier below.

When this final danger flashed upon me, I became nerve-shaken for the first time since setting foot on the mountains, and my mind seemed to fill with a stifling smoke. But this terrible eclipse lasted only a moment, when life blazed forth again with preternatural clearness. I seemed suddenly to become possessed of a new sense. The other self, bygone experiences, Instinct, or Guardian Angel—call it what you will—came forward and assumed control. Then my trembling muscles became firm again, every rift and flaw in the rock was seen as through a microscope, and my limbs moved with a positiveness and precision with which I seemed to have nothing at all to do. Had I been borne aloft upon wings, my deliverance could not have been more complete.

Above this memorable spot, the face of the mountain is still more savagely hacked and torn. It is a maze of yawning chasms and gullies, in the angles of which rise beetling crags and piles of detached boulders that seem to have been gotten ready to be launched below. But the strange influx of strength I had received seemed inexhaustible. I found a way without effort, and soon stood upon the topmost crag in the blessed light.

—*The Mountains of California*

A Perilous Night on Shasta's Summit

ON APRIL 30, 1875, against the advice of the innkeepers at the foot of the mountain, Justin and Lydia Sisson, John Muir, and a companion, Jerome Fay, set out to climb Mount Shasta, a 14,162-foot volcanic mountain in northern California with a dramatic conical summit. As before the Sissons predicted, the storm struck and Muir, who was making scientific observations of the summit, was reluctant to stop, even as it gathered. What follows qualifies as one of the all-time most thrilling adventure stories.

At two o'clock we rose, breakfasted on a warmed tin-cupful of coffee and a piece of frozen venison broiled on the coals, and started for the summit. Up to this time there was nothing in sight that betokened the approach of a storm. . . . It began to declare itself shortly after noon. . . . Jerome peered at short intervals over the ridge, contemplating the rising clouds with anxious gestures in the rough wind, and at length declared that if we did not make a speedy escape we should be compelled to pass the rest of the day and night on the summit. But anxiety to complete my observations stifled my own instinctive promptings to retreat, and held me to my work. No inexperienced person was depending on me, and I told Jerome that we two mountaineers should be able to make our way down through any storm likely to fall.

Presently thin, fibrous films of cloud began to blow directly over the summit from north to south, drawn out in long fairy webs like carded wool, forming and dissolving as if by magic. The wind twisted them into ringlets and whirled them in a succession of graceful convolutions like the outside sprays of Yosemite Falls in flood time; then, sailing out into the thin azure over the precipitous brink of the ridge they were drifted together like wreaths of foam on a river. These higher and finer cloud fabrics were evidently produced by the chilling of the air from its own expansion caused by the upward deflection of the wind against the slopes of the mountain. They steadily increased on the north rim of the cone, forming at length a thick, opaque, ill-defined embankment from the icy meshes of which snow-flowers began to fall, alternating with hail. The sky speedily darkened, and just as I had completed my last observation and boxed my instruments ready for the descent, the storm began in serious earnest. At first the cliffs were beaten with hail, every stone of which, as far as I could see, was regular in form, six-sided pyramids with rounded base, rich and sumptuous-looking, and fashioned with loving care, yet seemingly thrown away on those desolate crags down which they went rolling, falling, sliding in a network of curious streams.

After we had forced our way down the ridge and past the group of hissing fumaroles, the storm became inconceivably violent. The thermometer fell 22 degrees in a few minutes, and soon dropped below zero. The hail gave place to snow, and darkness came on like night. The wind, rising to the highest pitch of violence, boomed and surged amid the desolate crags; lightning flashes in quick succession cut the gloomy darkness; and the thunders, the most tremendously loud and appalling I ever heard, made an almost continuous roar, stroke following stroke in quick, passionate succession, as though the mountain were being rent to its foundations and the fires of the old volcano were breaking forth again.

Could we at once have begun to descend the snow slopes leading to the timber, we might have made good our escape, however dark and wild the storm. As it was, we had first to make our way along a dangerous ridge nearly a mile and a half long, flanked in many places by steep ice-slopes at the head of the Whitney Glacier on one side and by shattered precipices on the other. Apprehensive of this coming darkness, I had taken the precaution, when the storm began, to make the most dangerous points clear to my mind, and to mark their relations with reference to the direction of the wind. When, therefore, the darkness came on, and the bewildering drift, I felt confident that we could force our way through it with no other guidance. After passing the "Hot Springs" I halted in the lee of a lava-block to let Jerome, who had fallen a little behind, come up. Here he opened a council in which, under circumstances sufficiently exciting but without evincing any bewilderment, he maintained, in opposition to my views, that it was impossible to proceed. He firmly refused to make the venture to find the camp, while I, aware of the dangers that would necessarily attend our efforts, and conscious of being the cause of his present peril, decided not to leave him.

Our discussions ended, Jerome made a dash from the shelter of the lava-block and began forcing his way back against the wind to the "Hot Springs," wavering and struggling to resist being carried away, as if he were fording a rapid stream. After waiting and watching in vain for some flaw in the storm that might be urged as a new argument in favor of attempting the descent, I was compelled to follow. "Here," said Jerome, as we shivered in the midst of the hissing, sputtering fumaroles, "we shall be safe from frost." "Yes," said I, "we can lie in this mud and steam and sludge, warm at least on one side; but how can we protect our lungs from the acid gases, and how, after our clothing is saturated, shall we be able to reach camp without freezing, even after the storm is over? We shall have to wait for sunshine, and when will it come?"

The tempered area to which we had committed ourselves extended over about one fourth of an acre; but it was only about an eighth of an inch in thickness, for the scalding gas jets were shorn off close to the ground by the over-sweeping flood of frosty wind. And how lavishly the snow fell only mountaineers may know. The crisp crystal flowers seemed to touch one another and fairly to thicken the tremendous blast that carried them. This was the bloom-time, the summer of the cloud, and never before have I seen even a mountain cloud flowering so profusely. . . .

The snow fell without abatement until an hour or two after what seemed to be the natural darkness of the night. Up to the time the storm first broke on the summit its development was remarkably gentle. There was a deliberate growth of clouds, a weaving of translucent tissue above, then the roar of the wind and the thunder, and the darkening flight of snow. Its subsidence was not less sudden. The clouds broke and vanished, not a crystal was left in the sky, and the stars shone out with pure and tranquil radiance.

During the storm we lay on our backs so as to present as little surface as possible to the wind, and to let the drift pass over us. The mealy snow sifted into the folds of our clothing and in many places reached the skin. We were glad at first to see the snow packing about us, hoping it would deaden the force of the wind, but it soon froze into a stiff, crusty heap as the temperature fell, rather augmenting our novel misery.

When the heat became unendurable, on some spot where steam was escaping through the sludge, we tried to stop it with snow and mud, or shifted a little at a time by shoving with our heels; for to stand in blank exposure to the fearful wind in our frozen-and-broiled condition seemed certain death. The acrid incrustations sublimed from the escaping gases frequently gave way, opening new vents to scald us; and, fearing that if at any time the wind should fall, carbonic acid, which often formed a considerable portion of the gaseous exhalations of volcanoes, might collect in sufficient quantities to cause sleep and death, I warned Jerome against forgetting himself for a single moment, even should his sufferings admit of such a thing.

Accordingly, when during the long, dreary watches of the night we roused from a state of half-consciousness, we called each other by name in a frightened, startled way, each fearing the other might be benumbed or dead. The ordinary sensations of cold give but a faint conception of that which comes on after hard climbing with want of food and sleep in such exposure as this. Life is then seen to be a fire, that now smoulders, now brightens, and may be easily quenched. The weary hours wore away like dim half-forgotten years, so long and eventful they seemed, though we did nothing but suffer. Still the pain was not always of that bitter, intense kind that precludes thought and takes away all capacity for enjoyment. A sort of dreamy stupor came on at times in which we fancied we saw dry, resinous logs suitable for campfires, just as after going days without food men fancy they see bread.

Frozen, blistered, famished, benumbed, our bodies seemed lost to us at times—all dead but the eyes. For the duller and fainter we became the clearer was our vision, though only in momentary glimpses. Then, after the sky cleared, we gazed at the stars, blessed immortals of light, shining with marvelous brightness with long lance rays, near-looking and new-looking, as if never seen before. Again they would look familiar and remind us of stargazing at home. Oftentimes imagination coming into play would present charming pictures of the warm zone below, mingled with others near and far. Then the bitter wind and the drift would break the blissful vision and dreary pains cover us like clouds. "Are you suffering much?" Jerome would inquire with pitiful faintness. "Yes," I would say, striving to keep my voice brave, "frozen and burned; but never mind, Jerome, the night will wear away at last, and tomorrow we go a-Maying, and what campfires we will make, and what sunbaths we will take!"

The frost grew more and more intense, and we became icy and covered over with a crust of frozen snow, as if we had lain cast away in the drift all winter. In about thirteen hour—every hour like a year—day began to dawn, but it was long ere the summit's rocks were touched by the sun. No clouds were visible from where we lay, yet the morning was dull and blue, and bitterly frosty; and hour after hour passed by while we eagerly watched the pale light stealing down the ridge to the hollow where we lay. But there was not a trace of that warm, flushing sunrise splendor we so long had hoped for.

As the time drew near to make an effort to reach camp, we became concerned to know what strength was left us, and whether or no we could walk; for we had lain flat all this time without once rising to our feet. Mountaineers, however, always find in themselves a reserve of power after great exhaustion. It is a kind of second life, available only in emergencies like this; and, having proved its existence, I had no great fear that either of us would fail, though one of my arms was already benumbed and hung powerless.

At length, after the temperature was somewhat mitigated on this memorable first of May, we arose and began to struggle homeward. Our frozen trousers could scarcely be made to bend at the knee, and we waded the snow with difficulty. The summit ridge was fortunately wind-swept and nearly bare, so we were not compelled to lift our feet high, and on reaching the long home slopes laden with loose snow we made rapid progress, sliding and shuffling and pitching headlong, our feebleness accelerating rather than diminishing our speed. When we had descended some three thousand feet the sunshine warmed our backs and we began to revive. At 10 a.m. we reached the timber and were safe.

Half an hour later we heard Sisson shouting down among the firs, coming with horses to take us to the hotel. After breaking a trail through the snow as far as possible he had tied his animals and walked up. We had been so long without food that we cared but little about eating, but we eagerly drank the coffee he prepared for us. Our feet were frozen, and thawing them was painful, and had to be done very slowly by keeping them buried in soft snow for several hours, which avoided permanent damage. Five thousand feet below the summit we found only three inches of new snow, and at the base of the mountain only a slight shower of rain had fallen, showing how local our storm had been, notwithstanding its terrific fury. Our feet were wrapped in sacking, and we were soon mounted and on our way down into the thick sunshine—"God's Country," as Sisson calls the Chaparral Zone. In two hours' ride the last snowbank was left behind. Violets appeared along the edges of the trail, and the chaparral was coming into bloom, with young lilies and larkspurs about the open places in rich profusion. How beautiful seemed the golden sunbeams streaming through the woods between the warm brown boles of the cedars and pines! All my friends among the birds and plants seemed like OLD friends, and we felt like speaking to every one of them as we passed, as if we had been a long time away in some far, strange country. . . .

—*Steep Trails*

Stickeen: The Story of a Dog

MUIR TOLD THIS STORY MANY TIMES, and, finally, at the urging of his friends, he wrote it down in 1909, creating what has become a classic dog story. During Muir's second Alaskan trip, while exploring Brady Glacier, he and Stickeen, the little dog loaned to him for the expedition, were caught in a storm that divided the glacier from the mainland save for a narrow ice bridge over a chasm. Muir later recalled that, "This poor little apostle of Alaska, child-dog of the wilderness, taught me much. We were nearly killed and we both learned a lesson never to be forgotten, and are a better man and dog for it—learned that human love, hope and fear, are essentially the same, derived from the same source and fall on all alike like sunshine. . . . He enlarged my life, extended its boundaries. . . ."

I set off early the morning of August 30 before any one else in camp had stirred, not waiting for breakfast, but only eating a piece of bread. I had intended getting a cup of coffee, but a wild storm was blowing and calling, and I could not wait. Running out against the rain-laden gale and turning to catch my breath, I saw that the minister's little dog had left his bed in the tent and was coming boring through the storm, evidently determined to follow me. I told him to go back, that such a day as this had nothing for him. "Go back," I shouted, "and get your breakfast." But he simply stood with his head down, and when I began to urge my way again, looking around, I saw he was still following me. So I at last told him to come on if he must and gave him a piece of the bread I had in my pocket.

   Instead of falling, the rain, mixed with misty shreds of clouds, was flying in level sheets, and the wind was roaring as I had never heard wind roar before. Over the icy levels and over the woods, on the mountains, over the jagged rocks and spires and chasms of the glacier it boomed and moaned and roared, filling the fiord in even, gray, structureless gloom, inspiring and awful. I first struggled up in the face of the blast to the east end of the ice-wall, where a patch of forest had been carried away by the glacier when it was advancing. I noticed a few stumps well out on the moraine flat, showing that its present bare, raw condition was not the condition of fifty or a hundred years ago. In front of this part of the glacier there is a small moraine lake about half a mile in length, around the margin of which are a considerable number of trees standing knee-deep, and of course dead. This also is a result of the recent advance of the ice.

Pushing through the ragged edge of the woods on the left margin of the glacier, the storm seemed to increase in violence, so that it was difficult to draw breath in facing it; therefore I took shelter back of a tree to enjoy it and await, hoping that it would at last somewhat abate. Here the glacier, descending over an abrupt rock, falls forward in grand cascades, while a stream swollen by the rain was now a torrent,—wind, rain, ice-torrent, and water-torrent in one grand symphony.

At length the storm seemed to abate somewhat, and I took off my heavy rubber boots, with which I had waded the glacial streams on the flat, and laid them with my overcoat on a log, which I might mind them on my way back, knowing I would be drenched anyhow, and firmly tied my mountain shoes, tightened my belt, shouldered my ice-axe, and, thus free and ready for rough work, pushed on, regardless as possible of mere rain. Making my way up a steep granite slope, its projecting polished bosses encumbered here and there by boulders and the ground and bruised ruins of the ragged edge of the forest that had been uprooted by the glacier during its recent advance, I traced the side of the glacier for two or three miles, finding everywhere evidence of its having encroached on the woods, which here run back along its edge for fifteen or twenty miles. Under the projecting edge of this vast ice-river I could see down beneath it to a depth of fifty feet or so in some places, where logs and branches were bring crushed to pulp, some of it almost fine enough for paper, though most of it stringy and coarse.

After thus tracing the margin of the glacier for three or four miles, I chopped steps and climbed to the top, and as far as the eye could reach, the nearly level glacier stretched indefinitely away in the gray cloudy sky, a prairie of ice. The wind was now almost moderate, though rain continued to fall, which I did not mind, but a tendency to mist in the dropping draggled clouds made me hesitate about attempting to cross to the opposite shore. Although the distance was only six or seven miles, no traces at this time could be seen of the mountains on the other side, and in case the sky should grow darker, as it seemed inclined to do, I feared that when I got out of sight of land and perhaps into a maze of crevasses I might find difficulty in winning a way back.

Lingering a while and sauntering about in sight of the shore, I found this eastern side of the glacier remarkably free from large crevasses. Nearly all I met were so narrow I could step across them almost anywhere, while the few wide ones were easily avoided by going up or down along their sides to where they narrowed. The dismal cloud ceiling showed rifts here and there, and, thus encouraged, I struck out for the west shore, aiming to strike it five or six miles above the front wall, cautiously taking compass bearings at short intervals to enable me to find my way back should the weather darken again with mist or rain or snow. The structure lines of the glacier itself were, however, my main guide. All went well. I came to a deeply furrowed section about two miles in width where I had to zigzag in long, tedious tacks and make narrow doublings, tracing the edges of wide longitudinal furrows and chasms until I could find a bridge connecting their sides, oftentimes making the direct distance ten times over. . . . By dint of patient doubling and axe-work on dangerous places, I gained the opposite shore in about three hours, the width of the glacier at this point being about seven miles. Occasionally, while making my way, the clouds lifted a little, revealing a few bald, rough mountains sunk to the throat to the broad, icy sea which encompassed them on all sides, sweeping on forever and forever as we count time, wearing them away, giving them the shape they are destined to take when in the fullness of time they shall be parts of new landscapes.

Ere I lost sight of the east-side mountains, those on the west came in sight, so that holding my course was easy, and, though making haste, I halted for a moment to gaze down into the beautiful pure blue crevasses and to drink at the lovely blue wells, the most beautiful of all Nature's water-basins, or at the rills and streams outspread over the ice-land prairie, never ceasing to admire their lovely color and music as they glided and swirled in their blue crystal channels and potholes, and the rumbling of the moulins, or mills, where streams poured into blue-walled pits of unknown depth, some of them as regularly circular as if bored with augers. Interesting, too, were the cascades over blue cliffs, where streams fell into crevasses or slid almost noiselessly down slopes so, smooth and frictionless their motion was concealed. The round or oval wells, however, from one to ten feet wide, and from one to twenty or thirty feet deep, were perhaps the most beautiful of all, the water so pure as to be almost invisible. My widest views did not probably exceed fifteen miles, the rain and mist making distances seem greater.

On reaching the farther shore and tracing it a few miles to northward, I found a large portion of the glacier-current sweeping out westward in a bold and beautiful curve around the shoulder of a mountain as if going direct to the open sea. Leaving the main trunk, it breaks into a magnificent uproar of pinnacles and spires and up-heaving, splashing wave-shaped masses, a crystal cataract incomparably greater and wilder than a score of Niagaras. Tracing its channel three or four miles, I found that it fell into a lake, which it fills with bergs. The front of this branch of the glacier is about three miles wide. I first took the lake to be the head of an arm of the sea, but, going down to its shore and tasting it, I found it fresh, and perhaps less than a hundred feet above sea-level. It is probably separated from the sea only by a moraine dam. I had not time to go around its shores, as it was now near five o'clock and I was about fifteen miles from camp, and I had to make haste to recross the glacier before dark, which would come on about eight o'clock. I therefore made haste up to the main glacier, and, shaping my course by compass and the structure lines of the ice, set off from the land out on to the grand crystal prairie again. All was so silent and so concentred, owing to the low dragging mist, the beauty close about me was all the more keenly felt, though tinged with a dim sense of danger, as if coming events were casting shadows.

I was soon out of sight of land, and the evening dusk that on cloudy days precedes the real night gloom came stealing on and only ice was in sight, and the only sounds, save the low rumbling of the mills and the rattle of falling stones at long intervals, were the low, terribly earnest moanings of the wind or distant waterfalls coming through the thickening gloom. After two hours of hard work I came to a maze of crevasses of appalling depth and width which could not be passed apparently either up or down. I traced them with firm nerve developed by the danger, making wide jumps, poising cautiously on dizzy edges after cutting footholds, taking wide crevasses at a grand leap at once frightful and inspiring. Many a mile was thus traveled, mostly up and down the glacier, making but little real headway, running much of the time as the danger of having to pass the night on the ice became more and more imminent. This I could do, though with the weather and my rainsoaked condition it would be trying at best. In treading the mazes of this crevassed section I had frequently to cross bridges that were only knife-edges for twenty or thirty feet, cutting off the sharp tops and leaving them flat so that little Stickeen could follow me. These I had to straddle, cutting off the top as I progressed and hitching gradually ahead like a boy riding a rail fence. All this time the little dog followed me bravely, never hesitating on the brink of any crevasse that I had jumped, but now that it was becoming dark and the crevasses became more troublesome, he followed close at my heels instead of scampering far and wide, where the ice was at all smooth, as he had in the forenoon. No land was now in sight. The mist fell lower and darker and snow began to fly. I could not see far enough up and down the glacier to judge how best to work out of the bewildering labyrinth, and how hard I tried while there was yet hope of reaching camp that night! a hope which was fast growing dim like the sky. After dark, on such ground, to keep from freezing, I could only jump up and down until morning on a piece of flat ice between the crevasses, dance to the boding music of the winds and waters, and as I was already tired and hungry I would be in bad condition for such ice work. Many times I was put to my mettle, but with a firm-braced nerve, all the more unflinching as the dangers thickened, I worked out of that terrible ice-web, and with blood fairly up Stickeen and I ran over common danger without fatigue. Our very hardest trial was in getting across the very last of the sliver bridges. After examining the first of the two widest crevasses, I followed its edge half a mile or so up and down and discovered that its narrowest spot was about eight feet wide, which was the limit of what I was able to jump. Moreover, the side I was on—that is, the west side—was about a foot higher then the other, and I feared that in case I should be stopped by a still wider impassable crevasse ahead that I would hardly be able to take back that jump from its lower side. The ice beyond, however, as far as I could see it, looked temptingly smooth. Therefore, after carefully making a socket on my foot on the rounded brink, I jumped, but found that I had nothing to spare and more than ever dreaded having to retrace my way. Little Stickeen jumped this, however, without apparently taking a second look at it, and we ran ahead joyfully over smooth, level ice, hoping we were now leaving all danger behind us.

But hardly had we gone a hundred or two yards when to our dismay we found ourselves on the very widest of all the longitudinal crevasses we had yet encountered. It was about forty feet wide. I ran anxiously up the side of it to northward, eagerly hoping that I could get around its head, but my worst fears were realized when at a distance of about a mile or less it ran into the crevasse that I had just jumped. I then ran down the edge for a mile or more below the point where I had first met it, and found that its lower end also united with the crevasse I had jumped, showing dismally that we were on an island two or three hundred yards wide and about two miles long and the only way of escape from this island was by turning back and jumping again that crevasse which I dreaded, or venturing ahead across the giant crevasse by the very worst of the sliver bridges I had ever seen. It was so badly weathered and melted down that it formed a knife-edge, and extended across from side to side in a low, drooping curve like that made by a loose rope attached at each end at the same height. But the worst difficulty was that the ends of the down-curving sliver were attached to the sides at a depth of about eight or ten feet below the surface of the glacier. Getting down to the end of the bridge, and then after crossing it getting up the other side, seemed hardly possible. However, I decided to dare the dangers of the fearful sliver rather than to attempt to retrace my steps. Accordingly I dug a low groove in the rounded edge for my knees to rest in and, leaning over, began to cut a narrow foothold on the steep, smooth side. When I was doing this, Stickeen came up behind me, pushed his head over my shoulder, looked into the crevasses and along the narrow knife-edge, then turned and looked in my face, muttering and whining as if trying to say, "Surely you are not going down there." I said, "Yes, Stickeen, this is the only way." He then began to cry and ran wildly along the rim of the crevasse, searching for a better way, then, returning baffled, of course, he came behind me and lay down and cried louder and louder.

After getting down one step I cautiously stooped and cut another and another in succession until I reached the point where the sliver was attached to the wall. There, cautiously balancing, I chipped down the upcurved end of the bridge until I had formed a small level platform about a foot wide, then, bending forward, got astride of the end of the sliver, steadied myself with my knees, then cut off the top of the sliver, hitching myself forward an inch or two at a time, leaving it about four inches wide for Stickeen. Arrived at the farther end of the sliver, which was about seventy-five feet long, I chipped another little platform on its upcurved end, cautiously rose to my feet, and with infinite pains cut narrow notch steps and finger-holds in the wall and finally got safely across. All this dreadful time poor little Stickeen was crying as if his heart was broken, and when I called to him in as reassuring a voice as I could muster, he only cried the louder, as if trying to say that he never,

never could get down there—the only time that the brave little fellow appeared to know what danger was. After going away as if I was leaving him, he still howled and cried without venturing to try to follow me. Returning to the edge of the crevasse, I told him that I must go, that he could come if he only tried, and finally in despair he hushed his cries, slid his little feet slowly down into my footsteps out on the big sliver, walked slowly and cautiously along the sliver as if holding his breath, while the snow was falling and the wind was moaning and threatening to blow him off. When he arrived at the foot of the slope below me, I was kneeling on the brink ready to assist him in case he should be unable to reach the top. He looked up along the row of notched steps I had made, as if fixing them in his mind, then with a nervous spring he whizzed up and passed me out on to the level ice, and ran and cried and barked and rolled about fairly hysterical in the sudden revulsion from the depth of despair to triumphant joy.

I tried to catch him and pet him and tell him how good and brave he was, but he would not be caught. He ran round and round, swirling like autumn leaves in an eddy, lay down and rolled head over heels. I told him we still had far to go and that we must now stop all nonsense and get off the ice before dark. I knew by the ice-lines that every step was now taking me nearer the shore and soon it came in sight. The headland four or five miles back from the front, covered with spruce trees, loomed faintly but surely through the mist and light fall of snow not more than two miles away. The ice now proved good all the way across, and we reached the lateral moraine just at dusk, then with trembling limbs, now that the danger was over, we staggered and stumbled down the bouldery edge of the glacier and got over the dangerous rocks by the cascades while yet a faint light lingered. We were safe, and then, too, came limp weariness such as no ordinary work ever produces, however hard it may be.

Wearily we stumbled down through the woods, over logs and brush and roots, devil's-clubs pricking us at every faint blundering tumble. At last we got out on the smooth mud slope with only a mile of slow but sure dragging of weary limbs to camp. The Indians had been firing guns to guide me and had a fine supper and fire ready.... Stickeen and I were too tired to eat much, and, strange to say, too tired to sleep, both of us springing up in the night again and again, fancied we were still on that dreadful ice bridge in the shadow of death.

We arose next morning in newness of life. Never before had rocks and ice and trees seemed so beautiful and wonderful, even the cold, biting rainstorm that was blowing seemed full of loving-kindness, wonderful compensation for all that we had endured, and we sailed down the bay through the gray, driving rain rejoicing.

—*"Stickeen: The Story of a Dog," 1909*

chapter eight

Nature's Inexhaustible Abundance

Commentary

A CHANCE ENCOUNTER, a moment of insight, an accidental meeting, an hour, or
even a minute in time can radiate a beam of light—a brilliance that never fades—over
an entire lifespan. What is seen through the eyes enters into the heart, there to remain
to inform and inspire. Such was John Muir's first sight of the Sierra Nevada Mountains
in 1868 where they meet the Central Valley at Twenty Hill Hollow. In early 1869 he
recalled, "Never shall I forget my baptism in this font. It happened in January, a resur-
rection day for many a plant and for me. I suddenly . . . overflowed with light. . . . Light,
of unspeakable richness, was brooding the flowers. Truly, said I, is California the Golden
State—in metallic gold, in sun gold, and in plant gold. The sunshine for a whole summer
seemed condensed into the chambers of that one glowing day. Every trace of dimness
had been washed from the sky; the mountains were dusted and wiped clean with clouds;
. . . the grand Sierra stood along the plain, colored in four horizontal bands—the lowest,
rose purple; the next higher, dark purple; the next, blue; and, above all, the white row
of summits pointing to the heavens. . . . To lovers of the wild, these mountains are not a
hundred miles away. Their spiritual power and the goodness of the sky make them near,
as a circle of friends. . . . You bathe in these spirit-beams, turning round and round, as if
warming at a camp-fire. Presently you lose consciousness of your own separate existence:
you blend with the landscape, and become part and parcel of nature."[1]

   Whether it is was purple mountains, water pounding down a waterfall, luxuriant
golden wildflowers, swarms of bees, great flocks of migrating birds, thick expanses of
forests, sunrises and sunsets splashing a palate of reds and oranges across the heavens, or
the spring rains that awaken new life in every living being—John Muir was intoxicated
by their abundance; all was "fresh beauty at every step."[2]

But there was a caveat: Nature's bounty would continue only if everything was kept in balance. Muir was not so awestruck by nature's bounty as to be blind to its fragile balance. In the chapter of his first book, *The Mountains of California*, in which he shares his first glimpse of the lush, flowering Central Valley, he also laments that "of late years, plows and sheep have made sad havoc of these glorious pastures, destroying tens of thousands of the flowering acres like a fire and banishing many species."[3] Oh, if John Muir could see the Central Valley now, ravaged by industrial agriculture! He would weep.

A Heart Beating in Every Crystal and Cell

John Muir imagined his heart beating to the Divine rhythm of the universe, in which everything is connected in harmonious order. "Another big day, enough for a lifetime. . . . [I] am holding an easterly course, the deep canyon of Tenaya Creek on the right hand, Mt. Hoffman on the left, and the lake straight ahead about ten miles distant, the summit of Mt. Hoffman about three thousand feet above me."

> The rocks, the air, everything speaking with audible voice or silent; joyful, wonderful, enchanting, banishing weariness and sense of time. No longing for anything now or hereafter as we go home into the mountain's heart. The level sunbeams are touching the fir-tops, every leaf shining with dew. . . . On I sauntered in freedom complete; body without weight as far as I was aware. . . . No Sierra landscape that I have seen holds anything truly dead or dull, or any trace of what in manufactories is called rubbish or waste; everything is perfectly clean and pure and full of divine lessons. . . . When we try to pick out anything by itself, we find it hitched to everything else in the universe. One fancies a heart like our own must be beating in every crystal and cell, and we feel like stopping to speak to the plants and animals as friendly fellow-mountaineers. Nature as a poet . . . becomes more and more visible the farther and higher we go. . . .
>
> —JOURNAL ENTRY, JULY 27, 1869

Nature's Choicest Treasures

EXCEPT FOR ONE TRIP TO ALASKA, Muir had mostly stayed home during the 1880s, managing the family fruit farm. A wanderer at heart, when the offer came to write essays for a handsomely illustrated book, *Picturesque California,* he jumped at it. With his friend, the nature artist William Keith, Muir took off on a series of trips to Yosemite and the Pacific Northwest during 1887 and 1888. One of the essays contains this springtime description of Yosemite bathed in sunshine as all of nature sprang into bloom.

The far-famed Yosemite Valley lies well back on the western slope of the Sierra. . . . It is about seven miles long, from half a mile to a mile wide, and nearly a mile deep, carved in the solid granite flank of the range. Its majestic walls are sculptured into a bewildering variety of forms—domes and gables, towers and battlements, and sheer massive cliffs, separated by grooves and furrows and deep, shadowy canyons, and adorned with evergreen trees. The bottom is level and park-like, finely diversified with meadows and groves, and bright, sunny gardens; the River of Mercy [Merced], clear as crystal, sweeping in tranquil beauty through the midst, while the whole valley resounds with the music of its unrivaled waterfalls.

It is a place compactly filled with wild mountain beauty and grandeur, floods of sunshine, floods of snowy water, beautiful trees of many species, thickets of flowering shrubs, beds of flowers of every color, from the blue and white violets on the meadows, to the crimson pillars of the snow-flowers glowing among the brown needles beneath the firs. Ferns and mosses find grateful homes in a thousand moist nooks among the rocks, humming-birds are seen glinting about among the showy flowers, small singers enliven the under-brush, and wide-winged hawks and eagles float in the calm depths between the mighty walls; squirrels in the trees, bears in the canyons; all find peaceful homes, beautiful life of every form, things frail and fleeting and types of enduring strength meeting and blending, as if into this grand mountain mansion nature had gathered her choicest treasures, whether great or small.

—Picturesque California and the Region West of the
Rocky Mountains, from Alaska to Mexico, 1888

The Heart-Peace of Nature

THE PICTURE JOHN MUIR presents of Yosemite Creek with all its myriad of waterfalls that flow into it, is one of sheer abundance, divine light falling as spray and foam, whispering peace to all who will listen.

The Yosemite Creek is the most tranquil of all the larger streams that pour over the valley walls. . . . Issuing from their moraine fountains, each shining thread of water at once begins to sing, running gladly onward, over boulders, over rock-stairs, over dams of fallen trees; now groping in shadows, now gliding free in the light on glacier-planed pavements, not a leaf on their borders; diving under willows, fingering their red roots and low-dipping branches, then absorbed in green bogs; out again among mosaics of leaf, shadows and light, whirling in pools giddy and ruffled, then restful and calm, not a foambell in sight; whispering low, solemn in gestures as full grown rivers, slowly meandering through green velvet meadows, banks embossed with bryanthus and yet finer cassiope, white and blue violets blending with white and blue daisies in smooth, silky sods of the Alpine agrostis; out again on bare granite, flowing over gravel and sand mixed with mica and garnets and white crystal quartz, making tiny falls and cascades in rapid succession, until at length all the bright, rejoicing choir meet together to form the main stream which flows calmly down to its fate in the valley, sweeping over the tremendous verge beneath a mantle of diamond spray.

Amid the varied foams and fine ground mists of the mountain streams that are ever rising from a thousand waterfalls, there is an affluence and variety of rainbows. . . . Both day and night, winter and summer, this divine light may be seen wherever water is falling in spray and foam, a silent interpreter of the heart-peace of nature, amid the wildest displays of her power.

*—Picturesque California and the Region West of
the Rocky Mountains, from Alaska to Mexico, 1888*

Hundreds of Happy Sun-Plants

JOHN MUIR'S FIRST SIGHT of the luxuriant Central Valley remained with him always, and he described it many times in various letters to friends and in his journals, including this account in the essay "The Bee-Pastures," a chapter in his first book, *The Mountains of California.*

When I first saw this central garden, the most extensive and regular of all the bee-pastures of the State, it seemed all one sheet of plant gold, hazy and vanishing in the distance, distinct as a new map along the foot-hills at my feet.

Descending the eastern slopes of the Coast Range through beds of gilias and lupines, and around many a breezy hillock and bush-crowned headland, I at length waded out into the midst of it. All the ground was covered, not with grass and green leaves, but with radiant corollas, about ankle-deep next the foot-hills, knee-deep or more five or six miles out. Here were bahia, madia, madaria, burrielia, chrysopsis, corethrogyne, grindelia, etc., growing in close social congregations of various shades of yellow, blending finely with the purples of clarkia, orthocarpus, and oenothera [various herbs and wild flowers], whose delicate petals were drinking the vital sunbeams without giving back any sparkling glow.

Because so long a period of extreme drought succeeds the rainy season, most of the vegetation is composed of annuals, which spring up simultaneously, and bloom together at about the same height above the ground, the general surface being but slightly ruffled by the taller phacelias [blue bells], penstemons [commonly known as "beard tongue"], and groups of Salvia carduacea, the king of the mints.

Sauntering in any direction, hundreds of these happy sun-plants brushed against my feet at every step, and closed over them as if I were wading in liquid gold. The air was sweet with fragrance, the larks sang their blessed songs, rising on the wing as I advanced, then sinking out of sight in the polleny sod, while myriads of wild bees stirred the lower air with their monotonous hum—monotonous, yet forever fresh and sweet as every-day sunshine. Hares and spermophiles showed themselves in considerable numbers in shallow places, and small bands of ante-lopes were almost constantly in sight, gazing curiously from some slight elevation, and then bounding swiftly away with unrivaled grace of motion. Yet I could discover no crushed flowers to mark their track, nor, indeed, any destructive action of any wild foot or tooth whatever.

The great yellow days circled by uncounted, while I drifted toward the north, observing the countless forms of life thronging about me, lying down almost any-where on the approach of night. And what glorious botanical beds I had! Often-times on awaking I would find several new species leaning over me and looking me full in the face, so that my studies would begin before rising.

—*The Mountains of California*

Clouds in the Sky-Fields

HERE IS AN ILLUSTRATION OF John Muir's legendary pose-poetry at its best. He suc-cessfully invokes our powers of imagination in seeing the sky as a flowering field, called into being by the sun. Like most of John Muir's journal entries during his first summer in the Sierra, this was written at the close of a long day spent following the herd of sheep for which he was responsible.

> A slight sprinkle of rain—large drops far apart, falling with hearty pat and plash on leaves and stones and into the mouths of the flowers. Cumuli rising to the eastward. How beautiful their pearly bosses! How well they harmonize with the upswelling rocks beneath them. Mountains of the sky, solid-looking, finely sculptured, their richly varied topography wonderfully defined. Never before have I seen clouds so substantial looking in form and texture. Nearly every day toward noon they rise with visible swelling motion as if new worlds were being created. And how fondly they brood and hover over the gardens and forests with their cooling shadows and showers, keeping every petal and leaf in glad health and heart. One may fancy the clouds themselves are plants, springing up in the sky-fields at the call of the sun, growing in beauty until they reach their prime, scattering rain and hail like berries and seeds, then wilting and dying.
>
> —JOURNAL ENTRY, JUNE 12, 1869

Nature's Inexhaustible Abundance

THE DAYS OF LATE SUMMER were cooling, the nights shortening; day after day the sky had been almost cloudless. As darkness descends upon the sheep camp, John Muir contemplates the eternal cycle of life to death to life rising again. Nothing natural is ever wasted. Death nourishes life. As he mentioned the day before writing the journal entry below, "….another grand throb of Nature's heart, ripening late flowers and seeds for next summer, full of life and the thoughts and plans of life to come, and full of ripe and ready death beautiful as life, telling divine wisdom and goodness and immortality."

> One is constantly reminded of the infinite lavishness and fertility of Nature—inexhaustible abundance amid what seems enormous waste. And yet when we look

into any of her operations that lie within reach of our minds, we learn that no particle of her material is wasted or worn out. It is eternally flowing from use to use, beauty to yet higher beauty; and we soon cease to lament waste and death, and rather rejoice and exult in the imperishable, unspendable wealth of the universe, and faithfully watch and wait the reappearance of everything that melts and fades and dies about us, feeling sure that its next appearance will be better and more beautiful than the last.

—JOURNAL ENTRY, SEPTEMBER 2, 1868

Fresh Beauty at Every Step

IN THE SPRING OF 1887, John Muir took a second trip to Bloody Canyon, a lovely uplands canyon in the eastern Sierra. The canyon probably got its name from the damage the sharp rocks inflicted on the ankles of the horses traversing the canyon's steep ledges. Muir looked forward to the trip and he wasn't disappointed. "I made up a package of bread, tied my notebook to my belt, and strode away in the bracing air, every nerve and muscle tingling with eager indefinite hope, and ready to give welcome to all that wilderness might offer. The plushy lawns staffed with blue gentians and daisies soothed my morning haste, and made me linger; they were all so fresh, so sweet, so peaceful."

Climbing higher, as the day passed away, I traced the paths of the ancient glaciers over many a shining pavement, and marked the lanes in the upper forests that told the power of the winter avalanches. Still higher, I noted the gradual dwarfing of the pines in compliance with climate, and on the summit discovered creeping mats of the arctic willow, low as the lowliest grasses; and patches of dwarf vaccinium, with its round pink bells sprinkled over the sod as if they had fallen from the sky like hail; while in every direction the landscape stretched sublimely away in fresh wildness, a manuscript written by the hand of Nature alone. . . .

Here for the first time I met the Arctic daisies in all their perfection of pure spirituality—gentle mountaineers, face to face with the frosty sky, kept safe and warm, by a thousand miracles. I leaped lightly from rock to rock, glorying in the eternal freshness and sufficiency of nature, and in the rugged tenderness with which she nurtures her mountain darlings in the very homes and fountains of storms.

Fresh beauty appeared at every step, delicate rock-ferns, and tufts of the fairest flowers. Now another lake came to view, now a waterfall. Never fell light in brighter spangles, never fell water in whiter foam. I seemed to float through the canyon enchanted, feeling nothing of its roughness. . . .

Looking back from the shore of Moraine Lake, my morning ramble seemed all a dream. There curved Bloody Canyon, a mere glacier furrow two thousand and three thousand feet deep. . . . Here the lilies were higher than my head, and the sunshine was warm enough for palms. Yet the snow around the Arctic willows on the summit was plainly visible, only a few miles away.

—*Picturesque California and the Region West of
the Rocky Mountains, from Alaska to Mexico, 1888*

Rejoicing Everywhere

IN MUIR'S VIEW, only the beauty of the natural world—not philosophies, dogmas, or even literature—could nurture the soul. In his first summer in the Sierra, Muir's deep sense of sacred wilderness was awakened in him along with his ardent voice as a defender of the wilderness, a voice that was to awaken others to the idea that nature had value for itself, not just for its usefulness for grazing, timber, water, and mineral resources.

How deep our sleep last night in the mountain's heart, beneath the trees and stars, hushed by solemn-sounding waterfalls and many small soothing voices in sweet accord whispering peace! And our first pure mountain day, warm, calm, cloudless—

how immeasurable it seems, how serenely wild! I can scarcely remember its beginning. Along the river, over the hills, in the ground, in the sky, spring work is going
on with joyful enthusiasm, new life, new beauty, unfolding, unrolling in glorious
exuberant extravagance —new birds in their nests, new winged creatures in the air,
and new leaves, new flowers, spreading, shining, rejoicing everywhere.

—JOURNAL ENTRY, JUNE 9, 1869

Everything in Joyous Rhythmic Motion

IT WAS JOHN MUIR'S VIEW that creation was always creating—the crystal mountains,
gleaming rivers, flowering meadows, ferns, and forests were continually evolving in one
cosmic dance of life.

Warm, sunny day, thrilling plant and animals and rocks alike, making sap and blood
flow fast, and making every particle of the crystal mountains throb and swirl and
dance in glad accord like star-dust. No dullness anywhere visible or thinkable. No
stagnation, no death. Everything kept in joyful rhythmic motion in the pulses of
Nature's big heart.

—JOURNAL ENTRY, JULY 2, 1869

The History of a Single Raindrop

NOTHING WAS TOO SMALL or seemingly insignificant to claim John Muir's attention.
He saw beauty and utility even in a single raindrop.

How interesting to trace the history of a single raindrop! It is not long, geologically
speaking, as we have seen, since the first raindrops fell on the newborn leafless
Sierra landscapes. How different the lot of these falling now! Happy the showers
that fall on so fair a wilderness—scarce a single drop can fail to find a beautiful
spot—on the tops of the peaks, on the shining glacier pavements, on the great

smooth domes, on forests and gardens and brushy moraines, plashing, glinting, pattering, laving. Some go to the high snowy fountains to swell their well-saved stores; some into the lakes, washing the mountain windows, patting their smooth glassy levels, making dimples and bubbles and spray; some into the water-falls and cascades, as if eager to join in their dance and song and beat their foam yet finer; good luck and good work for the happy mountain raindrops, each one of them a high waterfall in itself, descending from the cliffs and hollows of the clouds to the cliffs and hollows of the rocks, out of the sky-thunder into the thunder of the falling rivers. Some, falling on meadows and bogs, creep silently out of sight to the grass roots, hiding softly as in a nest, slipping, oozing hither, thither, seeking and finding their appointed work. Some, descending through the spires of the woods, sift spray through the shining needles, whispering peace and good cheer to each one of them. Some drops with happy aim glint on the sides of crystals . . . . Some happy drops fall straight into the cups of flowers, kissing the lips of lilies. How far they have to go, how many cups to fill, great and small, cells too small to be seen, cups holding half a drop as well as lake basins between the hills, each replenished with equal care, every drop in all the blessed throng a silvery newborn star with lake and river, garden and grove, valley and mountain, all that the landscape holds reflected in its crystal depths, God's messenger, angel of love sent on its way with majesty and pomp and display of power. . . .

—JOURNAL ENTRY, JULY 19, 1869

Everything is Flowing

WATER IS BLOOD FOR THE UNIVERSE, flowing eternally through "Nature's warm heart."

Contemplating the lace-like fabric of streams outspread over the mountains, we are reminded that everything is flowing—going somewhere, animals and so-called lifeless rocks as well as water. Thus the snow flows fast or slow in grand beauty-making glaciers and avalanches; the air in majestic floods carrying minerals, plant leaves, seeds, spores, with streams of music and fragrance; water streams carrying rocks both in solution and in the form of mud particles, sand, pebbles, and boulders. Rocks flow from volcanoes like water from springs, and animals flock together and flow in currents modified by stepping, leaping, gliding, flying, swimming . . . while the stars go streaming through space pulsing on and on forever like blood globules in Nature's warm heart.

—JOURNAL ENTRY, AUGUST 27, 1869

chapter nine

Walking Lightly on the Land

Commentary

Prior to the discovery of gold in 1848, the Sierra Nevada were unknown except to the Native Americans whose forebearers had inhabited the land for some 6,000 years. From goldseekers to tourists, the word of Yosemite's great beauty rapidly spread as tourists began to arrive in the park. In l864 a group of influential Californians persuaded Congress and President Abraham Lincoln to set aside the Yosemite Valley as the nation's first public preserve. The grant deeded Yosemite Valley and the Mariposa Grove of Big Trees to the State of California. Unfortunately, no such protection existed for the vast wilderness surrounding the Valley with its majestic sequoia groves.

In 1889, John Muir was host and field guide to Robert Underwood Johnson, the politically well-connected and influential editor of the *Century Magazine*. The two established an immediate rapport. Johnson found, as Muir knew already, that the high country had been overrun with flocks of domestic sheep and it suffered from the ravages of lumbering and mining. As they camped together in Tuolumne Meadows, they decided to do something about it. Together they planned a campaign to add the high country surrounding Yosemite Valley into the proposed national park. Johnson would use his influence with key citizens and politicians in Washington to help preserve the region, and Muir would write two articles extolling the benefits of their preservation in the *Century Magazine:* "The Treasures of Yosemite" and "Features of the Proposed Yosemite National Park." Their efforts were handsomely rewarded, for in just one year, on October 1, 1890, the U.S. Congress set aside more than 1,500 square miles of "reserved forest lands" soon to be known as Yosemite National Park. It included the area surrounding Yosemite Valley and the Mariposa Grove of Giant Sequoias. During President Benjamin

Harrison's term (1889–1893), 13 million acres of forests were preserved. President Grover Cleveland (1893–1897) set aside another 21 million acres.

John Muir had his greatest influence with President Theodore Roosevelt (1901–1909). Roosevelt had read Muir's book *Our National Parks*, published in l901, and two years later he invited himself on a camping trip with the Great Naturalist. One can only imagine their conversation beneath Yosemite's towering pines, for Roosevelt emerged from the encounter with the foundation of his conservation programs. Following his meeting with Muir, he began a course of action that established 140 million acres of national forest, five national parks and 23 national monuments.

The Yosemite Valley and the Mariposa Grove were ceded from the State of California's control to become Yosemite National Park in 1906. In addition, Muir's influence led to the creation of Sequoia (1890), Mount Ranier (1897), and Petrified Forest (1906) National Parks during his lifetime, and Grand Canyon National Park five years after his death. Prior to Muir, neither the United States nor any other government in the world had recognized public lands for their own value and set them aside in perpetuity. This is uniquely the contribution of John Muir and his influence upon four American presidents. Ever a modest man, Muir wrote, "I have done the best I could to show forth the beauty, grandeur, and all embracing usefulness of our wild mountain forest reservations and parks, with the view to inciting people to come and enjoy them, and get them into their hearts, so that at length their preservation and right use might be made sure."[1]

Despite all these measures to preserve natural lands, Yosemite was not entirely safe from other interests. The year 1906 also saw the devastating earthquake and fire that shook and burned most of San Francisco. Awakened to the vulnerability of their water supplies which they feared could be limited in the future, the city supervisors looked for other water sources and identified the Hetch Hetchy Valley, part of the new Yosemite National Park, as the best candidate. The valley would be easy to dam, and the project could be completed more cheaply than other alternatives.

In l908 John Muir began his fight to save the Hetch Hetchy Valley, and, with the Sierra Club, he submitted a resolution to the U. S. Secretary of the Interior opposing damming of the Hetch Hetchy Valley. In 1908 he wrote to President Theodore Roosevelt regarding the project, "There is not in all the wonderful Sierra, or indeed in the world, another so grand and wonderful a block in Nature's handiwork. . . . These sacred mountain temples are the holiest ground that the heart of man has consecrated, and behoves us all faithfully to do our part in seeing that our wild mountain parks are passed on unspoiled to those who come after us."[2]

But the odds were against Muir. Chief U. S. Forester Gifford Pinchot urged that the valley be turned over to the City of San Francisco. Roosevelt left office in 1909 and was followed by William Howard Taft, who like Roosevelt, had been given a tour of Yosemite by John Muir. Nonetheless, conservation-minded Californians and their Washington supporters could do little to halt the damming of the Hetch Hetchy Valley. In December 1913, the U. S. Senate finally passed the enabling bill (Raker Bill), granting the City of San Francisco full rights to Hetch Hetchy—even though the valley lay within the National Park—and President Woodrow Wilson signed the bill into law on December 19.

The period between 1889 and 1905 was the time of John Muir's greatest flowering as a writer, explorer of wilderness areas, preservationist, and advocate for Yosemite. Muir was reaping the benefits of his earlier years during which he lived intensely in the mountains and prodigeously recorded every aspect of what he discovered—plants, animals, rock formations, seasons, the weather, days and nights in the Sierra Nevada. One president had gone camping with him and another would soon do so. He made the acquaintance of other notable individuals: Edward H. Harriman, the New York financier and railway magnate, and Robert Underwood Johnson, the associate editor of the *Century Magazine*. Muir continued to produce a steady stream of articles. His first two books were published—*The Mountains of California* (1894) and *Our National Parks* (1901), the book that had stirred President Roosevelt's interest in Yosemite.

In 1892 Muir was part of the small group that founded the Sierra Club, which began as a California group of mountain-lovers. He was the Sierra Club's first president, and he remained so until his death. In 1896 he received an honorary degree from

Harvard; a year later, he received another from the University of Wisconsin. The University of Wisconsin's honorary degree was particularly gratifying to Muir because, although he had attended the school, he never graduated. In l896 Muir was a member of a U. S. Forestry Commission trip to survey the forests of Yellowstone, the Black Hills of South Dakota, and forests in Idaho, Oregon, and Washington. During this period he also visited Boston, where he took a sentimental side trip to visit Emerson and Thoreau's graves in nearby Concord. He also went on a heartwarming visit to his boyhood home in Dunbar, Scotland.

As Muir's reputation and fame grew, so also did the losses in his personal life. Not only was Hetch Hetchy gone, but he endured the loss of both his parents and his father-in-law. Most significant was the death of his wife, Louie. Muir had been very worried about his younger daughter, Helen, who suffered from chronic respiratory problems. Believing the dry Arizona air would help, after one more severe attack of pneumonia, he took her there for a rest cure. Just as Helen began to improve through breathing in "the clean, pure as ice Arctic air," Muir received a telegram from home that Louie was gravely ill with lung cancer. He returned home at once, and she died a month later on August 6, l905. Muir was deeply shaken by her death. Although they had spent many months apart, Louie was perhaps the only person close to him who truly understood his need to be out and about, and she was his quiet and steady rock. John Muir was 64 years old, and finally he was feeling his age and the pain of all of his losses.

From this point on, John Muir would be a lonelier man. Still, he had wilderness lands to protect, more Alaskan glaciers to discover, more mountains to climb, far-off countries to visit, and trees of South America and Africa to see for himself.

Walking Lightly on the Land

BY THE TIME JOHN MUIR PUBLISHED *My First Summer in the Sierra*, his attitude towards America's First People had significantly evolved. There were not many Native people living near the Muir family farm in Wisconsin, and one of Muir's first encounters with one of them was unfavorable. It involved the theft of his favorite horse, Nob, by a Native youth, and although Muir was successful in reclaiming the horse, the experience left him wary.

When Muir first went to the Yosemite region, most of the Native population had been run out of the valley, so he had little contact with them; nonetheless, the settlers still talked about the Mariposa Indian War of 1850 to 1851.

White men flocked into the foothills of the Sierra in search of gold, and it was not long before difficulties arose between them and the Native Americans who struggled to keep possession of ancestral lands. An early white settler, James D. Savage, ran a trading post and mining camp on the Merced River 20 miles below Yosemite Valley, which was practically unknown to European-Americans. Savage traded with the Native Americans who brought him gold and pelts. What exactly precipitated the event is unknown, but during the spring of 1850, Native people came down the river and attacked the post, killing several settlers. Savage responded by forming a volunteer army in early 1851, and they had several indecisive skirmishes with the Indians. The governor of California was pursuaded to authorize the call-up of 200 militiamen who promptly rounded up the Native Americans, including the great Yosemite Chief Tenaya, and sent them to a reservation in the San Joaquin Valley. With the goal of capturing every Native person in the area, Savage took one of the young braves as a guide and marched north. On March 25, 1851, the trail led them to what is now known as Inspiration Point, affording the European-Americans their first view of the magnificent Yosemite Valley.

As is evident in the selection below, Muir grew into an appreciation of the First People's respect for the land, how they ". . . walk softly and hurt the landscape hardly more than the birds and the squirrels . . . ," and he later depended upon Native guides during his Alaskan explorations.

> Along the main ridges and larger branches of the [north fork of the Merced] river In-
> dian trails may be traced, but they are not nearly as distinct as one would expect to

find them. How many centuries Indians have roamed these woods nobody knows, probably a great many, extending far beyond the time that Columbus touched our shores, and it seems strange that heavier marks have not been made. Indians walk softly and hurt the landscape hardly more than the birds and squirrels, and their brush and bark huts last hardly longer than those of wood rats, while their more enduring monuments, excepting those wrought on the forests by the fires they made to improve their hunting grounds, vanish in a few centuries.

How different are most of those of the white man, especially on the lower gold region—roads blasted in the solid rock, wild streams dammed and tamed and turned out of their channels and led along the sides of canyons and valleys to work in mines like slaves. Crossing from ridge to ridge, high in the air, on long straddling trestles as if flowing on stilts, or down and up across valleys and hills, imprisoned in iron pipes to strike and wash away hills and miles of the skin of the mountain's face, riddling, stripping every gold gully and flat. These are the white man's marks made in a few feverish years, to say nothing of mills, fields, villages, scattered hundreds of miles along the flank of the Range. Long will it be ere these marks are effaced. . . .

—JOURNAL ENTRY, JULY 11, 1869

Vain Efforts to Save a Little Glacial Bog

ALTHOUGH JOHN MUIR FAILED in his lifetime to preserve his family's first farm, Fountain Lake Farm, it was declared a State of Wisconsin Natural Area in 1972. It was designated a National Historic Landmark in 1990. Also a portion of the 1,200-mile Wisconsin Ice Age National Scenic Trail runs through Fountain Lake Farm. Thus the "little glacial bog" Muir lamented of has now been restored.

The preservation of specimen sections of natural flora—bits of pure wildness—was a fond, favorite notion of mine long before I heard of national parks. When my father came from Scotland, he settled in a fine wild region in Wisconsin, beside a small glacier lake bordered with white pond-lilies. And on the north side of the lake, just below our house, there was a carex meadow full of charming flowers—cypripediums, pogonias, calopogons, asters, goldenrods, etc.—and around the margin of the meadow many nooks rich in flowering ferns and heathworts. And when I was about to wander away on my long rambles, I was sorry to leave that precious meadow unprotected; therefore, I said to my brother-in-law, who then owned it, "Sell me the forty acres of lake meadow, and keep it fenced, and never allow cattle or hogs to break into it, and I will gladly pay you whatever you say. I want to keep it untrampled for the sake of its ferns and flowers; and even if I should never see it again, the beauty of its lilies and orchids is so pressed into my mind I shall always enjoy looking back at them in imagination, even across seas and continents, and perhaps after I am dead." But he regarded my plan as a sentimental dream wholly impracticable. The fence he said would surely be broken down sooner or later, and all the work would be in vain.

Eighteen years later I found the deep-water pond lilies in fresh bloom, but the delicate garden-sod of the meadow was broken up, and I trampled into black mire. On the same Wisconsin farm there was a small flowery, ferny bog that I also tried to save. It was less than half an acre in area, and I said, "Surely you can at least keep for me this little bog." Yes, he would try. And when I had left home, and kept writing about it, he would say in reply, "Let your mind rest, my dear John; the mud hole is safe, and the frogs in it are singing right merrily." But in less than twenty years the beauty of this little glacier-bog also was trampled away [and destroyed].

—"THE NATIONAL PARKS AND FOREST RESERVATIONS,"

Sierra Club Bulletin, 1896

God's First Temples

ACCORDING TO THE "GOSPEL OF JOHN MUIR," God is revealed first through the natural world; every natural artifact is a reflection of the beauty, magnificence, and abundance of the Creator. Wood and stone churches bear no comparison; all are poor imitations of God's first temples. Human beings cannot improve on the pure work of the Creator, and, furthermore, the more people seek God in human-made structures, ". . . the farther off and dimmer seems the Lord himself."

> Clouds at noon occupying about half the sky gave half an hour of heavy rain to wash one of the cleanest landscapes in the world. How well it is washed! The sea is hardly less dusty than the ice-burnished pavements and ridges, domes and canyons, and summit peaks plashed with snow like waves with foam. How fresh the woods are and calm after the last films of clouds have been wiped from the sky! A few minutes ago every tree was excited, bowing to the roaring storm, waving, swirling, tossing their branches in glorious enthusiasm like worship. But though to the outer ear these trees are now silent, their songs never cease. Every hidden cell is throbbing with music and life, every fibre thrilling like harp strings, while incense is ever flowing from the balsam bells and leaves. No wonder the hills and groves were God's first temples, and the more they are cut down and hewn into cathedrals and churches, the farther off and dimmer seems the Lord himself. The same may be said of stone temples. Yonder, to the eastward of our camp grove, stands one of Nature's cathedrals, hewn from the living rock, almost conventional in form, about two thousand feet high, nobly adorned with spires and pinnacles, thrilling under floods of sunshine as if alive like a grove-temple, and well named "Cathedral Peak."
>
> —JOURNAL ENTRY, JULY 24, 1869

The Eternal Conflict between Right and Wrong

PEOPLE SOON REALIZED that Yosemite National Park still was not safe from commercial interests and more would be needed to ensure its protection. Thus, a group at the University of California led by Professor Henry Senger organized to make the Sierra Mountains, and especially the Yosemite region, better-known and more accessible to hikers and mountain-lovers. Others in the group were John Muir, the artist William Keith, attorney Warren Olney, professors Joseph LeConte and Cornelius Beach Bradley, and Stanford University President David Starr Jordan. Olney and Senger drew up articles of incorporation, and on May 28, 1892, the Sierra Club was incorporated "to explore, enjoy, and render accessible the mountain regions of the Pacific Coast; to publish authentic information concerning them," and "to enlist the support and cooperation of the people and government in preserving the forests and other natural features of the Sierra Nevada."

No sooner were the boundaries of the park established, than interested parties began to try to break through them. Last winter a determined effort was made to have the area of the park cut down nearly one-half. But the Sierra Club and other good friends of the forests on both sides of the continent made a good defense, and to-day the original boundaries are still unbroken.

The battle we have fought, and are still fighting, for the forests is a part of the eternal conflict between right and wrong, and we cannot expect to see the end of it. I trust, however, that our Club will not weary in this forest well-doing. The fight for the Yosemite Park and other forest parks and reserves is by no means over; nor would the fighting cease, however much the boundaries were contracted. Every good thing, great and small, needs defense. The smallest forest reserve, and the first I ever heard of, was in the Garden of Eden; and though its boundaries were drawn by the Lord, and embraced only one tree, yet even so moderate a reserve as this was attacked. And I doubt not, if only one of our grand trees in the Sierra were reserved as an example and type of all that is most noble and glorious in mountain trees, it would not be long before you would find a lumberman and a lawyer at the foot of it, eagerly proving by every law terrestrial and celestial that that tree must come down. So we must count on watching and striving for these trees, and should always be glad to find anything so surely good and noble to strive for.

—"THE NATIONAL PARKS AND FOREST RESERVATIONS,"
Sierra Club Bulletin, 1896

Dam Hetch Hetchy!

AFTER A STRUGGLE OF ALMOST 25 YEARS, the City of San Francisco was successful in taking for use as a reservoir the beautiful Hetch Hetchy Valley, a canyon within Yosemite National Park, regarded by some as prettier than the Yosemite Valley. Some say the loss broke Muir's heart, for he wrote to his friend C. Hart Merriam ten months before his death that ". . . it is a monumental mistake, but it is more, it is a monumental crime."

Yosemite is so wonderful that we are apt to regard it as an exceptional creation, the only valley of its kind in the world; but Nature is not so poor as to have only one of anything. Several other Yosemites have been discovered in the Sierra that occupy the same relative positions on the Range and were formed by the same forces in the same kind of granite. One of these, the Hetch Hetchy Valley, is in the Yosemite National Park about twenty miles from Yosemite. . . . After my first visit to it in the autumn of 1871, I have always called it the "Tuolumne Yosemite," for it is a wonderfully exact counterpart of the Merced Yosemite, not only in its sublime rocks and waterfalls but in the gardens, groves and meadows of its flowery park-like floor. . . .

Sad to say, this most precious and sublime feature of the Yosemite National Park, one of the greatest of all our natural resources for the uplifting joy and peace and health of the people, is in danger of being dammed and made into a reservoir to help supply San Francisco with water and light, thus flooding it from wall to wall and burying its gardens and groves one or two hundred feet deep. This grossly destructive commercial scheme has long been planned and urged (though water as pure and abundant can be got from outside of the people's park, in a dozen different places), because of the comparative cheapness of the dam and of the territory which it is sought to divert from the great uses to which it was dedicated in the Act of 1890 establishing the Yosemite National Park. . . . Nevertheless, like anything else worth while, from the very beginning, however well guarded, they have always been subject to attack by despoiling gainseekers and mischief-makers of every degree from Satan to Senators, eagerly trying to make everything immediately and selfishly commercial, with schemes disguised in smug-smiling philanthropy. . . . Thus long ago a few enterprising merchants utilized the Jerusalem temple as a place of business instead of a place of prayer, changing money, buying and selling cattle and sheep and doves. . . . Ever since the establishment of the Yosemite National Park, strife has been going on around its borders and I suppose this will go on as part of the universal battle between right and wrong, however much its boundaries may be shorn, or its wild beauty destroyed. . . .

Should Hetch Hetchy be submerged for a reservoir, as proposed, not only would it be utterly destroyed, but the sublime canyon way to the heart of the High Sierra would be hopelessly blocked. . . . That any one would try to destroy such a place seems incredible; but sad experience shows that there are people good enough and bad enough for anything. The proponents of the dam scheme bring forward a lot of bad arguments to prove that the only righteous thing to do with the people's parks is to destroy them bit by bit as they are able. Their arguments are curiously like those of the devil. . . . These temple destroyers, devotees of ravaging commercialism, seem to have a perfect contempt for Nature, and, instead of lifting their eyes to the God of the mountains, lift them to the Almighty Dollar. Dam Hetch Hetchy!

—The Yosemite

Barbarous Harvesting of Lumber

AMERICA WAS ONCE COVERED with one billion acres of lush, towering forests teeming with plants and animals of all kinds. In the past 500 years, aggressive logging and development have destroyed over 95 percent of America's original forests, and the costs to our wellbeing, and to the wellbeing of the planet, are staggering.

At first sight it would seem that the mighty granite temples could be injured little by anything that man may do. But it is surprising to find how much our impression in such cases depends upon the delicate bloom of the scenery, which in all the more accessible places is so easily rubbed off. I saw the King's River Valley in its midsummer glory sixteen years ago, when it was wild, and when the divine balanced beauty of the trees and flowers seemed to be reflected and doubled by the on-looking rocks and streams as though they were mirrors, while they in turn were mirrored in every garden and grove. In that year (1875) I saw the following ominous notice on a tree in the King's River Yosemite:

> "We, the undersigned, claim this valley for the purpose of raising stock.
>
> Mr. Thomas, Mr. Richards,
>
> Harvey & Co,"

and I feared that the vegetation would soon perish. This spring [1891] I made my fourth visit to the valley, to see what damage had been done, and to inspect the forests. . . . I left San Francisco on the 28th of May, accompanied by Mr. Robinson, the artist. At the new King's River Mills we found that the sequoia giants, as well as the pines and firs, were being ruthlessly turned into lumber. Sixteen years ago I saw five mills on or near the sequoia belt, all of which were cutting more or less of "big-tree" lumber. Now, as I am told, the number of mills along the belt in the basins of the King's, Kaweah, and Tule Rivers is doubled, and the capacity more than doubled. As if fearing restriction of some kind, particular attention is being devoted to the destruction of the sequoia groves owned by the mill companies, with the view to get them made into lumber and money before steps can be taken to save them.

Trees which compared with mature specimens are mere saplings are being cut down, as well as the giants, up to at least twelve to fifteen feet in diameter. Scaffolds are built around the great brown shafts above the swell of the base, and several men armed with long saws and axes gnaw and wedge them down with damnable industry. The logs found to be too large are blasted to manageable dimensions with powder.

It seems incredible that Government should have abandoned so much of the forest cover of the mountains to destruction. As well sell the rain-clouds, and the snow, and the rivers, to be cut up and carried away if that were possible. Surely it is high time that something be done to stop the extension of the present barbarous, indiscriminating method of harvesting the lumber crop.

—"A RIVAL OF THE YOSEMITE: THE CANYON OF THE SOUTH FORK OF KING'S RIVER, CALIFORNIA," *Century Magazine*, 1891

Any Fool Can Destroy Trees

SUCH IS THE POWER OF WORDS that when the essay "Any Fool Can Destroy Trees" was first published, it was enough to lead President Grover Cleveland to establish 13 forest reserves, comprising 21 million acres, and lay the foundation of the United States Forest Service. They are the final words in Muir's second book, *Our National Parks*, published in 1901. By the time the book came out, John Muir had been acknowledged as the country's most ardent defender of the American wilderness.

The axe and saw are insanely busy, chips are flying thick as snowflakes, and every summer thousands of acres of priceless forests, with their underbrush, soil, springs, climate, scenery, and religion, are vanishing away in clouds of smoke....

Any fool can destroy trees. They cannot run away; and if they could, they would still be destroyed—chased and hunted down as long as fun or a dollar could be got out of their bark hides, branching horns, or magnificent bole backbones. Few that fell trees plant them; nor would planting avail much towards getting back anything like the noble primeval forests. During a lifetime only saplings can be grown, in the place of the old trees—tens of centuries old—that have been destroyed.

It took more than three thousand years to make some of the trees of these Western woods—trees that are still standing in perfect strength and beauty—waving and singing in the mighty forests of the Sierra. Through all the wonderful, eventful centuries since Christ's time—and long before that—God has cared for these trees, saved them from drought, disease, avalanches, and a thousand straining, leveling tempests and floods; but he cannot save them from sawmills and fools. . . .

—*Our National Parks*

The Slaughter of Walruses

MUIR ACCEPTED THE NATIVE PEOPLES' killing of seals and walruses as they had done for millennia to provide their basic sustenance, but he found the wanton killing of such beautiful creatures—sometimes just for sport—totally unacceptable as recounted in this account taken from the journal of his 1881 trip to Alaska.

The 1972 Marine Mammal Act has partially protected the approximately 129,000 Pacific walruses, but further measures are needed because the walrus population has been disturbed by the recently vanishing ice packs. Thus in 2011 the U.S. Fish and Wildlife Service added them to the list of candidates for inclusion under the Endangered Species Act.

While sailing [off St. Lawrence Island in the Bering Sea] amid the loose blocks of ice that form the edge of the pack, we saw a walrus, and soon afterward a second one with its young. The Captain [Calvin L. Hooper] shot and killed the mother from the pilothouse. . . . After floating for eight or ten minutes she sank to the bottom and was lost—a sad fate and a luckless deed.

It was pitiful to see the young one swimming around its dying mother, heeding neither the ship nor the boat. They are said to be very affectionate and bold in the defense of one another against every enemy whatever. We have as yet seen but few, though in some places they are found in countless thousands. Many vessels are exclusively employed in killing them on the eastern Greenland coast, and along some portions of the coast of Asia. Here also, the whalers, when they have poor success in whaling, devote themselves to walrus hunting, both for the oil they yield and for the valuable ivory. The latter is worth from forty to seventy cents per pound in San Francisco, and a pair of large tusks weighs from eight to ten pounds.

. . . . These magnificent animals are killed oftentimes for their tusks alone, like buffaloes for their tongues, ostriches for their feathers, or for mere sport and exercise. In nothing does man, with his grand notions of heaven and charity, show forth his innate, low-bred, wild animalism more clearly than in his treatment of his brother beasts. From the shepherd with his lambs to the red handed hunter, it is the same; no recognition of rights—only murder in one form or another.

—The Cruise of the Corwin

Crimes in the Name of Vanity

IN A RELATED LETTER TO KATHERINE HITTELL, who was bringing political pressure to save the California songbirds, John Muir said, "We will save them yet. Keep on pegging away at the divine work until the public sympathy is aroused. Civilized people are still very nearly savage, and much work must be done 'ere they see the brutality of their ways. I consider the meadow lark the best, most influential, most characteristic of all California song birds—the least earthy, the most divine and I could say no more were I to speak till Doomsday."

If it be true that not a sparrow falls to the ground unnoted, what cumbersome records must be piling up to confront us! Watch the women that pass along the street and you will be appalled at the crimes that are committed in the name of vanity, for on nine hats out of ten balance the fragments of a drawn and quartered bird. . . . If the half-starved dogs and superfluous cats could be stuffed and used for millinery purposes, women might decorate themselves to the uttermost limits of their barbaric instincts, and not a protest would be raised; but these poor little airships of nature, who earn their own living and contribute more than their share to the beauty and harmony of the world, must they go?

That is not a merely rhetorical question. They are going fast, and if we want to save them, something must be done about it. Orioles are nearly extinct in California, humming birds are growing scarcer every year, and all the tribes who have been cursed with bright plumage are swiftly diminishing. As though it were not enough to lose those, the sweetest singers of all birdland are being slaughtered by thousands to serve the ignoble purpose of an entree. . . .

A number of individual attempts have been made in California to check this wholesale slaughter. Great efforts were made a year ago to protect at least the meadow larks, who came into the markets by the thousand as soon as the quail season was over. It would be as fitting to split up celestial harps for kindling wood, but the tiny musicians brought a dollar a dozen and nothing else mattered.

—"PROTECT OUR SONGBIRDS: SOME ACTION SHOULD BE TAKEN SOON

TO SAVE THE WARBLERS," *San Francisco Examiner*, 1895

chapter ten

The Scriptures of Ancient Glaciers

Commentary

JOHN MUIR LIKED SNOW AND ICE and the rich soil of glacial morains—the ac-
cumulated soil picked up and transported by glaciers creating new landscapes as the ice
eventually melts with the retreating glaciers. He never ceased to marvel at the beauty of
snowflakes and snow crystals, which he frequently called "snow flowers." To him these
were winter's versions of spring wild flowers. He first became acquainted with glaciers
at Fountain Lake Farm, the site of his family's first Wisconsin home. Fountain Lake is a
kettle pond, and there are dry kettles on the land through which he and his brother, David, would ride their horses. As he explained in *The Story of My Boyhood and Youth*, "These
so-called 'kettles' were formed by the melting of large detached blocks of ice that had
been buried in moraine material thousands of years ago when the ice-sheet that covered
all this region was receding. As the buried ice melted, of course the moraine material
above and about it fell in, forming hopper-shaped hollows."[1]

From his first arrival in Yosemite, John Muir was passionate about glaciers. "Prior
to the autumn of 1871 the glaciers of the Sierra were unknown. I was not expecting to
find any active glaciers so far south in the land of sunshine. In October of that year I
discovered the Black Mountain Glacier in a shadowy amphitheater between Black and
Red Mountains, two of the peaks of the Merced group."[2] Thus began Muir's quest to
learn all he could about these unique, colossal, moving masses of ice. He defined a glacier simply as ". . . a current of ice derived from snow," and by studying them he came
up with his moving-ice theory of the origins of the Yosemite glaciers.

A series of glaciations modified the region starting about two to three million years ago and ending sometime around 10,000 years ago. Glacial systems
reached depths of up to 4,000 feet, and their slowly moving floes of ice sculpted the

Yosemite Valley. The retreating glaciers left fertile moraines, glacial boulders, and magnificent upland lakes and ponds. The longest glacier in the Yosemite area ran down the Grand Canyon of the Tuolumne River for 60 miles. The Merced Glacier flowed out of Yosemite Valley and into the Merced River Gorge. Only Yosemite's highest peaks were not covered by glaciers.

Glorious Crystal Glaciers

GLACIAL ICE, ACCORDING TO MUIR, ". . . is only another form of terrestrial love," and the reader can almost picture Muir, enthralled by the crystalline beauty, posing like the writer of Genesis overlooking creation and declaring, "It is good."

No songs were so grand as those of the glaciers themselves, no falls so lofty as those poured from brows, and chasmed mountains of pure dark ice. Glaciers made the mountains and ground corn for all the flowers, and the forests of silver fir, made smooth paths for human feet until the sacred Sierras have become the most approachable of mountains. Glaciers came down from heaven, and they are angels with folded wings, white songs of snowy bloom, locked hand in hand the little spirits did nobly; the primary mountain waves, un-vital granite, were soon carved to beauty. They bared the lordly domes and fashioned the clustering spires; smoothed godlike mountains brows, and shaped like cups for crystal waters; wove myriads of mazy canyons, and spread them out like lace. They remembered the loud-songed rivers and every tinkling rill. The busy snowflakes saw all the coming flowers, and the grand predestined forests. They said, "We will crack this rock for cassiope [mountain heather] where she may sway her tiny urns. Here we'll smooth a plat for green mosses, and round a bank for bryanthus [red heather] bells." Thus labored the willing flake-souls linked in close congregations of ice, breaking rock for pines, as a bird crumbles bread for her young, spiced with dust of garnets and zircons and many a nameless gem; and where food was gathered for the forests and all their elected life, when every rock was finished, every monument raised, the willing messengers, un-wearied, un-wasted, heard God's "well done" from heaven calling them back to their homes in the sky.

—LETTER TO JEANNE C. CARR, DECEMBER 11, 1871

Learning Every Natural Lesson

THIS LETTER TO JEANNE C. CARR includes one of John Muir's first writings on his theory on the formation of glaciers. In the same letter he also wrote that "Professor [John Daniel] Runkle from [Massachusetts] Institute of Technology, was here last week and I preached my glacial theory to him for five days, taking him into the canyon of the valley and up among the grand glacier wombs and pathways of the summit. He was fully convinced of the truth of my readings and urged me to write out the glacial system of Yosemite and its tributaries for the Boston Academy of Science."

For the last three years I have been ploddingly making observations about this [Yosemite] Valley and the high mountain region to the east of it, drifting, brooding about and taking every natural lesson that I was fitted to absorb. In particular the great Valley has always kept a place in my mind. How did the Lord make it? What tools did He use? How did He apply them and when? I considered the sky above it and all of its opening canyons, and studied the forces that came in by every door that I saw standing open, but I could get no light. Then I said, "You are attempting what is not possible for you to accomplish. Yosemite is the end of the grand chapter; if you would learn to read it, go commence at the beginning. " Then I went above to the alphabet valleys of the summits, comparing canyon and canyon, with all their varieties of rock structure and cleavage and the comparative size and slope of the glaciers and waters which they contained; also the grand congregations of rock-creations was present to me, and I studied their forms and sculpture. I soon had the key to every Yosemite rock and perpendicular and sloping wall. The grandeur of these forces and their glorious results overpower me and inhabit my whole being. Waking or sleeping I have no rest. In dreams I read blurred sheets of glacial writing, or follow lines of cleavage, or struggle with the difficulties of some extraordinary rock form.

—LETTER TO JEANNE C. CARR, SEPTEMBER 8, [1871]

One Grand Wrinkled Sheet of Glacial Records

GLACIERS ARE THE INDELIBLE MARKERS of the ages. The eons of geological time never ceased to stir John Muir's imagination. As he said in his first published newspaper article in 1871, "There is sublimity in the life of a glacier. Water rivers work openly, and so the rains and the gentle dews, and the great sea also grasping all the world: and even the universal ocean of breath, though invisible, yet speaks aloud in a thousand voices, and proclaims its modes of working and its power: but glaciers work apart from men, exerting their tremendous energies in silence and darkness, outspread, spirit-like, brooding above predestined rocks unknown to light, unborn, working on unwearied through unmeasured times, unhalting as the stars, until at length, their creations complete, their mountains brought forth, homes made for the meadows and the lakes, and fields for waiting forests, earnest, calm as when they came as crystals from the sky, they depart."

The Sierra Nevada of California may be regarded as one grand wrinkled sheet of glacial records. For the scriptures of the ancient glaciers cover every rock, mountain, and valley of the range, and are in many places so well preserved, and are written in so plain a hand, they have long been recognized even by those who are not seeking for them, while the small living glaciers, lying hidden away among the dark recesses of the loftiest and most inaccessible summits, remain almost wholly unknown.

Looking from the summit of Mount Diablo across the San Joaquin Valley, the atmosphere has been washed with winter rains, the Sierra is beheld stretching along the plain in simple grandeur, like some immense wall, two and a half miles high, and colored almost as bright as a rainbow, in four horizontal bands—

the lowest rose purple, the next higher dark purple, the next blue, and the topmost pearly white—all beautifully interblended, and varying in tone with the time of day and the advance of the seasons. . . .

The Sierra granite is admirably fitted for the reception and preservation of glacial records, and from these it is plain that the Sierra ice once covered the whole range continuously as one sheet, which gradually broke up into individual glaciers, and these again into small residual glaciers arranged with reference to shadows. These last were very numerous. . . . The Transformation of snow into glacier ice varies as to place and rapidity with the climate and with the form of the basin in which the fountain snow is collected.

—*Harper's Monthly*, 1875

The Mighty Glaciers of the Sierra

JOHN MUIR IMAGINED the Divine Maker sending messengers down from the heavenly realm to "work in the mountain mines on errands of divine love." Just as a sculptor patiently carves away the stone to reveal the image within, so the Divine Maker peels away the ice to uncover the beauty of the Yosemite Valley.

[The march of creation continues as] plants and animals, biding their time, closely followed the retiring ice, bestowing quick and joyous animation on the new-born landscapes. Pine-trees marched up the sun-warmed moraines in long, hopeful files, taking the ground and establishing themselves as soon as it was ready for them; brown-spiked sedges fringed the shores of the newborn lakes; young rivers roared in the abandoned channels of the glaciers; flowers bloomed around the feet of the great burnished domes—while with quick fertility mellow beds of soil, settling and warming, offered food to multitudes of Nature's waiting children, great and small, animals as well as plants; mice, squirrels, marmots, deer, bears. . . . The ground burst into bloom with magical rapidity, and the young forests into birdsong: life in every form warming and sweetening and growing richer as the years passed away over the mighty Sierra.

Nature chose for a tool not the earthquake or lightning to rend and split asunder, not the stormy torrent or eroding rain, but the tender snowflowers noiselessly falling through unnumbered centuries, the offspring of the sun and sea. Laboring harmoniously in united strength they crushed and ground and wore away the rocks in their march, making vast beds of soil, and at the same time developed and fashioned the landscapes into the delightful variety of hill and dale and lordly mountain that mortals call beauty.... And our admiration must be excited again and again as we toil and study and learn that this vast job of rockwork, so far-reaching in its influences, was done by agents so fragile and small as are these flowers of the mountain clouds. Strong only by force of number, they carried away entire mountains, particle by particle, block by block, and cast them into the sea; sculptured, fashioned, modeled all the range, and developed its predestined beauty.

All these new Sierra landscapes were evidently predestined, for the physical structure of the rocks on which the features of the scenery depend was acquired while they lay at least a mile deep below the pre-glacial surface. And it was while these features were taking form in the depths of the range, the particles of the rocks marching to their appointed places in the dark with reference to the coming beauty, that the particles of icy vapor in the sky marching to the same music assembled to bring them to the light. Then, after their grand task was done, these bands of snow-flowers, these mighty glaciers, were melted and removed as if of no more importance than dew destined to last but an hour. Few of Nature's agents have left monuments so noble and enduring as they. The great granite domes a mile high, the canyons as deep, the noble peaks, the Yosemite valleys, these, and indeed nearly all other features of the Sierra scenery, are glacier monuments.

Contemplating the works of these flowers of the sky, one may easily fancy them endowed with life: messengers sent down to work in the mountain mines on errands of divine love. Silently flying through the darkened air, swirling, glinting, to their appointed places, they seem to have taken counsel together, saying,

"Come, we are feeble; let us help one another. We are many, and together we will be strong. Marching in close, deep ranks, let us roll away the stones from these mountain sepulchers, and set the landscapes free. Let us uncover these clustering domes. Here let us carve a lake basin; there, a Yosemite Valley; here, a channel for a river with fluted steps and brows for the plunge of songful cataracts. Yonder let us spread broad sheets of soil, that man and beast may be fed; and here pile trains of boulders for pines and giant Sequoias. Here make ground for a meadow; there, for a garden and grove, making it smooth and fine for small daisies and violets and beds of heathy bryanthus, spicing it well with crystals, garnet feldspar, and zircon." Nothing that I can write can possibly exaggerate the grandeur and beauty of their work. Like morning mist they have vanished in sunshine, all save the few small companies that still linger on the coolest mountainsides, and, as residual glaciers, are still busily at work completing the last of the lake basins, the last beds of soil, and the sculpture of some of the highest peaks.

—*The Mountains of California*

Tracing the Yosemite's Grand Old Glacier

THERE IS THE STORY OF the Zen master who asked the disciple if he could hear the murmuring of the mountain stream, and when he answered that he could, the master remarked, "Here is the way to enter. . . ." It only takes one stream to open up the wondrous world of water.

Early . . . I set out to trace the grand old glacier that had done so much for the beauty of the Yosemite region back to its farthest fountains, enjoying the charm that every explorer feels in Nature's untrodden wildernesses. The voices of the mountains were still asleep. The wind scarce stirred the pine-needles. The sun was up, but it was yet too cold for the birds and the few burrowing animals that dwell here. Only the stream, cascading from pool to pool, seemed to be wholly awake. Yet the spirit of the opening day called to action. The sunbeams came streaming gloriously through the jagged openings of the col, glancing on the burnished pavements and lighting the silvery lakes, while every sun-touched rock burned white on its edges like melting iron in a furnace. Passing round the north shore of my camp lake I followed the central stream past many cascades from lakelet to lakelet. The scenery became more rigidly arctic, the Dwarf Pines and Hemlocks disappeared, and the stream was bordered with icicles. As the sun rose higher rocks were loosened on shattered portions of the cliffs, and came down in rattling avalanches, echoing wildly from crag to crag. . . .

A series of rugged zigzags enabled me to make my way down into the weird under-world of the crevasse. Its chambered hollows were hung with a multitude of clustered icicles, amid which pale, subdued light pulsed and shimmered with inde-scribable loveliness. Water dripped and tinkled overhead, and from far below came strange, solemn murmurings from currents that were feeling their way through veins and fissures in the dark. The chambers of a glacier are perfectly enchanting, notwithstanding one feels out of place in their frosty beauty. I was soon cold in my shirt-sleeves, and the leaning wall threatened to engulf me; yet it was hard to leave the delicious music of the water and the lovely light. Coming again to the surface, I noticed boulders of every size on their journeys to the terminal moraine [the mass of rocks and debris deposited at the furthest advance of a glacier]—journeys of more than a hundred years, without a single stop, night or day, winter or summer.

The sun gave birth to a network of sweet-voiced rills that ran gracefully down the glacier, curling and swirling in their shining channels, and cutting clear sections through the porous surface-ice into the solid blue, where the structure of the glacier was beautifully illustrated. . . .

When the climatic changes came on that caused the melting and retreat of the main glacier that filled the amphitheater, a series of residual glaciers were left in the cliff shadows. . . . Then, as the snow became still less abundant, all of them van-ished in succession, except the one just described. . . . How much longer this little glacier will last depends on the amount of snow it receives from year to year.

—*The Mountains of California*

Luxuriant Butterfly-Filled Glacial Meadows

JOHN MUIR WAS OPEN to all that he would encounter as he set off on a hike to Lake Tenaya, a portion of which he describes in this diary entry. "Another big day, enough for a lifetime. The rocks, the air, everything speaking with audible voice or silent; joyful, wonderful, enchanting, banishing weariness and sense of time. No longing for anything now or hereafter as we go home into the mountain's heart." It was as if all of nature were encircling him, including butterflies that waltzed over his head, the "beautiful winged people."

[Some glacial] meadows hanging on ridge and mountain slopes, not in basins at all, but made and held in place by masses of boulders and fallen trees, which, forming dams one above another in close succession on small, outspread, channelless streams, have collected soil enough for the growth of grasses, carices, and many flowering plants, and being kept well watered, without being subject to currents sufficiently strong to carry them away, a hanging or sloping meadow is the result. Their surfaces are seldom so smooth as the others, being roughened more or less by the projecting tops of the dam rocks or logs; but at a little distance this roughness is not noticed, and the effect is very striking—bright green, fluent, down-sweeping flowery ribbons on gray slopes. The broad shallow streams these meadows belong to are mostly derived from banks of snow and because the soil is well drained in some places, while in others the dam rocks are packed close and caulked with bits of wood and leaves, making boggy patches; the vegetation, of course, is correspondingly varied. I saw patches of willow, bryanthus, and a fine show of lilies on some of them, not forming a margin, but scattered about among the carex and grass.

Most of these meadows are now in their prime. How wonderful must be the temper of the elastic leaves of grasses and sedges to make curves so perfect and fine. Tempered a little harder, they would stand erect, stiff and bristly, like strips of metal; a little softer, and every leaf would lie flat. And what fine painting and tinting there is on the glumes and pales, stamens and feathery pistils. Butterflies colored like the flowers waver above them in wonderful profusion, and many other beautiful winged people, numbered and known and loved only by the Lord, are waltzing together high over head, seemingly in pure play and hilarious enjoyment of their little sparks of life. How wonderful they are! How do they get a living, and endure the weather? How are their little bodies, with muscles, nerves, organs, kept warm and jolly in such admirable exuberant health? Regarded only as mechanical inventions, how wonderful they are! Compared with these, Godlike man's greatest machines are as nothing.

—JOURNAL ENTRY, JULY 27, 1869

Vanishing Glaciers

MUIR MAY HAVE BEEN the first naturalist to name what we now know as "global warming," for he identified the warming of the atmosphere as causing the contraction of glaciers. The glaciers cited here are located on Spitsbergen, a Norwegian island; Nova Zembla, a Canadian island in Baffin Bay; and Franz-Joseph-Land, an Arctic archipelago discovered by the Austro-Hungarian North Pole Expedition in 1873. Today this is Russian territory used exclusively by the Russian military.

The glaciers of Switzerland, like those of the Sierra, are mere wasting remnants of mighty ice-floods that once filled the great valleys and poured into the sea. So, also, are those of Norway, Asia, and South America. Even the grand continuous mantles of ice that still cover Greenland, Spitsbergen, Nova Zembla, Franz-Joseph-Land, parts of Alaska, and the south polar region are shallowing and shrinking. Every glacier in the world is smaller than it once was. All the world is growing warmer, or the crop of snow-flowers is diminishing. . . .

—*The Mountains of California*

chapter eleven

Land of the Midnight Sun

Commentary

YOSEMITE'S MAGNIFICENT VALLEYS, moraines, waterfalls, and upland pastures were sculptured by glaciers—mighty masses of ice that slowly cut through the landscape like the sharpest of knives. John Muir saw the effects of glacial action in Yosemite and how they fashioned the terrain; his sense of curiosity propelled his desire to seek living glaciers, glaciers that were still carving Earth's landscape. Alaska would be the location where the action of living glaciers could best be observed and studied. Thus Muir set his sights on traveling to the great white north.

> After eleven years of study and exploration in the Sierra Nevada of California and the mountain-ranges of the Great Basin, studying in particular their glaciers, forests, and wild life, above all their ancient glaciers and the influence they exerted in sculpturing the rocks over which they passed with tremendous pressure, making new landscapes, scenery, and beauty which so mysteriously influence every human being, and to some extent all life, I was anxious to gain some knowledge of the regions to the northward, about Puget Sound and Alaska. With this grand object in view I left San Francisco in May, 1879, on the steamer *Dakota*."[1]

His assignment was to write about what he saw for the San Francisco *Daily Evening Bulletin*. It's unlikely San Francisco's newspaper readers were interested in glaciers, but they were interested in newly discovered gold following discoveries in 1872 in Sitka and in Windham Bay in 1876. The seven-month trip took Muir through the Inland Passage and into long land fingers of fjords, past giant cliffs and towering mountains. As new vistas unfolded at the blending of the thin line between land and sea, Muir was rapturous.

"Never, before making this trip, have I found myself embosomed in scenery so hopelessly beyond description. . . . It seems as if we must surely at length reach the very paradise of poets, the abode of the blessed."[2] Here was Muir's new Yosemite, and the living glaciers he so longed to see did not disappoint him. It was a Yosemite Valley on a grander scale in the process of formation, the modeling and sculpturing of the cliffs not yet completed; no grooves had emerged on the raw, unfinished bottom of the valley. He wrote, "All the world seemed new-born. Everything, even the commonest, was seen in new light and looked at with interest as if never seen before."[3] At Fort Wrangell, Muir joined S. Hall Young, a Presbyterian missionary, and together they wandered all over the Inland Passage, to Sitka, the Stikine River, the Fairweather Mountains, Glacier Bay, and what was later to be named Muir Glacier.

Muir returned home in January 1880, and that summer he and Louie Strentzel were married at the Strentzel ranch in Martinez. In July, Muir left again for Alaska on his second trip, this one made memorable for his adventures in which he almost lost his life on the Taylor (now Brady) Glacier with the brave little dog, Stickeen. Their story is told in Chapter 7 of this book.

In May 1881, Muir took his third Alaskan trip, this time on the coal-burning steamship the Thomas Corwin: the destination was Point Barrow on Alaska's Arctic coast. The goal of the voyage was to find the *Jeannette* that had disappeared the previous year off Point Barrow. The Corwin threaded its way through the Bering Strait, passing the Diomede Islands with Russia's Siberian coast in the distance. The party stopped at Wrangell Island, believed to be the last place on earth inhabited by the woolly mammoth. The *Jeannette* was never found, but the remains of other shipwrecked whaling ships were located along with a few unwelcome surprises.

Muir's 1890 trip again took him through the Bering Strait and included a ten-day solo expedition by sled across Muir Glacier. He also traveled to Alaska in 1896, 1897, and 1899. Muir could not get enough of Alaska! He was 61 years old when he made his final trip, which was to join the Harriman Expedition to Prince William Sound, through the Bering Sea to Fort Wrangell and St. Lawrence Island. The wealthy owner of the Union

Pacific Railroad, Edward H. Harriman, assembled an illustrious party of scientists, naturalists, and his friends and family. He commissioned a custom-made steamer for the trip.

It had been 20 years since Muir's first trip through the Inland Waterway. In the intervening years "gold fever" had struck. Gold strikes in the Klondike and near Nome had brought prospectors to Alaska in the 1890s. Many of them took steamships to Skagway in Southeast Alaska where they began their trek by land to the Klondike. Wherever the gold miners went they left a wake of destruction. Muir was dismayed at the damage done by gold-struck visitors whose eyes were transfixed by the glitter of gold. Where land and sea had been pristine, there was evidence of clear-cutting, deforestation, and over-fishing. Muir was also taken aback by some of the members of Harriman's party who fished for sport and shot serene, beautiful bears for the fun of it. Nonetheless, the scientists aboard collected data on glaciers and other geological formations, First Nation people, fish, mammals, insects, and birds. The party claimed to have discovered 600 species. Fifty papers from the expedition were later published in Harriman's Alaska series.

If Muir could have blotted out the wanton slaughter of mammals for sport, the clear-cutting of the forests, the ravages to the land left by gold-mining, and the memory of the island where almost all the inhabitants had died of starvation in the winter of 1878–79, his impression of Alaska would have been that of a land as close to perfection as could be experienced this side of Heaven. Alaska was second only to Yosemite in his affections. Glaciers were aplenty, mountains and deep fjords abounded. In Alaska nature was extravagant, including the sunrises and sunsets and the dazzling auroras that shimmered across the spacious evening sky. On his 1880 voyage, Muir wrote, "How delightful it is, and how it makes one's pulses bound to get back into this reviving northland wilderness! How truly wild it is, and how joyously one's heart responds to the welcome it gives, its waters and mountains shining and glowing like enthusiastic human faces! Gliding along the shores of its network of channels, we may travel thousands of miles without seeing any mark of man. . . . Back a few yards from the beach the forests are as trackless as the sky, while the mountains, wrapped in their snow and ice and clouds, seem never before to have been even looked at."[4] Throughout John Muir's seven trips to Alaska, neither his enchantment with glaciers nor the wild glories of the Land of the Midnight Sun ever waned.

My First Campfire in Alaska

JOHN MUIR'S ALASKA ADVENTURES begin with his first campfire in the beguiling Land of the Midnight Sun.

Being anxious to see how the Alaska trees behave in storms and hear the songs they sing, I stole quietly away through the gray drenching blast to the hill back of the town, without being observed. Night was falling when I set out and it was pitch dark when I reached the top. The glad, rejoicing storm in glorious voice was singing through the woods, noble compensation for mere body discomfort. But I wanted a fire, a big one, to see as well as hear how the storm and trees were behaving. . . . Soon I had light enough to enable me to select the best dead branches and large sections of bark, which were set on end, gradually increasing the height and corresponding light of the hut fire. A considerable area was thus well lighted, from which I gathered abundance of wood, and kept adding to the fire until it had a strong, hot heart and sent up a pillar of flame thirty or forty feet high, illuminating a wide circle in spite of the rain, and casting a red glare into the flying clouds. Of all the thousands of camp-fires I have elsewhere built none was just like this one, rejoicing in triumphant strength and beauty in the heart of the rain-laden gale. It was wonderful—the illumined rain and clouds mingled together and the trees glowing against the jet background, the colors of the mossy, lichened trunks with sparkling streams pouring down the furrows of the bark, and the gray-bearded old patriarchs bowing low and chanting in passionate worship!

My fire was in all its glory about midnight, and, having made a bark shed to shelter me from the rain and partially dry my clothing, I had nothing to do but look and listen and join the trees in their hymns and prayers. . . .

I have enjoyed thousands of camp-fires in all sorts of weather and places, warm-hearted, short-flamed, friendly little beauties glowing in the dark on open spots in high Sierra gardens, daisies and lilies circled about them, gazing like enchanted children; and large fires in silver fir forests, with spires of flame towering like the trees about them, and sending up multitudes of starry sparks to enrich the sky; and still greater fires on the mountains in winter, changing camp climate to summer, and making the frosty snow look like beds of white flowers, and oftentimes mingling their swarms of swift-flying sparks with falling snow-crystals when the clouds were in bloom. But this Wrangell camp-fire, my first in Alaska, I shall always remember for its triumphant storm-defying grandeur, and the wondrous beauty of the psalm-singing, lichen-painted trees which it brought to light.

—Travels in Alaska

The Discovery of Glacier Bay

TRAVELING BY CANOE, John Muir, accompanied by Hall Young, an adventure-seeking missionary, and Native guides, finally reached Glacier Bay. The weather was rainy, cold, and forbidding, and at times the guides refused to accompany Muir. One of them, Toyatte, asked Muir what possible motive he could have in climbing mountains when storms were blowing. Muir replied that he was only seeking knowledge to which Toyatte remarked, "Muir must be a witch to seek knowledge in such a place as this and in such miserable weather!"

On October 24, [1879] we set sail for Guide Charley's ice-mountains. . . . We held a northwesterly course until long after dark, when we reached a small inlet that sets in near the mouth of Glacier Bay, on the west side. Here we made a cold camp on a desolate snow-covered beach in stormy sleet and darkness. At daybreak I looked eagerly in every direction to learn what kind of place we were in; but gloomy rain-clouds covered the mountains, and I could see nothing that would give me a clue. . . . Notwithstanding the rain, I was anxious to push on and grope our way beneath the clouds as best we could, in case worse weather should come; but Charley was ill at ease, and wanted one of the seal-hunters to go with us. . . . We got under way about 10 A.M. The wind was in our favor, but a cold rain pelted us, and we could see but little of the dreary, treeless wilderness which we had now fairly entered. The bitter blast, however, gave us good speed; our bedraggled canoe rose and fell on the waves as solemnly as a big ship. Our course was northwestward, up the southwest side of the bay, near the shore of what seemed to be the mainland, smooth marble islands being on our right. About noon we discovered the first of the great glaciers, the one I afterward named for James Geikie, the noted Scotch geologist. Its lofty blue cliffs, looming through the draggled skirts of the clouds, gave a tremendous impression of savage power, while the roar of the newborn icebergs thickened and emphasized the general roar of the storm.

The next day. . . . I set out on an excursion, and spent the day alone on the mountain-slopes above the camp, and northward, to see what I might learn. Pushing on through rain and mud and sludgy snow, crossing many brown, boulder-choked torrents, wading, jumping, and wallowing in snow up to my shoulders was mountaineering of the most trying kind. After crouching cramped and benumbed in the canoe, poulticed in wet or damp clothing night and day, my limbs had been asleep. . . . I reached a height of fifteen hundred feet, on the ridge that bounds the second of the great glaciers. All the landscape was smothered in clouds and I began to fear that as far as wide views were concerned I had climbed in vain. But at length the clouds lifted a little, and beneath their gray fringes I saw the berg-filled expanse of the bay, and the feet of the mountains that stand about it, and the imposing fronts of five huge glaciers, the nearest being immediately beneath me. This was my first general view of Glacier Bay, a solitude of ice and snow and newborn rocks, dim, dreary, mysterious. . . .

Next morning it was still raining and snowing, but the south wind swept us bravely forward and swept the bergs from our course. In about an hour we reached the second of the big glaciers, which I afterwards named for Hugh Miller. We rowed up its fiord and landed to make a slight examination of its grand frontal wall. The berg-producing portion we found to be about a mile and a half wide, and broken into an imposing array of jagged spires and pyramids, and flat-topped towers and battlements, of many shades of blue, from pale, shimmering, limpid tones in the crevasses and hollows, to the most startling, chilling, almost shrieking vitriol blue on the plain mural spaces from which bergs had just been discharged. Back from the front for a few miles the glacier rises in a series of wide steps, as if this portion of the glacier had sunk in successive sections as it reached deep water, and the sea had found its way beneath it. Beyond this it extends indefinitely in a gently rising prairie like expanse, and branches along the slopes and canyons of the Fairweather Range. . . .

While camp affairs were being attended to, I set out to climb a mountain for comprehensive views; and before I had reached a height of a thousand feet the rain ceased, and the clouds began to rise from the lower altitudes, slowly lifting their white skirts, and lingering in majestic, wing-shaped masses about the mountains that rise out of the broad, icy sea, the highest of all the white mountains, and the greatest of all the glaciers I had yet seen. Climbing higher for a still broader outlook, I made notes and sketched, improving the precious time while sunshine streamed through the luminous fringes of the clouds and fell on the green waters of the fiord, the glittering bergs, the crystal bluffs of the vast glacier, the intensely white, far-spreading fields of ice, and the ineffably chaste and spiritual heights of the Fairweather Range, which were now hidden, now partly revealed, the whole making a picture of icy wildness unspeakably pure and sublime. . . .

Dancing down the mountain to camp, my mind glowing like the sunbeaten glaciers. . . . How hopefully, peacefully bright that night were the stars in the frosty sky, and how impressive was the thunder of the icebergs, rolling, swelling, reverberating through the solemn stillness! I was too happy to sleep.

About daylight next morning we crossed the fiord and landed on the south side of the rock that divides the wall of the great glacier. . . . At one favorable place I descended about fifty feet below the side of the glacier, where its denuding, fashioning action was clearly shown. . . . A short time ago it was at least two thousand feet below the surface of the over-sweeping ice; and under present climatic conditions it will soon take its place as a glacier-polished island in the middle of the fiord, like a thousand others in the magnificent archipelago. Emerging from its icy sepulchre, it gives a most telling illustration of the birth of a marked feature of a landscape. In this instance it is not the mountain, but the glacier, that is in labor, and the mountain itself is being brought forth.

In the evening, after witnessing the unveiling of the majestic peaks and glaciers and their baptism in the down-pouring sunbeams, it seemed inconceivable that nature could have anything finer to show us.

—*Travels in Alaska*

Glorious Mountains, Glaciers, and Light

HAVING JUST COME into Glacier Bay thinking the glaciers couldn't get any better, Muir observed the sun rise over the Fairweather Mountains.

The calm dawn gave no promise of anything uncommon. Its most impressive features were the frosty clearness of the sky and a deep, brooding stillness made all the more striking by the thunder of the newborn bergs. The sunrise we did not see at all, for we were beneath the shadows of the fiord cliffs; but in the midst of our studies, while the Indians were getting ready to sail, we were startled by the sudden appearance of a red light burning with a strange unearthly splendor on the topmost peak of the Fairweather Mountains. Instead of vanishing as suddenly as it had appeared, it spread and spread until the whole range down to the level of the glaciers was filled with the celestial fire. In color it was at first a vivid crimson, with a thick, furred appearance, as fine as the alpenglow, yet indescribably rich and deep—not in the least like a garment or mere external flush or bloom through which one might expect to see the rocks or snow, but every mountain apparently was glowing from the heart like molten metal fresh from a furnace.

Beneath the frosty shadows of the fiord we stood hushed and awe-stricken, gazing at the holy vision; and had we seen the heavens opened and God made manifest, our attention could not have been more tremendously strained. When the highest peak began to burn, it did not seem to be steeped in sunshine, however glorious, but rather as if it had been thrust into the body of the sun itself. Then the supernal fire slowly descended, with a sharp line of demarcation separating it from the cold, shaded region beneath; peak after peak, with their spires and ridges and cascading glaciers, caught the heavenly glow, until all the mighty host stood transfigured, hushed, and thoughtful, as if awaiting the coming of the Lord. The white, rayless light of morning, seen when I was alone amid the peaks of the California Sierra, had always seemed to me the most telling of all the terrestrial manifestations of God. But here the mountains themselves were made divine, and declared His glory in terms still more impressive.

How long we gazed I never knew. The glorious vision passed away in a gradual, fading change through a thousand tones of color to pale yellow and white, and then the work of the ice-world went on again in everyday beauty. The green waters of the fiord were filled with sun-spangles; the fleet of icebergs set forth on their voyages with the upspringing breeze; and on the innumerable mirrors and prisms of these bergs, and on those of the shattered crystal walls of the glaciers, common white light and rainbow light began to burn, while the mountains shone in their frosty jewelry, and loomed again in the thin azure in serene terrestrial majesty. We turned and sailed away, joining the outgoing bergs, while "Gloria in excelsis" still seemed to be sounding over all the white landscape, and our burning hearts were ready for any fate, feeling that, whatever the future might have in store, the treasures we had gained this glorious morning would enrich our lives forever.

—Travels in Alaska

An Alaskan Midsummer Day

HERE IS AN ACCOUNT of a midsummer day from Muir's first trip to Alaska in 1879. The steamer was heading north through the archipelagoes between Nanaimo and Fort Wrangell.

An Alaskan midsummer day is a day without night. In the extreme northern part of the territory the sun does not set for weeks…the colors of the sunset blend with those of the sunrise, leaving no gap of night darkness between. . . . The thin clouds are colored orange and red, marking in a very striking way the progress of the sun around the northern horizon.

Now we may contemplate the life and motion about us. It comes to mind of itself—the tides, the rivers, the flow of the light through the satiny sky, the marvelous abundance of fishes feeding in the lower ocean, misty flocks of insects in the air, the wild sheep and goats on a thousand grassy ridges above the forests, the beaver and mink and otter far back on many a rushing stream, Indians floating and basking along the shores, the leaves of the forests drinking the light, and the glaciers on the mountains tracing valleys for rivers and grinding earth-meal for every living creature. Through the afternoon all the way down to the sunset the day grows in beauty. The light seems to thicken and become more generously fruitful without loosing its softness or smooth translucent glow. Everything appears to settle into conscious repose, while the winds breathe gently or are wholly at rest. The few clouds visible are downy and luminous and combed out fine on the edges. A white gull here and there winnows the air on easy wing, and Indian hunters in their canoes are seen gliding about the islands, every stroke of their paddles told by a quick glancing flash—sky, land and water meeting and blending in one inseparable scene of enchantment. Then comes the sunset with its purple and gold, not a narrow arch on the horizon but filling the sky....

—MUIR'S JOURNAL ENTRY FOR JULY 10, 1879, FROM *Picturesque California and the Region West of the Rocky Mountains, from Alaska to Mexico*, 1888

Though Made, The World Is Still Being Made

THIS IS MUIR'S JOURNAL account of his first visit to an Alaskan glacier during the summer of 1879. He canoed to a glacier between the head of the Wrangell Narrows and Cape Fanshaw, where he was entranced by the beauty that surrounded him on every side. This passage illustrates Muir's unique ability to describe landscapes and seascapes so vividly that readers feel as though they are by his side, seeing the same the image.

[Approached by canoe] at length we reached the glorious crystal wall, along the foot of which we passed, admiring [the glacier's] marvelous architecture, the play of light in the blue riffs and angles, and the structure of the ice as displayed in the less fractured sections, finding fresh, exultant, rejoicing beauty at every step. By dint of patient zigzagging and doubling among the crevasses and a vigorous use of an axe in cutting steps on the ice-blades and ridges, we made our way up the terminal wall and back a mile or so above the cascading brow to a height of about seven hundred feet above the base of the wall. Here we obtained a glorious view.

The whole front and brow of the glacier is gashed and sculptured into a maze of yawning chasms and crevasses and a bewildering variety of strange forms appalling to the strongest nerves but beautiful beyond description—clusters of glittering lance-shaped spires, gables and obelisks; bold outstanding bastions, and plain mural cliffs adorned along the top with fretted cornice and battlement; while every gorge and crevasse, pit and hollow, was filled with light, pulsing and shimmering in pale blue tones of ineffable tenderness and beauty.... Where crevasses were less common, small streams of pure water were outspread in a complicated network, gleaming and glancing in frictionless channels worn into the solid blue ice, and flowing with a grace of motion and a glad ring of gurgle and flashing light to be found on the crystal hills and dales of the glacier. Every feature glowed with intention, reflecting the earth-plans of God.

Along the sides we could see the mighty flood grinding against its granite walls with tremendous pressure . . . deepening and widening its grand valley channel and fashioning every portion of its mountain walls into the forms they are destined to have in the fullness of time, when all the ice-work accomplished, the glacier, like a tool no longer required, shall be withdrawn from its place by the sun.

[One] learns that the world, though made, is being made; that this is still the morning of creation, that mountains and valleys long since conceived and now being born, channels traced for rivers, basins hollowed for lakes; that moraine soil is being ground and outspread for coming grasses. . . . building particle on particle, cementing and crystallizing to make mountains, and valleys and plains. . . . which like fluent, pulsing water, rise and fall and pass on through the ages in endless rhythm and beauty.

—MUIR'S JOURNAL ENTRY FOR JULY 10, 1879, FROM *Picturesque California and the Region West of the Rocky Mountains, from Alaska to Mexico*, 1888

A Gentle Arctic Day

HERE IS JOHN MUIR'S luminous account of one summer evening in the open world of the Arctic, recorded somewhere north of St. Lawrence Bay.

This has been by far the most beautiful and gentle of our Arctic days, the water perfectly glassy and with no swell, mirroring the sky, which shows a few blue cloudless spots, white as satin near the horizon, of beautiful luster, trying to the eyes. . . . Gulls skimming the glassy level. Innumerable multitudes of eider ducks, the snowy shore, and all the highest mountains cloud-capped—a rare picture and perfectly tranquil and peaceful! God's love is manifest in the landscape as in a face. How unlike yesterday! In the evening a long approach to sunset, a red sky mingling with brown and white of the ice-blink. Growing colder towards midnight. There is no night at all now; only a partial gloaming; never, even in cloudy midnights, too dark to read. . . .

—JOURNAL ENTRY, JUNE 4, 1881

Long Nightless Days

MUIR WAS REFRESHED by the long days in the far North at the thin line between Russia and the United States. "Sunshine now in the Far North, sunshine all the long, nightless days! . . . How bright the lily-spangles that flashed on the glassy water! With what rapture we gazed into the crimson and gold of the midnight sunsets!"

The fourth of June was the most beautiful of the days we spent in the Arctic Ocean. The water was smooth, reflecting a tranquil, pearl-gray sky with spots of pure azure near the zenith and a belt of white around the horizon that shone with a bright, satiny luster, trying to the eyes like clear sunshine. . . . gulls, auks, eider ducks, and other water birds in countless multitudes skimmed the glassy level, while in the background of this Arctic picture the Siberian coast, white as snow could make it, was seen sweeping back in fine, fluent, undulating lines to a chain of mountains, the tops of which were veiled in the shining sky. A few snow crystals were shaken down from a black cloud towards midnight, but most of the day was one of deep peace, in which God's love was manifest as in a countenance.

—JOURNAL ENTRY, JUNE 4, 1881

A Baby's Smile

ANCHORING OFF OF ST. LAWRENCE ISLAND, crew members bartered with the local people. As John Muir recorded, "Several canoe loads of Eskimos came aboard, and there was a brisk trade in furs, mostly reindeer hides and parkas for winter use; also fox [skins] and some whalebone and walrus ivory. Flour and molasses were the articles most in demand. Some of the women, heedless of the weather, brought their boys, girls, and babies." One baby in particular claimed Muir's attention.

> One little thing, that the proud mother held up for our admiration, smiled delightfully, exposing her two precious new teeth. No happier baby could be found in warm parlors, where loving attendants anticipate every want and the looms of the world afford their best in the way of soft fabrics. She looked gayly out at the strange colors about her from her bit of a fur bag, and when she fell asleep; her mother laid her upon three oars that were set side by side across the canoe. The snowflakes fell on her face, yet she slept soundly for hours while I watched her, and she never cried. . . . The smile, or, rather, broad grin of that Eskimo baby went directly to my heart, and I shall remember it as long as I live. When its features had subsided into perfect repose, the laugh gone from its dark eyes, and the lips closed over its two teeth, I could make its sweet smile bloom out again as often as I nodded and chirruped to it. Heaven bless it!
>
> —JOURNAL ENTRY, JUNE 9, 1881

Golgotha

THE PURPOSE OF THE 1881 JOURNEY to Alaska was to ascertain the fate of the *Jeannette*, a ship carrying a group of north polar explorers that had disappeared in the Arctic Ocean in the spring of 1881. While the remains of the *Jeannette*'s crew were never found, the Corwin group stumbled upon the macabre scene described here. It was the most wrenching sight John Muir had ever witnessed. Nothing else in all of Muir's writings deals so strikingly with the dark side of nature.

> St. Lawrence Island, the largest in Bering Sea.... [is] a dreary, cheerless-looking mass of black lava, dotted with volcanoes, covered with snow, without a single tree, and rigidly bound in ocean ice for more than half the year....
>
> Three years ago there were about fifteen hundred inhabitants on the island, chiefly Eskimos, living in ten villages located around the shores, and subsisting on the seals, walruses, whales, and water birds that abound here. Now there are only about five hundred people, most of them in one village on the northwest end of the island, nearly two thirds of the population having died of starvation during the winter of 1878–79. In seven of the villages not a single soul was left alive....
>
> We stopped an hour or so this morning at one of the smallest of the dead villages. Mr. [Edward William] Nelson went ashore and obtained a lot of skulls and specimens of one sort and another for the Smithsonian Institution. Twenty-five skeletons were seen.
>
> A few miles farther on we anchored before a larger village . . . which I visited in company with Mr. Nelson, the Captain, and the Surgeon. We found twelve desolate huts close to the beach with about two hundred skeletons in them or strewn about on the rocks and rubbish heaps within a few yards of the doors. The scene was indescribably ghastly and desolate, though laid in a country purified by frost as by fire. Gulls, plovers, and ducks were swimming and flying about in happy life, the pure salt sea was dashing white against the shore, the blooming tundra swept back to the snow-clad volcanoes, and the wide azure sky bent kindly over all—nature intensely fresh and sweet, the village lying in the foulest and most glaring death. The shrunken bodies, with rotting furs on them, or white, bleaching skeletons, picked bare by the crows, were lying mixed with kitchen-rubbish where they had been cast out by surviving relatives while they yet had strength to carry them.

In the huts those who had been the last to perish were found in bed, lying evenly side by side, beneath their rotting deerskins. A grinning skull might be seen looking out here and there, and a pile of skeletons in a corner, laid there no doubt when no one was left strong enough to carry them through the narrow underground passage to the door. Thirty were found in one house, about half of them piled like fire-wood in a corner, the other half in bed, seeming as if they had met their fate with tranquil apathy. Evidently these people did not suffer from cold, however rigorous the winter may have been, as some of the huts had in them piles of deerskins that had not been in use. Nor, although their survivors and neighbors all say that hunger was the sole cause of their death, could they have battled with famine to the bitter end, because a considerable amount of walrus rawhide and skins of other animals was found in the huts. These would have sustained life at least a week or two longer.

The facts all tend to show that the winter of 1878–79 was, from whatever cause, one of great scarcity, and as these people never lay up any considerable supply of food from one season to another, they began to perish. The first to succumb were carried out of the huts to the ordinary ground for the dead, about half a mile from the village. Then, as the survivors became weaker, they carried the dead a shorter distance, and made no effort to mark their positions or to lay their effects beside them, as they customarily do. At length the bodies were only dragged to the doors of the huts, or laid in a corner, and the last survivors lay down in despair without making any struggle to prolong their wretched lives by eating the last scraps of skin.

Mr. Nelson went into this Golgotha with hearty enthusiasm, gathering the fine white harvest of skulls spread before him, and throwing them in heaps like a boy gathering pumpkins. He brought nearly a hundred on board, which will be shipped with specimens of bone armor, weapons, utensils, etc., on the Alaska Commercial Company's steamer St. Paul.

We also landed at the village on the southwest corner of the island and interviewed the fifteen survivors. When we inquired where the other people of the village were, one of the group, who speaks a few words of English, answered with a happy, heedless smile, "All mucky." "All gone!" "Dead?" "Yes, dead, all dead!" Then he led us a few yards back of his hut and pointed to twelve or fourteen skeletons lying on the brown grass, repeating in almost a merry tone of voice, "Dead, yes, all dead, all mucky, all gone!"

About two hundred perished here, and unless some aid be extended by our government which claims these people, in a few years at most every soul of them will have vanished from the face of the earth.

—JOURNAL ENTRY, JULY 3, 1881

The Midnight Sun

ROUNDING POINT BARROW, John Muir was arrested by the sky and its myriad dazzling colors, the shimmering, fluctuating sea, the light, the coolness of the air. All his senses were alive to the moment.

The sun is low in the northwest at nine o'clock. A lovely evening, bracing, cool, with a light breeze blowing over the polar pack. The ice is marvelously distorted and miraged; thousands of blocks seem suspended in the air; some even poised on slender black poles and pinnacles; a bridge of ice with innumerable piers, the ice and water wavering with quick, glancing motion. At midnight the sun is still above the horizon about two diameters; purple to west and east, gradually fading to dark slate color in the south with a few banks of cloud. A bar of gold in the path of the sun lay on the water and across the pack, the large blocks in the line [of vision] burning like huge coals of fire.

—JOURNAL ENTRY, JULY 23, 1881

Sky Wonders of the Glorious Night

WEARY AFTER THREE DAYS of strenuous hiking into the base of Mount Fairweather, Muir was just about to go to bed when one of his companions glanced out of the cabin door and shouted, "Muir, come look here. Here's something fine." Immediately, Muir forgot his tiredness and spent the night outside enraptured by the splendor of the Northern Lights.

Here was an aurora—a glowing silver bow spanning the Muir Inlet in a magnificent arch right under the zenith, or a little to the south of it, the ends resting on the top of the mountain-walls. And though colorless and steadfast, its intense, solid, white splendor, noble proportions, and fineness of finish excited boundless admiration. In form and proportion it was like a rainbow, a bridge of one span five miles wide; and so brilliant, so fine and solid and homogeneous in every part, I fancy that if all the stars were raked together into one windrow, fused and welded and run through some celestial rolling-mill, all would be required to make this one glowing white colossal bridge.

After my last visitor went to bed, I lay down on the moraine in front of the cabin and gazed and watched. Hour after hour the wonderful arch stood perfectly motionless, sharply defined and substantial-looking as if it were a permanent addition to the furniture of the sky. At length while it yet spanned the inlet in serene unchanging splendor, a band of fluffy, pale gray, quivering ringlets came suddenly all in a row over the eastern mountain-top, glided in nervous haste up and down the under side of the bow and over the western mountain-wall. They were about one and a half times the apparent diameter of the bow in length, maintained a vertical posture all the way across, and slipped swiftly along as if they were suspended like a curtain on rings. Had these lively auroral fairies marched across the fiord on the top of the bow instead of shuffling along the under side of it, one might have fancied they were a happy band of spirit people on a journey making use of the splendid bow for a bridge. There must have been hundreds of miles of them; for the time required for each to cross from one end of the bridge to the other seemed only a minute or less, while nearly an hour elapsed from their first appearance until the last of the rushing throng vanished behind the western mountain, leaving the bridge as bright and solid and steadfast as before they arrived. But later, half an hour or so, it began to fade. Fissures or cracks crossed it diagonally through which a few stars were seen, and gradually it became thin and nebulous until it looked like the Milky Way, and at last vanished, leaving no visible monument of any sort to mark its place.

I now returned to my cabin, replenished the fire, warmed myself, and prepared to go to bed, though too aurorally rich and happy to go to sleep. But just as I was about to retire, I thought I had better take another look at the sky, to make sure that the glorious show was over; and, contrary to all reasonable expectations, I found that the pale foundation for another bow was being laid right overhead like the first. Then losing all thought of sleep, I ran back to my cabin, carried out blankets and lay down on the moraine to keep watch until daybreak, that none of the sky wonders of the glorious night within reach of my eyes might be lost.

—Travels in Alaska

Midnight on Herald Island

"THE ENTIRE ISLAND IS A MASS of granite, with the exception of a patch of metamorphic slate near the center," Muir wrote. ". . .This little island, standing as it does alone out in the Polar Sea, is a fine glacial monument." Some might have considered Herald Island a desolate wasteland, but John Muir found beauty everywhere in the natural world, and this rock was no exception.

The midnight hour I spent alone on the highest summit—one of the most impressive hours of my life. The deepest silence seemed to press down on all the vast, immeasurable, virgin landscape. The sun near the horizon reddened the edges of belted cloud-bars near the base of the sky, and the jagged ice-boulders crowded together over the frozen ocean stretching indefinitely northward, while perhaps a hundred miles of that mysterious Wrangell Land was seen blue in the northwest—a wavering line of hill and dale over the white and blue ice-prairie! Pale gray mountains loomed beyond, well calculated to fix the eye of a mountaineer. But it was to the far north that I ever found myself turning, to where the ice met the sky. I would fain have watched here all the strange night, but was compelled to remember the charge given me by the Captain, to make haste and return to the ship as soon as I should find it possible, as there was ten miles of shifting, drifting ice between us and the open sea.

—JOURNAL ENTRY, JULY 31, 1881

chapter twelve

Peace to Every Living Thing

Commentary

JOHN MUIR WAS MOST ALIVE when he was traveling, and as the years passed his journeys took him further and further from his adopted homeland of California. Muir's most recent biographer, Donald Worster, writes in *A Passion for Nature: The Life of John Muir,* "In his later years, as he wandered farther from home and moved more rapidly through a lot of places, the pleasures became more shallow and the pains more pronounced."[1] So what, we may ask, was motivating John Muir during the last chapter of his life?

We may speculate. Muir was a widower; he missed Louie, the steadying force and supporter who encouraged his explorations. Without her, his 16-room Martinez ranch house seemed too large. He camped out in it, squirreling himself away in his "scribbling room" to work on his articles and books.

Still, for a man who spent so much time without human company in the wilderness, Muir could not be described as a loner. He enjoyed the company of others, and when they invited him on trips, such as the Harriman Expedition to Alaska in 1899, he accepted. Edward Harriman also offered Muir train and steamer tickets for additional adventures such as the immense trip he started with Charles Sargent, the Harvard botany professor, and his family in 1903 and 1904, and completed on his own. With the Sargents he visited London, Paris, Russia, Finland, and Siberia. On his own he went to the Orient and Oceana. In a letter to his friend Henry Fairfield Osborn following the trip he said, "At Shanghai [I] left the Sargents and set out on a grand trip alone and free to India, Egypt, Ceylon, Australia, New Zealand. Thence by way of Port Darwin, Timor, through the Malay Archipelago to Manila. Thence to Hong Kong again and Japan and home by Honolulu. Had perfectly glorious times in India, Australia, and New Zealand.

The flora of Australia and New Zealand is so novel and exciting I had to begin botanical studies over again, working night and day with endless enthusiasm. And what wondrous beasts and birds, too, are there!"[2] It was an exhaustive and exhausting journey but Muir was invigorated by it.

Another factor may have been Muir's abiding, unquenchable desire to learn as much as he could about the natural world; the same quest that drove him when he was a boy searching for what he called "wildness" along the shore of his home in Scotland and over the hillside behind his house. Perhaps it was this native curiosity that continued to drive him. Even though he had experienced more of the world than most people of his generation could even imagine, there were still vistas to gaze upon, mountains to climb, and, most importantly, more trees to see.

John Muir had seen the mighty sequoia, but he not yet set eyes on the giant trees he had dreamed about ever since he was a teenager—the araucaria of South America and the baobab of Africa. At age 73 John Muir set out on his last journey to find them. Like his first extended trip, the 1,000-mile walk to the Gulf, this journey was a solo trip. In August 1911, Muir left New York headed for South America. He went up to the source of the Amazon River; he visited some of South America's most renowned cities: Rio de Janeiro, Valparaiso, Santiago, Mendoza, Buenos Aires, and Montevideo. At every port he headed to botanical gardens, and finally he found the araucaria of his dreams. As he wrote to his daughter Helen from Buenos Aires on November 29, 1911, "I found a glorious wild Araucaria forest. . . guess how happy I was and how I'd stared at and admired those ancient trees I'd so long dreamed of."[3]

Now only one of the world's great trees remained for Muir to experience—the giant African baobab. It would have been a direct eastward voyage of 4,000 miles from Montevideo to Cape Town, but apparently no steamer was in port and headed that way. The best he could do was to obtain passage on the *Kurakina*, a ship going north to the Canary Islands. He departed on December 9 for the 17-day trip. His journal entries suggest he enjoyed it. The calm days were punctuated by spotting flying fish, the occasional albatross, and gazing at the wide-open skies. On December 23 he recorded observing ". . . a few flying fish, some of them making vigorous flights of fifty to a hundred yards against the wind at a speed of ten to twelve miles an hour. Others glinting, flashing from wave-top to wave-top."[4] He enjoyed the panoramic view of the sky and recorded that it was, "Dazzling before noon, beneath the sun, but dim around the horizon toward evening. Clear overhead with most beautiful lace pattern of cirrus, delicate beyond description, pure white on azure, with bits of mackerel form here and there. The sun yellow and dull red half an hour before night, lost in dark shapeless cloud mass. . . ."[5] Toward midnight on Christmas Eve, Muir's heart was moved by the voices of the ship's crew singing Christmas carols. The day after Christmas the ship reached Tenerife, and Muir immediately booked passage on the Dutch East Indian steamship, the *Windhuk*, heading for South Africa.

After another 17 days at sea the ship arrived in Cape Town on January 13, 1912, and on January 16 he boarded a train in the direction of Victoria Falls via Bulawayo. He noted monkeys and ostriches along the route while "the stars shone bright as we sped on over the apparently boundless plain" (Journal entry for January 16, 1912).[6] Finally on January 20 Muir found the long-anticipated baobab. He reports many anxious inquiries and finally finding a young guide who led him to a grove of baobabs located about a mile and a half from the head of Victoria Falls. "I discovered specimens showing their different forms, varying from twelve to twenty-four feet in diameter. . . . most of them about seventy-five to ninety feet high and very wide-spreading. . . . So striking in size and form, it is easily recognized at a distance of several miles. . . . Altogether I measured and sketched about a dozen specimens."[7]

His goal achieved, Muir could now start his homeward journey, by steamer, train, and small boat, taking in some of Africa's finest landscapes along the way and continuing to take every opportunity to visit botanical gardens and groves of baobab trees at every stop. On the morning of February 17, he reported seeing antelopes, zebras, and ostriches along with magnificent views of Mount Kilimanjaro. At Mombasa, Muir boarded the first of a series of steamers that would carry him through the Indian Ocean, the Gulf of Aden, the Red Sea, the Suez Canal, the Mediterranean Sea, and across the Atlantic to New York, where he arrived on March 27—an odyssey of seven months and 40 thousand miles. As he recounted in a letter to an old friend, Katharine Hooker, "I've had a most glorious time on this trip, dreamed of nearly half a century—have seen more than a thousand miles of the noblest of Earth's streams, and gained far more telling views of the wonderful forests than I ever hoped for."[8]

Arriving home in California, John Muir continued his battles against the destruction of the wilderness by axe, plough, fire, mining, and the cunning maneuvers of power barons. He endured the last hurdles of the Hetch Hetchy as the City of San Francisco set about to dam it. His books *The Yosemite* and *The Story of My Boyhood and Youth* were published in 1912 and 1913, and he was awarded an honorary degree from the University of California.

Hard times were ahead for the world. The summer of 1914 saw the opening volleys of the First World War; and times were becoming hard personally for the old man of the mountains. Back home alone at his Martinez ranch Muir worked diligently on his Alaska journals. As he wrote to his friend Mina Merrill, "I'm now at work on an Alaska book, and as soon as it is off my hands I mean to continue the autobiography from leaving the University to botanical excursions in the northern woods, around Indianapolis, and thence to Florida, Cuba, and California. This will be volume number two. It is now seven years since my beloved wife vanished in the land of the leal [hypothetical land of happiness]. Both of my girls are happily married and have homes and children of their own. Wanda has three lively boys, Helen has two and is living at Daggett, California. Wanda is living on the ranch in the old adobe, while I am alone in my library den in the big house on the hill."[9]

Muir had a sense of his own aging and a feeling that he needed to complete the autobiography and finish the task of turning his Alaska journals into a book. He had found his place as a naturalist and explorer; he had discovered the "wildness" he dreamed of as a young boy in Scotland, and his life was transformed by it. Muir wanted the same for others. His desire was to spend his remaining time by helping future generations to learn to appreciate the marvels of the natural world. In a letter to a friend who urged him to work on his autobiography, he said, "I am not anxious to tell what I have done, but what Nature has done—an infinitely more important story."[10]

Marion Randall Parsons, his kindly secretary, reported that he worked on his manuscripts from dawn to dusk, rarely stopping for a meal. She recalled, "His rare critical faculty was unimpaired to the end. So too was the freshness and vigor of his whole outlook on life. No trace of pessimism or despondency, even in the defeat of his most cherished hopes, ever darkened his beautiful philosophy."[11] In mid-December Muir's persistent respiratory problems worsened. Thinking the dry air would help, he set off for the Mojave Desert to visit his younger daughter, Helen. The condition turned into double pneumonia, and Helen put him on the train to seek treatment in a hospital in Los Angeles.

There he died alone on Christmas Eve, 1914, with remnants of his unfinished *Travels in Alaska* manuscript scattered around the room. One of its pages recounts a perfect day during which he climbed to Glenora Peak, a 5,224-foot mountain in British Columbia, on his first Alaskan trip in 1879: "As I lingered, gazing on the vast show, luminous shadowy clouds seemed to increase in glory of color and motion, now fondling the highest peaks with infinite tenderness of touch, now hovering above them like eagles over their nests. When night was drawing near, I ran down the flowery slopes exhilarated, thanking God for the gift of this great day. The setting sun fired the clouds. All the world seemed new-born. Every thing, even the commonest, was seen in new light and was looked at with new interest as if never seen before. The plant people seemed glad, as if rejoicing with me, the little ones as well as the trees, while every feature of the peak and its traveled boulders seemed to know what I had been about and the depth of my joy. . . ."[12]

Morning Opens on a Field of Lilies

CARRYING HIS CUSTOMARY BAG of tea and hard bread, John Muir walked till the sun set, choosing pine boughs for his bed. In the morning he awakened to the scene described below.

In the morning everything is joyous and bright, the delicious purple of the dawn changes softly to daffodil yellow and white; while the sunbeams pouring through the passes between the peaks give a margin of gold to each of them. Then the spires of the firs in the hollows of the middle region catch the glow, and your camp grove is filled with light. The birds begin to stir, seeking sunny branches on the edge of the meadow for sun-baths after the cold night, and looking for their breakfasts, every one of them as fresh as a lily and as charmingly arrayed. Innumerable insects begin to dance, the deer withdraw from the open glades and ridge-tops to their leafy hiding-places in the chaparral, the flowers open and straighten their petals as the dew vanishes, every pulse beats high, every life-cell rejoices, the very rocks seem to tingle with life, and God is felt brooding over everything great and small.

—The Mountains of California

Daybreak and Sunrise

ONE WOULD BE RELUCTANT to attach labels to a man who would have disdained them himself, but from the perspective of almost a century after his death, the modern reader of John Muir's writings sees a holy man—a St. Francis of the Sierra—living in a timeless world communing ecstatically with creation. Like St. Francis, Muir made friends with what he called the "bird people," the "plant people," and even the "butterfly people." He called the bears, deer, squirrels, and chipmunks of the forest his friends; he found inspiration in mountains, glaciers, and trees. Even rocks revealed their mysteries to him.

Watching the daybreak and sunrise. The pale rose and purple sky changing softly to daffodil yellow and white, sunbeams pouring through the passes between the peaks and over the Yosemite domes, making their edges burn; the silver firs in the middle ground catching the glow on their spiry tops, and our camp grove fills and

thrills with the glorious light. Everything awakening alert and joyful; the birds begin to stir and innumerable insect people. Deer quietly withdraw into leafy hiding-
places in the chaparral; the dew vanishes, flowers spread their petals, every pulse
beats high, every life cell rejoices, the very rocks seem to thrill with life. The whole
landscape glows like a human face in a glory of enthusiasm, and the blue sky, pale
around the horizon, bends peacefully down over all like one vast flower.

—JOURNAL ENTRY, JULY 19, 1869

Nature's Peace

WHEN JOHN MUIR WROTE *Our National Parks*, made up of sketches first published in
the *Atlantic Monthly*, he wrote in the preface, "I have done the best I could to show forth
the beauty, grandeur, and all-embracing usefulness of our wild mountain forest reservations and parks, with a view to inciting the people to come and enjoy them, and get them
into their hearts, that so at length their preservation and right use might be made sure."
Muir's words are reminiscent of those of Henry David Thoreau, who reminded us, "In
wilderness is the preservation of the world."

> Walk away quietly in any direction and taste the freedom of the mountaineer. Camp
> out among the grass and gentians of glacier meadows, in craggy garden nooks
> full of Nature's darlings. Climb the mountains and get their good tidings. Nature's
> peace will flow into you as sunshine flows into trees. The winds will blow their own
> freshness into you, and the storms their energy, while cares will drop off like au-
> tumn leaves. As age comes on, one source of enjoyment after another is closed,
> but Nature's sources never fail. Like a generous host, she offers here brimming cups
> in endless variety, served in a grand hall, the sky its ceiling, the mountains its walls,
> decorated with glorious paintings and enlivened with bands of music ever play-
> ing. The petty discomforts that beset the awkward guest, the unskilled camper, are

quickly forgotten, while all that is precious remains. Fears vanish as soon as one is fairly free in the wilderness.

—Our National Parks

Going Home

LIFE AND DEATH TO MUIR were one interrelated, continuous cycle participated in by all living beings, both plant and animal. Though undated, this journal entry was probably written near the time of Muir's death. "Death," he said, "is a kind nurse saying, 'Come, children, to bed and get up in the morning'—a gracious Mother calling her children home."

The rugged old Norsemen spoke of death as Heimgang—going home. So the snow-flowers go home when they melt and flow to the sea, and the rock ferns, after unrolling their fronds to the light and beautifying the rocks, roll them up again in the autumn and blend with the soil.

Myriads of rejoicing living creatures, daily, hourly, perhaps every moment sink into death's arms, dust to dust, spirit to spirit—waited on, watched over, noticed only by their Maker, each arriving at its own heaven-dealt destiny.

All the merry dwellers of the trees and streams, and the myriad swarms of the air, called into life by the sunbeam of a summer morning, go home through death, wings folded perhaps as in the last red rays of sunset of the day they had first tried. Trees towering into the sky, braving storms for centuries, flowers turning faces to the light for a single day or hour, having enjoyed their share of life's feast—all alike pass on and away under the law of death and love. Yet all are brothers and they enjoy their life as we do, share heaven's blessings with us, die and are buried in hallowed ground, come with us out of eternity and return into eternity. . . .

—JOURNAL ENTRY/NO DATE

One Love-Harmony of the Universe

IN 1866, WHEN JOHN MUIR went to Indianapolis to work at a carriage factory, his mentor from his days at the University of Wisconsin, Professor James Butler, felt that Muir needed something to offset what he felt was the coarseness of factory life. Thus he urged Muir to meet his friends, the cultured Merrill family, who had moved from Vermont to Indianapolis so that Samuel Merrill could further his entrepreneurial interests. Merrill had two lovely daughters, Catherine and Julia. When Muir had his devastating factory accident in 1867 that temporarily blinded him, the family offered him comfort and companionship. When he regained his sight, Julia's 11-year old son, Merrill Moores, accompanied Muir back home to Wisconsin.

Janet Moores, Julia's daughter, turned up in Oakland. Muir had not seen her since he left Indianapolis, and he looked forward to meeting her and perhaps taking her on a tour of Yosemite. In anticipation, Muir shares this recollection in this letter to her.

> Twenty years! How long and how short a time that seems to-day! How many times the seas have ebbed—and flowed—with their breaking waves around the edges of the continents and islands in this score of years, how many times the sky has been light and dark, and the ground between us been shining with rain, and sun, and snow: and how many times the flowers have bloomed, but . . . you seem just the same to me, and time and space and events hide you less than the thinnest veil. Marvelous indeed is the permanence of the impressions of those sunrise days, more enduring than granite mountains. Through all the landscapes I have looked into, with all their wealth of forests, rivers, lakes, and glaciers, and happy living faces, your face, Janet, is still seen as clear and keenly outlined as on the day I went away on my long walk. Aye, the auld lang syne is indeed young. Time seems of no avail to make us old except in mere outer aspects. To-day you appear the same little fairy girl, following me in my walks with short steps as best you can, stopping now and then to gather buttercups, and anemones, and erigenias, sometimes taking

my hand in climbing over a fallen tree, threading your way through tall grasses and ferns, and pushing through very small spaces in thickets of underbrush. Surely you must remember those holiday walks, and also your coming into my dark-room with light when I was blind!

And what light has filled me since that time.....the richest sun-gold flooding these California valleys, the spiritual alpenglow steeping the high peaks, silver light on the sea, the white glancing sunspangles on rivers and lakes, light on the myriad stars of the snow, light sifting through the angles of sun-beaten icebergs, light in glacier caves, irised spray wafting from white waterfalls, and the light of calm starry nights beheld from mountain-tops dipping deep into the clear air.

It is a blessed thing to go free in the light of this beautiful world, to see God playing upon everything, as a man would play on an instrument, His fingers upon the lightning and torrent, on every wave of sea and sky, and every living thing, making all together sing and shine in sweet accord, the one love-harmony of the Universe.

—LETTER TO JANET DOUGLASS MOORES, FEBRUARY 23, 1887

Streams of the River of Life

ALTHOUGH THEIR LIVES went separate ways, Muir had always maintained an affection for Janet Moores and was saddened when he learned of her death, as is illustrated by this letter of condolence to her mother.

Death is as natural as life, sorrow as joy. Through pain and death come all our blessings, life and immortality. However clear our faith and hope and love, we must suffer—but with glorious compensation. While death separates, it unites, and the sense of loneliness grows less and less as we become accustomed to the new light, communing with those who have gone on ahead in spirit, and feeling their influence as if again present in the flesh.... The Source of all Good turns even sorrow and seeming separation to our advantage, makes us better, drawing us closer together in love, enlarging, strengthening, brightening our views of the spirit world and our hopes of immortal union. Blessed it is to know and feel, even at this cost, that neither distance nor death can truly separate those who love.

My friends, whether living or dead, have always been with me in my so-called lonely wanderings, so kind and wonderful are God's compensations. . . . In His strength we must live on, work on, doing the good that comes to heart and hand, looking forward to meeting in that City which the streams of the River of Life make glad.

—LETTER TO JULIA MERRILL MOORES, JULY 25, 1900

Peace to Every Living Thing

WHILE JOHN MUIR SUFFERED HARDSHIPS in his early life and deep disappointments later in life—notably the loss of the Hetch Hetchy Valley and the death of his wife, Louie, and several friends—he never lost his open, positive outlook. He never lost his sense of awe and wonder in the natural world, nor did his fame in his latter years change his nature. His appreciation for the natural world only expanded over the years.

How fine the weather is! Nothing more celestial can I conceive. How gently the winds blow! Scarce can these tranquil air-currents be called winds. They seem the very breath of Nature, whispering peace to every living thing.

—JOURNAL ENTRY FOR JUNE 11, L869

This grand show is eternal. It is always sunrise somewhere; the dew is never dried all at once; a shower is forever falling; vapor ever rising. Eternal sunrise, eternal sunset, eternal dawn and gloaming, on seas and continents and islands, each in turn, as the round earth rolls.

—*John of the Mountains: The Unpublished Journals of John Muir*

appendix one

Notes

The notes have been simplified in order to facilitate the reading of this book. Unless otherwise indicated, subsequent quotations from John Muir's works included in each commentary are taken from the reference first cited. Most of John Muir's writings are in the public domain and are available on the Sierra Club website.

INTRODUCTION

1. John Muir, Letter to Jean C. Carr, December 25, 1872, in *The Life and Letters of John Muir, Vol. II*, Ed. by William Frederic Badè (Boston: Houghton Mifflin Co., 1924).

2. Richard Louv, *Last Child in the Woods* (Chapel Hill: Algonquin Books of Chapel Hill, 2008), p. 10.

3. Louv, p. 36.

4. Wendell Berry, Quoted in Louv, p. 113.

5. Luther Standing Bear, *Land of the Spotted Eagle* (Lincoln and London: University of Nebraska Books, 1978). Original publication date: 1933.

6. Robert Michael Pyle, *The Thunder Tree* (Boston and New York: Houghton, Mifflin Co., 1993), p. 145.

7. David Toolan, *At Home in the Cosmos* (Maryknoll, NY: Orbis Books, 2003), p. 226.

8. John Muir, *The Mountains of California*, 1894, Chapter 5. Courtesy of the Sierra Club.

Chapter 1: EARTH-PLANET, UNIVERSE

COMMENTARY

1. John Muir, *The Story of My Boyhood and Youth*, 1913, Chapter 6. Courtesy of the Sierra Club.

2. John Muir, *The Story of My Boyhood and Youth*, 1913, Chapter 6. Courtesy of the Sierra Club.

3. William Frederic Badè, Ed., *The Life and Letters of John Muir, Vol. I*, (Boston: Houghton Mifflin Co., 1924), Chapter 6. Copyright 1924 by Houghton Mifflin Harcourt Publishing Company,

renewed 1952 by John Muir Hanna. Reprinted by permission of Houghton Mifflin Harcourt Publishing Company. All rights reserved.

4. Badè, Vol. 1, Chapter 6. Copyright 1924 by Houghton Mifflin Harcourt Publishing Company, renewed 1952 by John Muir Hanna. Reprinted by permission of Houghton Mifflin Harcourt Publishing Company. All rights reserved.

5. John Muir, *A Thousand Mile Walk to the Gulf* (Boston: Houghton Mifflin Co, 1916), Chapter 8.

SELECTIONS

The Beginnings of Lifelong Wanderings: John Muir, *The Story of My Boyhood and Youth*, 1913, Chapter 1. Courtesy of the Sierra Club.

Everything New and Pure: John Muir, *The Story of My Boyhood and Youth*, 1913, Chapter 2. Courtesy of the Sierra Club.

Leaving for the University of the Wilderness: John Muir, *The Story of My Boyhood and Youth*, 1913, Chapter 8. Courtesy of the Sierra Club.

Joyful and Free: John Muir, *A Thousand-Mile Walk to the Gulf*, 1916, Chapter 1.

Life and Death in a Graveyard: John Muir, Letter to Jeanne C. Carr, Sept.–Oct., 1867, *California Illustrated Magazine*, Vol. 2, June, 1892. Courtesy of the Sierra Club.

Imperishable Impressions that Vibrate Our Lives: John Muir, *A Thousand Mile Walk to the Gulf*, 1916, Chapter 7, Journal entry for Oct. 23, 1867.

Chapter 2: THE MORNING OF CREATION

COMMENTARY

1. Frederick Turner, Foreword, *My First Summer in the Sierra* (San Francisco: Sierra Club Books, 1988), p. 10.

2. John Muir, *My First Summer in the Sierra* (Boston: Houghton Mifflin, 1911), Chapter 2, Journal entry for June 16, 1869.

3. John Muir, *My First Summer in the Sierra*, Chapter 1, Journal entry for June 6, 1869.

4. John Muir, *My First Summer in the Sierra*, Chapter 8, Journal entry for August 14, 1869.

SELECTIONS

Arriving in the Enchanting World of the Sierra Nevada: John Muir, Letter to Jeanne C. Carr, Written from Merced County, CA, July 26, [1868]. In *John Muir: Letters to a Friend Written to Mrs. Ezra S. Carr 1866-1879* (Boston and New York: Houghton Mifflin Company, 1915). Courtesy of the Sierra Club.

A New Earth Every Day: John Muir, *My First Summer in the Sierra*, 1911, Chapter 8, Journal entry for August 14, 1869.

A Window Opening Into Heaven: John Muir, *My First Summer in the Sierra*, 19ll, Chapter 6, Journal entry for July 27, 1868.

The Sun's Glorious Greeting: John Muir, *The Mountains of California*, 1894, Chapter 4.

Deep Summer Joy: John Muir, *The Mountains of California*, 1894, Chapter 7.

In the Morning: John Muir, *The Mountains of California*, 1894, Chapter 8.

In the Cool of the Evening: John Muir, Letter to Jeanne C. Carr, Undated, estimated as September, 1874. George Wharton James, "A Letter from the Yosemite Valley," *The Craftsman*, 7, (March, l905), 654-655. John Muir Papers, A3: 01431, Holt-Atherton Special Collections, University of the Pacific Library. Copyright 1984 Muir-Hanna Trust. Used by permission.

An Evening Under the Stars and Moon: John Muir, Letter to Jeanne C. Carr, Estimated date of April 3, l871, John Muir Papers, A2:00906, Holt-Atherton Special Collections, University of the Pacific Library. Copyright 1984 Muir-Hanna Trust. Used by permission.

A Picturesque Snow Storm: John Muir, "Yosemite in Winter," *New York Tribune*, January 1, 1872. Courtesy of the Sierra Club.

Chapter 3: THE POWER OF BEAUTY

COMMENTARY

1. Linnie Marsh Wolfe, *John of the Mountains: The Unpublished Journals of John Muir* (Boston: Houghton Mifflin, 1938.), page 439. Copyright renewed © 1966 by John Muir Hanna and Eugene Wolfe. Used by permission of Houghton Mifflin Harcourt Publishing Company. All rights reserved.

2. John Muir, *My First Summer in the Sierra*, 1911, Chapter 1, Journal entry for June 5, 1869.

3. Linnie Marsh Wolfe, *John of the Mountains: The Unpublished Journals of John Muir* (Boston: Houghton Mifflin, 1938.) page 438. Copyright renewed © 1966 by John Muir Hanna and Eugene Wolfe. Used by permission of Houghton Mifflin Harcourt Publishing Company. All rights reserved.

4. William Frederic Badè, Ed., *The Life and Letters of John Muir, Vol. 1* (Boston: Houghton Mifflin Co., 1924), Chapter 9, Letter to Catherine Merrill, June 9, 1872.

5. John Muir, *My First Summer in the Sierra*, 1911, Chapter 9, Journal entry for July 19, 1869.

6. John Muir, Letter to Jeanne C. Carr, October 7, 1874, John Muir Papers, 3: 1445, Holt-Atherton Special Collections, University of the Pacific Library. Copyright 1984 Muir-Hanna Trust. Used by permission.

SELECTIONS

Nature's Cathedral: John Muir, *My First Summer in the Sierra*, l911, Chapter 10, Journal entry for September 7, 1868.

The Power of Beauty: John Muir, *My First Summer in the Sierra*, 1911, Chapter 1, Journal entry for June 5, 1869.

A Peaceful Joyful Stream of Beauty: John Muir, *My First Summer in the Sierra*, 1911, Chapter 2, Journal entry for June 30, 1869.

Opening a Thousand Windows: John Muir, *My First Summer in the Sierra*, 1911, Chapter 2, Journal entry for June 23, 1869.

Enduring Beauty: John Muir, *My First Summer in the Sierra*, 1911, Chapter 3, Journal entry for July 7, 1869.

Illilouette Falls: John Muir, "The Treasurers of Yosemite," *The Century Magazine*, Vol. XL. August, 1890. No. 4. Courtesy of the Sierra Club.

A Beautiful Crystal Hill: John Muir, "The Treasurers of Yosemite," *The Century Magazine*, Vol. XL. August, 1890, No. 4. Courtesy of the Sierra Club.

One Grand Canyon of Canyons: John Muir, *Steep Trails*, l918, Chapter 24. Courtesy of the Sierra Club.

Leaf Shadows: John Muir, *My First Summer in the Sierra*, 1911, Chapter 2, Journal entry for June 19, 1869.

Reflections of the Creator: John Muir, *My First Summer in the Sierra*, 1911, Chapter 6, Journal entry for July 26, 1869.

Chapter 4: **TREES OF LIFE**

COMMENTARY

1. Charles Sprague Sargent, "Muir's Love for Trees," in *John Muir: His Life and Letters and Other Writings*, Ed. by Terry Gifford (Seattle: The Mountaineers, 1996), p. 887.

SELECTIONS

American Forests! The Glory of the World! John Muir, "The National Forests," *Our National Parks*, 1901, Chapter 10. Originally published in the *Atlantic Monthly*, August, 1897. Commentary note: *The Spell of the Rockies* (Boston: Houghton, Mifflin, 1911.), p. 123. Courtesy of the Sierra Club.

Pruning by Rain: John Muir, *The Story of My Boyhood and Youth*, 1913, Chapter 6.

Sugar Pines: John Muir, *Steep Trails*, 1918, Chapter 22. Courtesy of the Sierra Club.

King Sequoia: John Muir, Letter to Jeanne C. Carr, approximate date, Autumn, 1870, John Muir Papers, A2: 00883. Holt-Atherton Special Collections, University of the Pacific Library. Copyright 1984 Muir-Hanna Trust. Used by permission.

The Big Tree: John Muir, *Our National Parks*, 1901, Chapter 9. Courtesy of the Sierra Club.

Wind Storm in the Forest: John Muir, *The Mountains of California*, 1894, Chapter 10. Courtesy of the Sierra Club.

Music of the Treetops: John Muir, *The Mountains of California*, 1894, Chapter 8. Courtesy of the Sierra Club.

Chapter 5: **COMPANIONS AND FELLOW MORTALS**

COMMENTARY

1. John Muir, *The Story of My Childhood and Youth*, 1913, Chapter 5. Courtesy of the Sierra Club.

2. John Muir, *The Story of My Childhood and Youth*, 1913, Chapter 3. Courtesy of the Sierra Club.

3. John Muir, *Travels in Alaska*, 1915, Chapter 15. Courtesy of the Sierra Club.

4. John Muir, *A Thousand Mile Walk to the Gulf* (Boston: Houghton Mifflin Co, 1916), Chapter 5.

SELECTIONS

Humanity's Place in the Cosmos: John Muir, *A Thousand Mile Walk to the Gulf*, 1916, Chapter 6.

Kinship with the Oxen Team and Cows: John Muir, *The Story of My Boyhood and Youth*, 1913, Chapter 3. Courtesy of the Sierra Club.

Reflection after the Death of Nob: John Muir, *The Story of My Boyhood and Youth*, 1913, Chapter 3. Courtesy of the Sierra Club.

A Terrible, Beautiful Reptile: John Muir, *The Story of My Boyhood and Youth*, 1913, Chapter 3. Courtesy of the Sierra Club.

Lament for the Passenger Pigeon: John Muir, *The Story of My Boyhood and Youth*, 1913, Chapter 4. Courtesy of the Sierra Club.

The Bravest of All Sierra Mountaineers: John Muir, *The Mountains of California*, 1894, Chapter 14. Courtesy of the Sierra Club.

Our Sympathy is Widened: John Muir, *My First Summer in the Sierra*, 1911, Chapter 6, Journal entry for July 26, 1869.

The Sure-Footed, Fearless Chipmunk: John Muir, *My First Summer in the Sierra*, 1911, Chapter 6, journal entry for July 31, 1869.

Deer—The Very Poetry of Manners and Motion: John Muir, *My First Summer in the Sierra*, 1911, Chapter 5, Journal entry for July 22, 1869.

Master-Spirit of the Tree Top: John Muir, Letter to Jeanne C. Carr, approximate date, Autumn, 1870, John Muir Papers, A2: 00883, Holt-Atherton Special Collections, University of the Pacific Library. Copyright 1984 Muir-Hanna Trust. Used by permission.

Look into Nature's Warm Heart: John Muir, *Our National Parks*, 1901, Chapter 7. Courtesy of the Sierra Club.

Chapter 6: RENEW YOURSELF IN NATURE

COMMENTARY

1. John Muir, *Our National Parks*, 1901, Chapter 4. Courtesy of the Sierra Club.

2. John Muir, Letter to Jeanne C. Carr [September, 1824], *The Life and Letters of John Muir*, Ed. By William Frederic Badè (Boston: Houghton Mifflin co., 1924), Chapter 11.

3. John Muir, *Our National Parks*, 1901, Chapter 1. Courtesy of the Sierra Club.

4. John Muir, *Our National Parks*, 1901, Chapter 1. Courtesy of the Sierra Club.

5. John Muir, "Twenty Hill Hollow," appended to *A Thousand-Mile Walk to the Gulf*, 1916, Chapter 9.

SELECTIONS

Nature is a Good Mother: John Muir, *Steep Trails*, 1918, Chapter 1. Courtesy of the Sierra Club.

We Dream of Bread: John Muir, *My First Summer in the Sierra*, 1911, Chapter 3, Journal entry for July 7, 1869.

The Influences of Pure Nature: John Muir, *The Mountains of California*, 1894, Chapter 7. Courtesy of the Sierra Club.

No Pain Here: John Muir, *My First Summer in the Sierra*, 1911, Chapter 5, Journal entry for July 20, 1869.

A Thousand Yellowstone Wonders Are Calling: John Muir, *Our National Parks*, 1901, Chapter 2. Courtesy of the Sierra Club.

Wander Here a Whole Summer: John Muir, *Our National Parks*, 1901, Chapter 1. Courtesy of the Sierra Club.

Reflections on a Nighttime Walk in the Thin White Light: John Muir, letter to Jeanne C. Carr, Estimated date of April 3, 1871, John Muir Papers, A2:00906, Holt-Atherton Special Collections, University of the Pacific Library. Copyright 1984 Muir-Hanna Trust. Used by permission.

Stand Beside Me: John Muir, *The Yosemite*, 1912, Chapter 4. Courtesy of the Sierra Club.

Renew Yourself in Nature's Eternal Beauty: John Muir, *Steep Trails*, 1918, Chapter 5.

Emerson's Visit to Yosemite: John Muir, *Our National Parks*, 1901, Chapter 4. Commentary: From his letter home to Louie Muir, June 13, 1893, in William Frederic Badè, *The Life and Letters of John Muir* (Boston: Houghton Mifflin Co., 1924), Vol. 2, Chapter 16.

Softly Comes Night to the Mountains: John Muir, "Yosemite Glaciers," *New York Tribune*, December 5, 1871. Courtesy of the Sierra Club.

Chapter 7: STORMS, DANGER, AND SURVIVAL

COMMENTARY

1. John Muir, *The Mountains of California*, 1894, Chapter 10. Courtesy of the Sierra Club.

SELECTIONS

A Dangerous Hike in the High Sierra: John Muir, *My First Summer in the Sierra*, 1911, Chapter 5, Journal entry for July 15, 1869.

Nerve-Shaken on Mount Ritter: John Muir, *The Mountains of California*, 1894, Chapter 4. Courtesy of the Sierra Club.

A Perilous Night on Shasta's Summit: John Muir, *Steep Trails*, 1918, Chapter 4. Courtesy of the Sierra Club.

Stickeen: The Story of a Dog: John Muir, "Stickeen: The Story of a Dog" (1909)

Chapter 8: NATURE'S INEXHAUSTIBLE ABUNDANCE

COMMENTARY

1. John Muir, *Twenty Hill Hollow*, in *A Thousand Mile Walk to the Gulf* (Boston: Houghton Mifflin, 1916), Chapter 9.

2. John Muir, Chapter 2, *Picturesque California and the Region West of the Rocky Mountains, from Alaska to Mexico, 1888.* Courtesy of the Sierra Club.

3. John Muir, *The Mountains of California* (Boston: Houghton Mifflin, 1894), Chapter 16. Courtesy of the Sierra Club.

SELECTIONS

A Heart Beating in Every Crystal and Cell: John Muir, *My First Summer in the Sierra*, 1911, Chapter 6, Journal entry for July 27, 1869.

Nature's Choicest Treasurers: John Muir, Chapter 4, *Picturesque California and the Region West of the Rocky Mountains, from Alaska to Mexico, 1888.* Courtesy of the Sierra Club.

The Heart-Peace of Nature: John Muir, Chapter 4, *Picturesque California and the Region West of the Rocky Mountains, from Alaska to Mexico, 1888.* Courtesy of the Sierra Club.

Hundreds of Happy Sun-Plants: John Muir, *The Mountains of California*, 1894, Chapter 16. Courtesy of the Sierra Club.

Clouds in the Sky-Fields: John Muir, *My First Summer in the Sierra*, 1911, Chapter 2, Journal entry for June 12, 1869.

Nature's Inexhaustible Abundance: John Muir, *My First Summer in the Sierra*, 1911, Chapter 10, Journal entry for September 2, 1868. Courtesy of the Sierra Club.

Fresh Beauty at Every Step: John Muir, Chapter 2, *Picturesque California and the Region West of the Rocky Mountains, from Alaska to Mexico, 1888.* Courtesy of the Sierra Club.

Rejoicing Everywhere: John Muir, *My First Summer in the Sierra*, 1911, Chapter 2, Journal entry for June 9, 1869.

Everything in Joyous Rhythmic Motion: John Muir, *My First Summer in the Sierra*, 1911, Chapter 2, Journal entry for July 2, 1869.

The History of a Single Raindrop: John Muir, *My First Summer in the Sierra*, 1911, Chapter 5, Journal entry for July 19, 1869.

Everything is Flowing: John Muir, *My First Summer in the Sierra*, 1911, Chapter 10, Journal entry for August 27, 1869.

Chapter 9: WALKING LIGHTLY ON THE LAND

COMMENTARY

1. John Muir, *Any Fool Can Destroy Trees*: *Sierra Club Bulletin*, January, 1920. Courtesy of the Sierra Club.

2. John Muir, Letter to Theodore Roosevelt [July 21, 1908], William Frederic Badè, The Life and Letters of John Muir (Boston: Houghton Mifflin Co., l924), Vol. 2, Chapter 18.

SELECTIONS

Walking Lightly on the Land: John Muir, *My First Summer in the Sierra*, 19ll, Chapter 2, Journal entry for July 11, 1869.

Vain Efforts to Save a Little Glacial Bog: John Muir, "The National Parks and Forest Reservations," Proceedings of the Meeting of the Sierra Club, held November 23, 1895, published in *Sierra Club Bulletin*, 1896. Courtesy of the Sierra Club.

God's First Temples: John Muir, *My First Summer in the Sierra*, 1911, Chapter 5, Journal entry for July 24, 1869.

The Eternal Conflict between Right and Wrong: John Muir, "The National Parks and Forest Reservations," Proceedings of the Meeting of the Sierra Club Held November 23, 1895, published in *Sierra Club Bulletin*, 1896. Courtesy of the Sierra Club.

Dam Hetch Hetchy! John Muir, *The Yosemite*, 1912, Chapter 16. Commentary note: Letter to C. Hart Merriam, February 11, l914, *The Life and Letters of John Muir, Vol. II*, Ed. by William Frederic Badè, (Boston: Houghton Mifflin Co., l924), Chapter 17.

Barbarous Harvesting of Lumber: John Muir, "A Rival of the Yosemite: The Canyon of the South Fork of King's River, California," *Century Magazine*, November, l891. Courtesy of the Sierra Club.

Any Fool Can Destroy Trees: John Muir, *Our National Parks*, 1901, Chapter 10.; Also in John Muir, *Sierra Club Bulletin*, January, 1920.

The Slaughter of Walruses: John Muir, *The Cruise of the Corwin*, 1917, Chapters 6 and 12. Courtesy of the Sierra Club.

Crimes in the Name of Vanity: John Muir, "Protect our Songbirds: Some Action Should be Taken Soon to Save the Warblers," A clipping found in John Muir's files. It may have been an article published in *The San Francisco Examiner* in the Spring of 1895. Commentary note: *Letter to Katherine Hittell*, April 30, 1875. Clipping from the John Muir Collection, Reprinted from the *John Muir Newsletter*, Vol. 1, No. 4, Fall 1991. Holt-Atherton Special Collections, University of the Pacific Library. Copyright 1984 Muir-Hanna Trust. Used by permission.

Chapter 10: THE SCRIPTURES OF ANCIENT GLACIERS

COMMENTARY

1. John Muir, *The Story of My Boyhood and Youth*, 1913, Chapter 6. Courtesy of the Sierra Club.

2. John Muir, *The Mountains of California*, 1892, Chapter 2. Courtesy of the Sierra Club.

SELECTIONS

Glorious Crystal Glaciers: John Muir, Letter to Jeanne C. Carr, December 11, l871, in *Letters to a Friend: Written to Mrs. Ezra Carr, l866-1879*. (Boston: Houghton Mifflin Co., l915; reprint, Dunwoody, Georgia: Norman Berg, l973).

Learning Every Natural Lesson: John Muir, Letter from Yosemite to Jeanne C. Carr, Dated September 8 (with the probably year of 1871), John Muir. *Letters to a Friend: Written to Mrs. Ezra Carr, 1866-1879.* (Boston: Houghton Mifflin Co., 1915; reprint, Dunwoody, Georgia: Norman Berg, 1973).

One Grand Wrinkled Sheet of Glacial Records: John Muir, *Harper's Monthly*, November, 1875. Commentary note: "Yosemite Glaciers," *New York Tribune*, December 5, 1871. Courtesy of the Sierra Club.

The Mighty Glaciers of the Sierra: John Muir, *The Mountains of California*, 1894, Chapter 1. Courtesy of the Sierra Club.

Tracing the Yosemite's Grand Old Glacier: John Muir, *The Mountains of California*, 1894, Chapter 2. Courtesy of the Sierra Club.

Luxuriant Butterfly-Filled Glacial Meadows: John Muir, *My First Summer in the Sierra*, 1911, Chapter 6, Journal entry for July 17, 1869.

Vanishing Glaciers: John Muir, *The Mountains of California*, 1894, Chapter 2. Courtesy of the Sierra Club.

Chapter 11: LAND OF THE MIDNIGHT SUN

COMMENTARY

1. John Muir, *Travels in Alaska*, 1915, Chapter 2. Courtesy of the Sierra Club.

2. John Muir, *Travels in Alaska*, 1915, Chapter 2. Courtesy of the Sierra Club.

3. John Muir, *Travels in Alaska*, 1915, Chapter 7. Courtesy of the Sierra Club.

4. John Muir, *Travels in Alaska*, 1915, Chapter 14. Courtesy of the Sierra Club.

SELECTIONS

My First Campfire in Alaska: John Muir, *Travels in Alaska*, 1915, Chapter 2. Courtesy of the Sierra Club.

The Discovery of Glacier Bay: John Muir, *Travels in Alaska*, 1915, Chapter 10. Courtesy of the Sierra Club.

Glorious Mountains, Glaciers, and Light: John Muir, *Travels in Alaska*, 1915, Chapter 10. Courtesy of the Sierra Club.

An Alaskan Midsummer Day: John Muir, Journal entry for July 10, 1879, *Picturesque California and the Region West of the Rocky Mountains, from Alaska to Mexico, 1888.* Courtesy of the Sierra Club.

Though Made, The World Is Still Being Made: John Muir, *Picturesque California and the Region West of the Rocky Mountains, from Alaska to Mexico, 1888.* Courtesy of the Sierra Club.

A Gentle Arctic Day: John Muir, *The Cruise of the Corwin*, 1917, Chapter 4, Journal entry for June 4, 1881. Courtesy of the Sierra Club.

Long, Nightless Days: John Muir, *The Cruise of the Corwin*, 1917, Chapter 7, Journal entry for June 4, 1881. Courtesy of the Sierra Club.

A Baby's Smile: John Muir, *The Cruise of the Corwin*, 1917, Chapter 6, Journal entry for June 9, 1881. Courtesy of the Sierra Club.

Golgotha: John Muir, *Cruise of the Corwin*, 1917, Chapter 9, Journal entry for July 3, 1881. Courtesy of the Sierra Club.

The Midnight Sun: John Muir, *The Cruise of the Corwin*, 1917, Chapter 12, Journal entry for July 23, 1881. Courtesy of the Sierra Club.

Sky Wonders of the Glorious Night: John Muir, *Travels in Alaska*, 1915, Chapter 19. Courtesy of the Sierra Club.

Midnight on Herald Island: John Muir, *The Cruise of the Corwin*, 1917, Chapter 13, Journal entry for July 31, 1881. Courtesy of the Sierra Club.

Chapter 12: PEACE TO EVERY LIVING THING

COMMENTARY

1. Donald Worster, *A Passion for Nature: The Life of John Muir* (New York: Oxford University Press, 2008), p. 377.

2. John Muir, *Letter to Henry Fairfield Osborn*, July 16, 1904, William Frederic Badè, *The Life and Letters of John Muir, Vol. II* (Boston: Houghton Mifflin Co., 1924), Chapter 17.

3. John Muir, *Letter to Helen Muir Funk*, November 29, 1911, in *John Muir's Last Journey: South to the Amazon and East to Africa*, Ed. By Michael P. Branch: Washington, D. C.: Island Press, 2001), p. 121.

4. John Muir, *Journal entry*, December 23, 1911, in *John Muir's Last Journey: South to the Amazon and East to Africa*, Ed. By Michael P. Branch: Washington, D. C.: Island Press, 2001), p. 139.

5. John Muir, same as above: *Journal entry*, December 23, 1911, in *John Muir's Last Journey: South to the Amazon and East to Africa*, Ed. By Michael P. Branch: Washington, D. C.: Island Press, 2001), p. 139.

6. John Muir, *Journal entry*, January 16, 1912, in *John Muir's Last Journey: South to the Amazon and East to Africa*, Ed. By Michael P. Branch: Washington, D. C.: Island Press, 2001), p. 145.

7. John Muir, *Journal entry*, January 20, 1912, in *John Muir's Last Journey: South to the Amazon and East to Africa*, Ed. By Michael P. Branch: Washington, D. C.: Island Press, 2001), p. 147.

8. John Muir, *Letter to Katherine Hooker*, [March 27, 1912]. Holt-Atherton Special Collections, University of the Pacific Library. Copyright 1984 Muir-Hanna Trust. Used by permission.

9. John Muir, *Letter to Mina Merrill*, May 31, 1913, William Frederic Badè, *The Life and Letters of John Muir* (Boston: Houghton Mifflin Co., 1924), Vol. 2, Chapter 17.

10. John Muir, Letter to Charles Sprague Sargent, William Frederic Badè, *The Life and Letters of John Muir* (Boston: Houghton Mifflin Co., 1924), p. 317. Digital copy.

11. Marion Randall Parsons, "John Muir and the Alaska Book," in *John Muir: His Life and Letters and Other Writings*, Ed. Terry Gifford (Seattle: The Mountaineers, 1986), p. 885.

12. John Muir, *Travels in Alaska* (Boston: Houghton Mifflin, 1924), Chapter 7.

SELECTIONS

Morning Opens on a Field of Lilies: John Muir, *The Mountains of California*, 1894, Chapter 8. Courtesy of the Sierra Club.

Daybreak and Sunrise: John Muir, *My First Summer in the Sierra*, 1911, Chapter 5, Journal entry for July 19, 1869.

Nature's Peace: John Muir, *Our National Parks*, "Yellowstone National Park," 1901, Chapter 2. Courtesy of the Sierra Club.Commentary note: Henry David Thoreau, "Walking," *Atlantic Monthly*, June, 1862.

Going Home: John Muir, *John of the Mountains: Unpublished Journals of John Muir*, Ed. by Linnie Marsh Wolfe, (Boston: Houghton Mifflin Co., 1938.), Journal entry/no date, pp. 439-440. Copyright 1938 by Wanda Muir Hanna; copyright renewed © 1966 by John Muir Hanna and Ralph Eugene Wolfe. Used by permission of Houghton Mifflin Harcourt Publishing Company. All rights reserved.

One Love-Harmony of the Universe: John Muir, from a letter to Janet Douglass Moores, February

23, 1887, In, *The Life and Letters of John Muir, Vol. II*, Ed. William Frederic Badè, (Boston: Houghton Mifflin Co., 1924), Chapter 15.

Streams of the River of Life: John Muir, from a letter to Julia Merrill Moores, July 25, 1900 after the death of her daughter, Janet Moores. In, *The Life and Letters of John Muir, Vol. II*, Ed. William Frederic Badè, (Boston: Houghton Mifflin Co., 1924)., Chapter 17.

Peace to Every Living Thing: John Muir, *My First Summer in the Sierra*, 1911, Chapter 2, Journal entry for June 11, 1869. Courtesy of the Sierra Club. John Muir in: Linnie Marsh Wolfe, *John of the Mountains: The Unpublished Journals of John Muir* (Boston: Houghton Mifflin Co., 1938.), page 438. Copyright 1938 by Wanda Muir Hanna; copyright renewed © 1966 by John Muir Hanna and Ralph Eugene Wolfe. Used by permission of Houghton Mifflin Harcourt Publishing Company. All rights reserved.

Chronology of John Muir's Life and Work

1838 On April 21, John Muir was born in Dunbar, Scotland, the son of Daniel and Ann Gilrye Muir. His older siblings were: Margaret (b. 1834) and Sarah (b. 1836).

1845 Muir entered Dunbar Grammar School where he was taught Latin, French, English, mathematics, and geography. He learned about natural history in a school reader, and was especially fascinated by America's fauna as described by John Audubon and Alexander Wilson. Seven-year-old Muir spent his free time exploring the local coastline and countryside.

1849 In February at age 11, John Muir, along with his father and siblings David and Sarah emigrated from Glasgow to New York by sailing ship, then via the Great Lakes and wagon to Fountain Lake, the family's first farm near Portage, Wisconsin. After they built their house, Muir's mother along with the children—Margaret, Dan, Mary, and Annie arrived. A year later, a final child, Joanna, was born. From age 11 to 21 John Muir worked on his father's farms. He received no formal schooling but taught himself mathematics, geometry, literature, and philosophy. Muir constructed all manner of clocks, barometers, hydrometers, and saws.

1856 When John Muir was 18, the Muir family moved from Fountain Lake Farm to Hickory Hill Farm nearby. Muir nearly died from toxic gases while digging a well on the new farm.

1860 Muir, at age 22, left home to exhibit his inventions at the State Fair in Madison, Wisconsin. He received his first public recognition as "An Ingenious Whittler." Here he met Jeanne C. Carr, a judge of the exhibition and wife of Ezra Carr, a professor at University of Wisconsin. Jeanne C. Carr would exert a lifelong influence on Muir.

1861 John Muir enrolled at the University of Wisconsin and attended for almost two-and-a-half years. He supported himself by teaching school. Muir learned geology from Dr. Ezra Carr. He also became interested in botany. The U.S. Civil War began.

1863 Muir left the university and returned to Fountain Lake to await possible draft in the Civil War. He took his first botany field trip along the Wisconsin River to the Mississippi.

1864 Muir went to Canada for two years during of the Civil War, where he worked at a sawmill and broom and rake factory at Meaford, Ontario. He took botany trips in Ontario and discovered the rare orchid, Calypso borealis.

1866 On February 22, the Meaford, Ontario, factory where Muir had been working, burned down. With the Civil War over, he returned to the United States. and went to Indianapolis, where he found employment as foreman and engineer at a factory making wagon parts.

1867 On March 5, Muir was temporarily blinded in a factory accident. He decided to quit factory work, and after recuperation and an extended visit at home, Muir set out on September 1 on a 1,000-mile walk to Florida and Cuba, with South America as his ultimate goal.

1868 In January, when Muir was 30 years old, he traveled to California via Cuba, New York, and the Isthmus of Panama, arriving in San Francisco on March 28. In April he had his first glimpse of the Sierra Nevada Mountains.

1869 This year Muir considered his "first summer in the Sierra" because it afforded him the opportunity to explore the Sierra ranges and glaciers. He made his first ascent of Cathedral Peak in what is now Yosemite National Park.

1870 Muir spent his first winter in Yosemite Valley working at James M. Hutchings's sawmill, and he began guiding tours of Yosemite.

1871 In May Ralph Waldo Emerson visited Muir in Yosemite. In the autumn Muir first visited the Hetch Hetchy Valley, which he called the "Tuolumne Yosemite." In December the *New York Tribune* published Muir's first article from California, titled "Yosemite Glaciers."

1872 Muir spent the winter writing articles. "Yosemite Valley in Flood," "Twenty Hill Hollow," and "Living Glaciers of California" were published in *The Overland Monthly.* Muir made his first ascent of Mount Ritter (13,000 feet).

1873 Muir climbed Mount Whitney (14,500 feet), the first recorded ascent by an eastern route, and took his first excursion to Kings River Canyon. He began wintering in Oakland in order to write articles on Yosemite, and he ended his full-time residence in the Valley.

1874   Muir made a solo ascent of Mount Shasta (14,400 feet). *The Overland Monthly* started publishing Muir's series, "Studies in the Sierra." Through Jeanne C. Carr, Muir met the woman who would become his wife, Louie Wanda Strentzel, the 27-year-old daughter of Louisiana Irwin Strentzel and Dr. John Theophil Strentzel, a prosperous Polish immigrant who owned a large fruit farm near Martinez.

1876   Muir began to lobby in public for forest protection and conservation. The *Sacramento Record-Union* published his article "God's First Temples," urging government protection of the forests.

1879   Muir became engaged to Louisa Wanda (Louie) Strentzel. He discovered Glacier Bay and Muir Glacier during his first trip to Alaska.

1880   On April 14, at age 42, Muir married Louie Strentzel, age 33. In July he made his second trip to Alaska, where he had his perilous adventure with the dog Stickeen, creating what has become a classic dog story

1881   Muir took his third trip to Alaska aboard the *Corwin*. On March 25, his first daughter, Wanda, was born.

1882   At the age of 44 with a family to support, Muir spent 1882 and the next eight years running the family fruit farm in Martinez, California. His article, "Bee-Pastures of California," was published in *Century Magazine* and later in his book *Our National Parks*.

1886   Muir's second child, Helen, was born on January 23.

1887   Muir began work as editor and author of *Picturesque California and the Region West of the Rocky Mountains, from Alaska to Mexico*, 1888.

1888   On a trip to Puget Sound and Mount Shasta, Muir climbed Mount Rainier (14,500 feet). He visited many sites in the Pacific Northwest, including Portland Oregon, Columbia Gorge, Mount Rainier, Snoqualmie Falls, Spokane Falls, and Crater Lake. This trip provided material for articles about Oregon and Washington published in *Picturesque California and the Region West of the Rocky Mountains, from Alaska to Mexico*, and later in *Steep Trails*.

1889   Around the campfire at Soda Springs, in Tuolumne Meadows in Yosemite, the influential editor of the *Century Magazine*, Robert Underwood Johnson, persuaded Muir to write articles urging protection of Yosemite.

1890   Muir took his fourth trip to Alaska, which included a 10-day, solo expedition by sled across Muir Glacier. His articles on Yosemite, "The Treasures of Yosemite" and "Features of the Proposed Yosemite National Park," were published in *Century Magazine*, which greatly aided the campaign to establish Yosemite National Park.

1892   Muir co-founded the Sierra Club and served as its president for the rest of his life.

1893   On June 8, Muir visited Concord, Massachusetts, and laid flowers on Thoreau's and Emerson's graves. He took a trip to Europe and visited his hometown of Dunbar in Scotland as well as London, Ireland, Norway, Switzerland, France, and Italy. He campaigned for the creation of Mount Rainier National Park.

1894   Muir's first book, *The Mountains of California*, was published when he was 56 years old.

1896   Muir joined the U.S. Forestry Commission to survey of the forests of Yellowstone, the Black Hills, Idaho, Oregon, and Washington; also the Cascades, the Santa Lucia coastal ranges, the mountains of southern California, the Grand Canyon, and the southern Sierra Nevada. He took his fifth trip to Alaska and received an honorary degree from Harvard University.

1897   Muir was awarded an honorary doctorate degree from the University of Wisconsin. He took his sixth trip to Alaska—five weeks via Banff and the Canadian Rockies. Muir's articles on forest preservation, published in *Harper's Weekly* and *Atlantic Monthly*, created popular support for protecting forestlands.

1899   Muir took his seventh and final trip to Alaska with the Harriman Expedition to Wrangell, Glacier Bay, Sitka, and Prince William Sound.

1901   Muir's second book, *Our National Parks*, was published.

1903   From May 15–17 Muir hosted President Theodore Roosevelt on a camping trip in Yosemite. Muir began a world tour of London, Paris, Berlin, Russia, Finland, Siberia, Korea, Japan, China, India, Egypt, Ceylon, Australia, New Zealand, Malaya, Indonesia, Philippines, Hong Kong, and Hawaii. At age 65, he climbed Mueller Glacier on Mount Cook, New Zealand.

1904   On May 27 Muir returned home at the end of his world tour and intensified his campaign to return the Yosemite Valley back to federal control.

1905   On August 6, Muir's wife, Louie Strentzel Muir, died.

1906   The great San Francisco earthquake and fire occurred, fueling the city's desire to dam the Hetch Hetchy Valley for a new water supply.

1907 Muir and the Sierra Club began in earnest the fight to save the Hetch Hetchy Valley from damming.

1909 *Stickeen* was published, and John Muir led President Taft on a tour through the Sierra Nevada.

1911 On June 21 Muir was awarded an honorary doctorate degree by Yale University, and his book *My First Summer in the Sierra* was published. On August 12 he left New York for a year-long trip to South America and Africa, fulfilling his 40-year dream to explore the Amazon and the great araucaria trees in the forests of Brazil and Chile, and the baobab trees of Africa.

1912 On March 27 Muir arrived in New York after his 30-week, 40,000-mile-long voyage. At home in California, he continued the fight against the destruction of wilderness by lumber, mining, and power barons, and the plan to dam the Hetch Hetchy Valley. His book *The Yosemite* was published.

1913 The battle for Hetch Hetchy was lost; the Hetch Hetchy Valley was granted to San Francisco for a reservoir. Muir's autobiographical book *The Story of My Boyhood and Youth* was published. He was awarded an honorary doctorate degree by the University of California.

1914 On Christmas Eve, John Muir, at the age of 76, died of pneumonia in Los Angeles, with drafts of *Travels in Alaska* scattered around his hospital room. He was buried in the Strentzel family cemetery in Martinez, California.

1915 *Travels in Alaska* was published by Muir's literary executor, William F. Badè

1916 *A Thousand-Mile Walk to the Gulf* was published, and the U.S. Congress established the U.S. National Park Service, fulfilling one of Muir's dreams.

1917 *The Cruise of the Corwin* was published.

1918 *Steep Trails*, Muir's final book, was published.

1964 Muir's house in Martinez, California, was designated as the John Muir National Historic Site.

Selected Resources

BOOKS WRITTEN BY JOHN MUIR DURING HIS LIFETIME

The Mountains of California (1894)

Our National Parks (1901)

Stickeen: The Story of a Dog (a short story, 1909)

My First Summer in the Sierra (1911)

The Yosemite (1912)

The Story of My Boyhood and Youth (1913)

BOOKS WRITTEN BY JOHN MUIR AND PUBLISHED POSTHUMOUSLY

Travels in Alaska (1915)

A Thousand-Mile Walk to the Gulf (1916)

The Cruise of the Corwin (1917)

Steep Trails (1919)

All of the books written by John Muir were published by Houghton Mifflin Co.

JOHN MUIR'S LETTERS

Badè, William Frederic, Ed., *The Life and Letters of John Muir*. Boston: Houghton, Mifflin Co., 1924.

Branch, Michael P., Ed., *John Muir's Last Journey: South to the Amazon and East to Africa*. Washington, DC: Island Books, 2001.

Gifford, Terry, Ed., *John Muir: His Letters and Other Writings*. Seattle: The Mountaineers, 1996.

Gisel, Bonnie Johanna, Ed., *Kindred and Related Spirits: The Letters of John Muir and Jeanne C. Carr*. Salt Lake City: University of Utah Press, 2001.

BIOGRAPHIES OF JOHN MUIR

Turner, Frederick, *John Muir: Rediscovering America.* Cambridge, MA: Perseus Publishing, 1985.

Wolfe, Linnie Marsh, *John Muir: John of the Mountains: The Unpublished Journals of John Muir.* Boston: Houghton, Mifflin Co., 1938.

Worster, Donald. *A Passion for Nature: The Life of John Muir.* New York: Oxford University Press, 2008.

JOHN MUIR FOR CHILDREN

Cornell, Joseph, *John Muir: My Life with Nature*. Nevada City, CA: Dawn Publications, 2000.

VISUAL RESOURCES

John Muir: In the New World, DVD, Part of the American Masters series, produced for PBS, 2011.

The National Parks: America's Best Idea, DVD series produced for PBS, with photography by Ken Burns, 2009.

index

y

Jeffery Rowthorn

About the Author

ANNE ROWTHORN has written and compiled 11 books on diverse topics, but ecological spirituality has become her specialty. Rowthorn is a passionate, life-long environmentalist. She has taken her pen and notebook all over the United States, and to Asia, Latin America, Oceania, and Europe. Wherever she goes, following John Muir's example, she seeks out the wildest hiking trails, mountains, and coastlines. Along the way she collects evocative ecological literature from the great cultures and religions of the world. She and her husband, the hymn writer Jeffery Rowthorn, live in rural eastern Connecticut.